History of the Future of Economic Growth

The future of economic growth is one of the decisive questions of the twenty-first century. Alarmed by declining growth rates in industrialized countries, climate change, and rising socio-economic inequalities, among other challenges, more and more people demand to look for alternatives beyond growth. However, so far these current debates about sustainability, post-growth or degrowth lack a thorough historical perspective.

This edited volume brings together original contributions on different aspects of the history of economic growth as a central and near-ubiquitous tenet of developmental strategies. The book addresses the origins and evolution of the growth paradigm from the seventeenth century up to the present day and also looks at sustainable development, sustainable growth, and degrowth as examples of alternative developmental models. By focusing on the mixed legacy of growth, both as a major source of expanded life expectancies and increased comfort, and as a destructive force harming personal livelihoods and threatening entire societies in the future, the editors seek to provide historical depth to the ongoing discussion on suitable principles of present and future global development.

History of the Future of Economic Growth is aimed at students and academics in environmental, social, economic and international history, political science, environmental studies, and economics, as well as those interested in ongoing discussions about growth, sustainable development, degrowth, and, more generally, the future.

Iris Borowy is Distinguished Professor at Shanghai University, China.

Matthias Schmelzer works at the Konzeptwerk Neue Ökonomie in Leipzig and is a Permanent Fellow at the Research Group on Post-Growth Societies at the University of Jena, Germany.

Routledge Studies in Ecological Economics

For a full list of titles in this series, please visit www.routledge.com/series/RSEE

36. Redefining Prosperity
Edited by Isabelle Cassiers

37. Environmental Challenges and Governance
Diverse Perspectives from Asia
Edited by Sacchidananda Mukherjee and Debashis Chakraborty

38. Green Growth and Low Carbon Development in East Asia
Edited by Fumikazu Yoshida and Akihisa Mori

39. Biodiversity in the Green Economy
Edited by Alexandros Gasparatos and Katherine J. Willis

40. The Economics of Green Growth
New indicators for sustainable societies
Edited by Shunsuke Managi

41. Green Jobs for Sustainable Development
Ana-Maria Boromisa, Sanja Tišma and Anastasya Raditya Ležaić

42. Sustainability and the Political Economy of Welfare
Edited by Max Koch and
Oksana Mont

43. Creating Sustainable Bioeconomies
The Bioscience Revolution in Europe and Africa
Edited by Ivar Virgin and E. Jane Morris

44. History of the Future of Economic Growth
Historical Roots of Current Debates on Sustainable Degrowth
Edited by Iris Borowy and Matthias Schmelzer

History of the Future of Economic Growth

Historical Roots of Current Debates on Sustainable Degrowth

Edited by
Iris Borowy and Matthias Schmelzer

LONDON AND NEW YORK

First published 2017
by Routledge
2 Park Square, Milton Park, Abingdon, Oxon OX14 4RN

and by Routledge
711 Third Avenue, New York, NY 10017

First issued in paperback 2018

Routledge is an imprint of the Taylor & Francis Group, an informa business

British Library Cataloguing in Publication Data
A catalogue record for this book is available from the British Library

Library of Congress Cataloging in Publication Data
Names: Borowy, Iris, 1962- editor. | Schmelzer, Matthias, editor.
Title: History of the future of economic growth : historical roots of current debates on sustainable degrowth / edited by Iris Borowy and Matthias Schmelzer.
Description: Abingdon, Oxon ; New York, NY : Routledge, 2017. | Includes bibliographical references and index.
Identifiers: LCCN 2016039041 | ISBN 9781138685802 (hardback) | ISBN 9781315543000 (ebook)
Subjects: LCSH: Economic development--History. | Sustainable development. | Economic history.
Classification: LCC HD78 .H57 2017 | DDC 338.9/27--dc23
LC record available at https://lccn.loc.gov/2016039041

ISBN 13: 978-1-138-49967-6 (pbk)
ISBN 13: 978-1-138-68580-2 (hbk)

Typeset in Times New Roman
by Taylor & Francis Books

Contents

Figures

Contributors

Christophe Bonneuil is a Senior Researcher in the history of science and environmental history at the Centre National de la Recherche Scientifique and teaches at the École des Hautes Études en Sciences Sociales, Paris. His research explores the co-evolution of ways of knowing about and of governing nature. He has recently published a global environmental history of the Anthropocene (*The Shock of the Anthropocene: The Earth, History and Us*, Verso, 2015, with J.-B. Fressoz) and edited the volume *The Anthropocene and the Global Environmental Crisis: Rethinking Modernity in a new Epoch* (Routledge, 2015, with Clive Hamilton and François Gemenne).

Iris Borowy is Distinguished Professor at Shanghai University. She obtained her Ph.D. in Modern History from the University of Rostock in 1997. Since then, she has taught and done research, among other places, at the University of Rostock, the Centre Alexandre Koyré (Paris), the Casa Oswaldo Cruz/FIOCRUZ (Rio de Janeiro), and at Birkbeck University (London). She has published widely on the history of international health and international organizations, including *Defining Sustainable Development for Our Common Future: A history of the World Commission on Environment and Development* (Routledge, 2014). Her current research interests focus on interrelated developments in environmental and economic history.

Jeremy L. Caradonna received his Ph.D. in history from The Johns Hopkins University in 2007. After teaching history for nearly 10 years at the University of Alberta, he now teaches Environmental Studies at the University of Victoria. He is the author of two books, including *Sustainability: A History* (Oxford University Press, 2014). His research interests include the history of environmental consciousness, degrowth and ecological economics, and the history and practice of sustainable agricultural systems.

Gareth Dale teaches politics at Brunel University. His publications include *Green Growth: Ideology, Political Economy and the Alternatives* (Zed, 2016), *Reconstructing Karl Polanyi: Excavation and Critique* (Pluto, 2016), *Karl Polanyi: A Life on the Left* (Columbia UP, 2016), *Karl Polanyi: The*

Hungarian Writings (Manchester University Press, 2016), and *The Politics of East European Area Studies* (Routledge, 2016).

Lorenzo Fioramonti is Professor of Political Economy at the University of Pretoria (South Africa), where he directs the Centre for the Study of Governance Innovation. Among other prestigious international positions, he is the Jean Monnet Chair in Africa and also holds the UNESCO-UNU Chair in Regional Integration, Migration, and Free Movement of People. His most recent books are *How Numbers Rule the World: The Use and Abuse of Statistics in Global Politics* (Zed Books, 2014) and *Gross Domestic Problem: The Politics Behind the World's Most Powerful Number* (Zed Books, 2013, recipient of the UP Best Book of the Year Award 2014). He is the founder of the action research network for a Wellbeing Economy in Africa.

Jean-Baptiste Fressoz's research is at the crossroads between history of science, history of technology, and environmental history. Formerly lecturer at Imperial College London, he is now a Senior Researcher at the Centre National de la Recherche Scientifique (Centre Alexandre Koyré). He is the author of *The Shock of the Anthropocene: The Earth, History and Us* (Verso, 2016, with Christophe Bonneuil) and *L'Apocalypse joyeuse: Une histoire du risque technologique* (Le Seuil, 2012). He is currently working on a global history of climatic knowledge since the sixteenth century.

Stephen Macekura is Assistant Professor of International Studies in the School of Global and International Studies at Indiana University. Stephen received his Ph.D. in History from the University of Virginia in 2013. He has held post-doctoral fellowships at the Institute for Advanced Studies in Culture at the University of Virginia and the Dickey Center for International Understanding at Dartmouth of College. His first book, *Of Limits and Growth: The Rise of Global Sustainable Development in the Twentieth Century*, was published by Cambridge University Press in 2015. He is a scholar of U.S. and global history, with a particular focus on political economy, international development, environmentalism, and U.S. foreign relations.

Barbara Muraca is Assistant Professor for Environmental and Social Philosophy at Oregon State University, Corvallis. She obtained her Ph.D. in environmental ethics and moral philosophy from the University of Greifswald, Germany. Her dissertation on Process Philosophy as a theoretical foundation for a theory of strong sustainability, *Denken in Grenzgebiet*, was published in 2010 with Alber and awarded with the Karl-Alber Prize. She was Senior Researcher at the Advanced Research Group on Post-Growth Societies of the University of Jena. She has published several articles on degrowth, relational values of nature, and sustainability in international journals and books. Her most recent book in German is *Gut Leben. Eine Gesellschaft jenseits des Wachstums* (Wagenbach, 2014).

Matthias Schmelzer works at the Konzeptwerk Neue Ökonomie in Leipzig and is a Permanent Fellow at the Research Group on Post-Growth Societies at the University of Jena. He obtained his Ph.D. in Economic History at the European University Viadrina in Frankfurt (Oder) in 2013. Since then, he has taught and done research at the University of Geneva, at Humboldt-University Berlin, and at the University of Zürich. His most recent book is *The Hegemony of Growth: The OECD and the Making of the Economic Growth Paradigm* (Cambridge University Press, 2016). His research interests include economic and transnational history, alternative economics, and social movements.

Andrea Westermann is Lecturer at the History Department of the University of Zurich. In her studies, she combines the history of science and technology with the history of material culture and environmental history. She obtained her Ph.D. from Bielefeld University with a study on the history of plastic and political culture in West Germany (2007), worked at ETH Zurich, and was a guest scholar at University of California, San Diego and the Max Planck Institute for the History of Science in Berlin. She is currently finishing a book on Alpine research, the making of global tectonics, and the societal impact of geological knowledge in late nineteenth-century Europe.

Acknowledgments

The idea for this book goes back to a special session at the Fourth International Degrowth Conference for Ecological Sustainability and Social Equity that took place in Leipzig in September 2014. Entitled "Degrowth and History – Economics, Sustainability, Power," the session aimed at introducing a historical perspective into the burgeoning research field on sustainability, no-growth alternatives, and degrowth, and to open up a new research agenda for ecological, cultural, social, and economic history. Our collective discussions and the comments by economic historian and proponent of degrowth, Joan Martinez-Alier, encouraged us that the endeavor was worth pursuing further. Therefore, we asked panel participants and additional authors to contribute original research articles, and the present volume is the result.

This book – as all intellectual endeavors – is the product of and rests on the work of many, to whom we would like to address our sincerest thanks. In particular, we would like to thank the authors, who contributed fascinating and original historical chapters and put up with our demanding process of editing and revisions. For helpful comments on the conceptualization of this book, we would like to thank in particular John McNeill, Jan-Hendrik Meyer, Joan Martinez-Alier, Andrea Vetter, Anna-Katharina Wöbse, and Giorgos Kallis. Furthermore, we also want to thank the staff of Routledge for their professional and rigorous help in finishing this book project, in particular Elanor Best and Andy Humphries.

Iris Borowy changed positions during work on this volume and wishes to thank both the Institute for the History, Theory and Ethics of Medicine at Aachen University and the College of Liberal Arts at Shanghai University for making work possible as well as enjoyable. Other than that, she is thankful to Norbert for many reasons, including for maintaining a healthy skepticism about degrowth. And Matthias Schmelzer would like to thank the Research Center for Social and Economic History at the University of Zürich for enabling this project financially. And, last but not least, his special thanks go to Nina – you made every day wonderful during the time this book evolved.

Introduction

The end of economic growth in long-term perspective

Iris Borowy and Matthias Schmelzer

The future of economic growth is one of the decisive challenges of the twenty-first century. Since approximately 1820, global economic growth has profoundly transformed human life and the planet, and current societies, economies, and cultures are fundamentally built on the expectation of continuing future growth. However, given the exceptional and non-reproducible circumstances, which have given rise to the unprecedented economic expansion of recent history, it seems essentially clear that, irrespective of local or regional developments to the contrary, on a global scale future growth rates will be nowhere near what they have been in the recent past. What is unclear, however, is how societies will react to the end of growth and related crises. What is the significance of economic growth in current societies? How did humanity come to develop this dependence on a growth-centered economy? And what possible alternatives are there and how have they evolved historically? These, among others, are the questions addressed in *History of the Future of Economic Growth*.

Although a highly ambivalent and elusive term, the semantic core of economic growth is statistically fixed. It is generally defined as the annual increase in the Gross National Product (GNP) or Gross Domestic Product (GDP). GNP and GDP measure the monetary value of all the final goods and services produced within a country, including the costs of producing all the services provided by the government.[1] Since production and services are provided and consumed by the inhabitants of a country, GNP/GDP is related to population. Using per capita GNP/GDP allows comparing the economies of countries of different population sizes. While this definition has always stayed at the core of what is meant by economic growth, the concept has become charged with a multitude of contested and shifting meanings, assumptions, and connotations. Often, economic growth is equated with development (in itself a contested concept), social progress, economic improvement, or the expansion of material through-put. This diversity of meaning is hardly surprising since, as the various contributions to this book make clear, the concept of economic quantification – or even of a recognizable "economy" – has been contingent on circumstances, is highly contested among various social groups, has evolved over time, and is likely to continue to do so in the future (for more details, see Fioramonti 2013; Speich-Chassé 2013; Schmelzer 2016).

For a long time, economic growth drew its legitimacy from its promise of providing the means both for improvements of individual living conditions and for social progress. This may explain why the idea of continuing economic growth has been broadly endorsed, readily taken for granted, and rarely questioned. The concept proved attractive both in those high-income countries, which had experienced substantial economic growth already, and in low-income countries, where people were hoping to get their share of the benefits of increased income in the future. However, the advantages of economic growth have always come at a social and/or environmental price, giving rise to concerns, which have repeatedly been articulated on the fringes of academia and society. As prospects for future growth seem bleaker than they have been in the past, discussions about the future of economic growth have gained strength and are beginning to spread into the mainstream of public discussions. In the process, the debate makes use of historical arguments, making claims about alleged past records and their meaning for the future, but frequently these claims remain unreflected and untested against a body of studies on often very complex phenomena and their short- and long-term causes and effects. Nevertheless, even though historical knowledge would clearly benefit the debate, up to now, historians have been curiously absent from it. This volume is an attempt to add historians' voices to considerations about the nature of challenges related to the costs and possible end of economic growth, about the historical developments leading up to these challenges, and about the degree to which past experience can or cannot serve as orientation for the future. History never really repeats itself, so it is a truism that the future cannot be a simple continuation of the past. This volume argues that today, in the second decade of the twenty-first century, this truism is more true than usual.

In order to give historical context to current debates about the future challenges of growth, in this Introduction we take a long-term view: We start by discussing the *external limits* to economic growth, in particular resources, climate change, and land; then explore what might be conceptualized as *internal limits* related to secular stagnation, prosperity, and equality; and finally present some historical perspectives on current debates about societies beyond economic growth by drawing out key arguments of the contributions to this volume.

External limits: resources, climate change, and land

Historically, the economic development since the late nineteenth century and, particularly, the high rates of economic growth during this period, represent an anomaly, which only appears normal to many people today because it has characterized circumstances in living memory. Between 1890 and 1990, global population increased four-fold, global energy consumption and GDP increased approximately 14-fold, and industrial production 40-fold. Of all the years ever lived by *homo sapiens* and his predecessors during the past four million years, probably one-fifth were lived during the twentieth century (Krausmann et al. 2013; McNeill 2002; McNeill 2000). How and when global economic growth will decline and possibly end is unclear, but the fact that a repetition of the experience of the twentieth century is impossible for any extended period of time should be obvious even to the most enthusiastic cornucopianists.

Much of this growth happened in the second half of the twentieth century during the "golden age" of exceptionally high GDP growth rates between 1950 and 1970 in industrialized countries and in emerging market economies since. Named the "1950s Syndrome" or "Great Acceleration," it has also been a period characterized by rapidly increasing consumption of fossil fuel energy and production of material goods, of increasing exploitation of natural resources, and of various forms of environmental degradation (Pfister 2010; Steffen et al. 2007).

This development reflected exceptional circumstances, based primarily on an unprecedented exploitation of cheap fossil fuels. They allowed humanity to break out of the bounds of energy restrictions, which had severely limited the possibilities of economic activities so far (McNeill 2002; Crosby 2006). This liberation from energy constraints due to fossil fuels will necessarily be temporary. Coal, oil, and gas will not be able to keep sustaining economic growth (or even the existing high level of economic activity) endlessly into the future. One reason is the simple fact that they are finite and, though it is impossible to define this moment in time, at some point they will be used up. Much earlier, they will be so expensive and energy-intensive to mine as to make exploitation useless (Exner et al. 2013). Second, even if there was an endless supply of coal, oil, and gas, burning them results in climatic changes of intolerable dimensions, making their use increasingly objectionable. According to some studies, current reserves of fossil fuels, which are still in the ground, are tantamount to five times the amount that can be burned, if humanity is to stay within the internationally agreed limit of two degree global warming (Klein 2014, 148). There is already tangible opposition against forms of energy with a high negative impact on climate change and on local and regional environments, observable as public resistance against fracking, oil, lignite mining, or tar sands, and it is likely to increase with growing awareness of the effects of climate change and of the role of fossil fuels in causing it.

After all, the prospects regarding climate change are, indeed, dire. Scientists warn that "[i]ndirect effects of global climate change threaten the health of hundreds of millions of people" (Myers and Bernstein 2011). Predicted results include heat waves and changes in extreme weather conditions and in water resources, leading to harvest failures, changes in disease spectrum, damage and loss of property and livelihoods, loss of ecosystem services, and increases in violence and hostilities, all of which will disproportionately affect the most vulnerable groups in the world and within each society, i.e. the poor, the elderly, and the marginalized. Even more disturbingly, they include the risk of reaching and going beyond tipping points such as the melting of the Northern permafrost or the loss of wood cover, which will provoke irreversible and auto-catalyzing run-away changes that may take the entire process of climate change to a new and really unimaginable level (World Bank 2014; IPCC 2014). Ironically, the relation goes both ways: not only does fossil fuel–based economic growth jeopardize climate stability, but climate change also imperils the future of economic growth. In 2007, the Stern Review famously calculated that the cost of not acting against climate change could be equivalent to losing between 5 and 20 percent of GDP each year, indefinitely (Stern 2007). Thus, it seems that, unless some entirely new form of energy will be found that is powerful, environmentally friendly, cheap, and rapidly available in large quantities, both a shift away from fossil fuels in order to mitigate climate change and the failure to do so will seriously depress economic growth rates.

There can simply be no doubt that eventually, humanity will need to face a change in its energy regime. In theory, this fact is easy enough to comprehend, but its full impact is nowhere near adequately appreciated. In spite of robust increases and improvements in the use of alternative energy such as solar, wind, or hydropower, at the time of writing it is difficult to imagine that these efforts will fully replace fossil fuels anytime soon. Regardless of how and when it will come about, a change in energy sources will truly be something that "changes everything" (Klein 2014), ranging from how we eat, live, dress, work, go on holiday, and spend our free time. It will also change social relations and hierarchies of inequality. Inevitably, it will also prevent a simple continuation of the present global economic system, which is predicated on continued economic growth.

Nevertheless, even though centrally important, the connection between fossil fuels and climate change is only one of the factors that contradict an endless continuation of economic growth. The impediments are multifaceted and inter-related and are connected to various building blocks of what constitutes our current economic system. Again, on a simple level, constraints result from the sheer physicality of economic growth. Though expressed in quasi-ethereal monetary GDP terms, the underlying developments are eminently material. This point may be most evident with regard to population growth, a powerful driver of economic growth. As McNeill (2002: 12) has graphically pointed out: "If twentieth-century growth rates were to persist, within a few centuries the earth would be encased in a mass of human flesh expanding outward with a radial velocity greater than the speed of light." Similar fictitious scenarios could be imagined about urban construction, industrial and agricultural production, or plastic waste, to name just a few. Obviously, this will not happen. Something will change between now and, say, the twenty-third century, which will curtail growth rates of the physical economy.

While it is thus clear that the material throughput – the non-renewable energy and the material resources consumed by the economic process and the emissions and waste generated by it – cannot continue to expand for long, some claim that GDP could still increase due to technological improvements. Proponents of continued economic growth maintain that equating GDP growth and improving living standards with increasing physical pressure on the environment is simplistic. In as much as the natural world (resources, space, waste sinks, etc.) does not enter economic processes directly but after transformation through constantly changing technological processes and social frameworks it is supposedly possible, indeed normal, that rising GDP coincides with decreasing environmental degradation. The idea that innovations could "help to decouple growth from natural capital depletion and environmental pollution" (Dutz and Sharma 2012, 2) forms the basis of "green growth" as a concept designed to reconcile the continuation of the existing economic system with changes in the ecological burdens of this system. Thus, green growth can be seen as an extension of the Environmental Kuznets Curve, which gained prominence during the 1990s, spurred by its adoption by the World Bank (World Bank 1992, 41). This curve purported to show that environmental pressure rises during the early phases of industrial development but declines during its later, mature part, as further increases in national income give rise to more sophisticated, resource-efficient, and cleaner technology, and as, with basic needs met, public concern about the environment increases, resulting in protective policies.

This view has some merit. Some empirical data do, indeed, indicate that some progress has been made to separate GDP growth from environmental pressure. Thus, OECD calculations suggest that the world has experienced relative decoupling of GDP growth from the ecological footprint since the 1980s (OECD 2008). However, these improvements have remained limited. Decoupling has been relative rather than absolute, so that GDP growth still entails a rising ecological footprint, albeit less so than during earlier times. It is unclear, whether a combination of technological and social development will ever sufficiently decouple GDP from ecological pressure, making possible, for example, increases in GDP while radically reducing CO_2 emissions as is necessary to mitigate climate change. As of now, 40 years after the Stockholm Conference of 1972 and 20 years after the Earth Summit, both of which called for continued economic development with less environmental degradation, no member state of the United Nations has achieved a significant decoupling of economic growth from environmental pressure. In fact, even though the United Nations Framework Convention on Climate Change, signed in 1992 at the Earth Summit in Rio de Janeiro, called for a stabilization of greenhouse gas concentrations in the atmosphere, CO_2 emissions in 2012 were 58 percent higher than those in 1990 (Peters et al. 2013). On the contrary, the only times that global or regional CO_2 emissions declined were related to periods of economic decline: the oil price shock and US recession in the early 1980s, the collapse of the former Soviet Union, the Asian financial crisis, and the economic decline following the world financial crisis in 2009 (Peters et al. 2012).

Similarly, the Environmental Kuznets Curve has lost a lot of its promise. Subsequent studies showed that it seems to hold true for only a limited selection of pollutants and often it is unclear to what extent improvements in one country are the result of the transfer of polluting industries to other, usually low-income countries, a strategy which could obviously not be imitated on a global scale (Stagl 1999; Dinda 2004).

Besides, some key industries have strengthened their "coupling." A case in point is cement, whose production has doubled since 1990, surpassing global GDP growth by some 70 percent while causing substantial degradation for river beds, beaches, and the ocean floor as the origin of sand (Jackson 2009, 75; UNEP 2014).

Taking a broader view of the changing societal uses of products and their repercussions shows that frequently a large part of technological efficiency improvements are compensated by more resource usage. This so-called Jevon's Paradox has been known to economists since 1865, when William Jevons pointed out that efficiency improvements in steam power had led to increased coal consumption, and it was revived as the "rebound effect" in the 1990s (Polimeni et al. 2009; Sorrell 2009). For instance, the money saved through a more energy-efficient car is often spent either on driving more often and longer distances (direct rebound effect), or it is spent on other energy-intensive consumption (indirect rebound effect; Santarius 2015; Paech 2012). Assessments for the size of the rebound effects are notoriously difficult and differ enormously. A widely cited study of the UK Energy Research Council calculated an average of 26 percent for the different sectors of the UK economy (UKERC 2008). Recent metastudies found a range of between 34 to 96 percent, depending on country, time period, and economic sector (Chakravarty et al. 2013) or a broad variety of effects under 60 percent (Gillingham 2014). At any rate, the effect is real and sufficiently large to question efficiency improvements as viable options for decoupling.

Inevitably, if economic growth is tied to environmental degradation, continued growth will lead to continually increasing burdens on complex ecological processes. Indeed, a growing number of studies seem to bear out this connection and point to a dangerous approach of global limits. The best-known early publication of this type, the 1972 *Limits to Growth* report commissioned by the Club of Rome, which presented a total of 12 scenarios for possible future developments, was widely read and discussed. Yet subsequent criticism, especially by economists and often on the basis of misrepresentations of what the study had actually said, succeeded in establishing a view of the book as having been "wrong" in its "predictions" (Bardi 2011). Subsequent studies have proved more difficult to dismiss. In 2005, the Millennium Ecosystem Asssessment, which included contributions from more than 1,000 scientists worldwide, concluded that 15 out of 24 crucial ecosystem services were degraded or being used unsustainably, including fresh water, air and water purification, climate regulation, and pest control (MEA 2005). No study of a similar dimension has been conducted since. More recent studies indicate that global development has overstepped three out of nine planetary boundaries (Rockström et al. 2009; WWF 2014, 67).[2] At present, the world is using the resources and waste absorption capacities of 1.6 planets per time unit, and, if present trends continue, this number will rise to two planets by 2030, less than a generation from now (Footprintnetwork 2016).

Even seemingly reassuring news are only warnings in disguise and apparent solutions to environmental problems often merely seem to shift the burden in time and space, thus transferring the costs to the future or to other regions. In 1986, Peter Vitousek, Paul and Anne Ehrlich, and Pamela Matson calculated that all the productivity of lands devoted entirely to human activities amounted to 30.7 percent of terrestrial and 2.2 percent of aquatic net primary production. This calculation referred to biomasss, which provides humans as well as other beings with food, fiber, and fuel. Thus, according to this calculation, almost one-third of everything that grew on land was used strictly for human purposes (Vitousek et al. 1986). It was a result that was bound to alarm anyone whose vision of the world included the continued existence of animals and plants that were not meant to be eaten and of land that was not cultivated, mined, or built over. Indeed, given the highly constructed nature of the concept of human appropriated net primary production (HANPP), the many assumptions necessary to calculate it, and the wide margin of error resulting from the combination of many possible errors in individual sectors, such a number can clearly not be taken at face value. But even Vaclav Smil in his highly critical review of Vitousek et al.'s and several subsequent similar attempts concedes that the human appropriated NPP "does tell us something important [...] about the human claim on the biosphere's primary resource" (Smil 2013, 197). In the latest attempt so far, Krausmann et al. came to a more optimistic result, estimating that unlike the manifold increases in population and industrial output, the HANPP only doubled between 1910 and 2005, rising from 13 percent to 25 percent of the NPP of potential vegetation. Depending on future policies, it is estimated to rise to between 27 and 44 percent. This astounding increase in efficiency in making use of HANPP has only been possible because a of the changing energy regime experienced during this period: as fuel wood and draft animals were replaced by fossil fuels, humanity makes fewer demands on biomass. Given the potentially devastating effect of climate change noted above, this is not so much positive news as it demonstrates the extent to which physical limitations have not been overcome but transferred into future challenges (Krausmann et al. 2013).

Arguably, the most disturbing warning may be based on an analysis of the degree to which the present developmental system has failed to provide even the basic service of sufficient food for all inhabitants of planet Earth even while exploiting its carrying capacity beyond its limits. This record raises the scary question of what will happen when the good times are over and humanity will have to face the challenge of feeding its members with only the diminished capacities of a thoroughly exploited world:

> A freeze frame of the present reveals a civilization at the peak of its power. Within the space of a few decades, humanity will have experienced peak population, peak oil, peak water, peak land, and perhaps even peak crop yields. Yet, even at the height of power, having taken virtual control of the biosphere and having turned the arable Earth into a vast feeding

> lot for our species, it still has not been enough. In what amounts to the greatest perpetual famine in human history, nearly three billion people are without proper food and water [...] Now, with deteriorating conditions of planetary forests, soil, water, oil, climate, and ecosystems, we are expecting to improve the quality of life for billions of more people in the coming decades. There is a flaw with the logic of our expectations – one which may well translate into billions of additional malnourished people by mid-century, or, indeed, could even augur a painful population crash.
>
> (Schade and Pimentel 2010, 254)

This vision is, indeed, alarming, because Schade and Pimentel's reference to the "height of power" relates to the fact that the world has never fed as many people as today using food production which has never been as plentiful as today. Indeed, since the nineteenth century, a combination of improved agricultural methods, better transportation (notably by trains), a substantially strengthened network of small and large food shops, the industrialization of food production, notably the development of canning technology, the mechanization of food production and improved purchasing power of large parts of the populations resulted in tangibly improving diets of many people. Not all of these factors were directly tied to economic growth, but all were in some way related to it. The effect was not only a drastic reduction of hunger and an end to periodic famine but also an increase in population and an unprecedented equalization of food quality and quantity between different classes of society (Fernández-Armesto 2001, 194–205; Hirschfelder 2001, 189–205).

However, for all its achievements in feeding a growing global population, economic growth has failed to solve the problem of malnutrition and hunger on a global scale. Indeed, it can be argued that some aspects have increasingly been counterproductive to this goal. For instance, economic growth has entailed spurring – though not inventing – a form of agriculture that exacerbates soil erosion (Montgomery 2007) and by contributing to food waste. The latter is hardly a negligible aspect of this issue. According to a recent study published by the FAO, at present approximately one-third of all food produced for human consumption gets lost or wasted globally, is allowed to rot, or discarded at some stage of the supply chain between cultivation, storage, processing, transportation, and consumer usage. While waste occurs everywhere, the extent seems to be a function of wealth. It is estimated that consumers in Europe and North America waste 95–115 kg per year while in sub-Saharan Africa and South/Southeast Asia food waste is a mere 6–11 kg per capita and year (FAO 2011, v).

Even more complicated, economic growth has, at the very least, failed to solve and possibly exacerbated the global injustice in global food distribution, strengthening a system in which food was treated like any other marketable good instead of an essential human right to be protected from normal trade exigencies. Unfortunately, there is little indication that these problems of global injustice and inefficiency will be more intelligently and more humanely addressed in the future under conditions of increasing absolute scarcity. In fact, recent developments of "land grabbing" in low-income countries, which were triggered by a spike in food prices in 2008 but also reflect efforts to safeguard food security (especially in the Gulf States) and the replacement of fossil fuels with biofuels (especially in Europe), suggest the opposite (Smaller and Mann 2009; Future Agricultures 2011). Nevertheless, given the shrinking possibilities for economic growth, distributional justice may be humanity's best bet for the future. Clearly, relying on further growth as a solution is not a promising strategy. A different strategy will be required in the coming decades and centuries.

Internal limits: stagnation, prosperity, and equality

However, external limitations arising from the scarcity of resources, sinks, and land are not the only reason why continued economic growth in the future is far from certain. Even independently from these environmental concerns, there are good reasons to question the possibility, but also the desirability of continued growth in the future. In the wake of the recent economic crisis at the end of the first decade of the twenty-first century, several economists have suggested that early industrialized economies have entered a new stage in the history of economic development. Based on the finding that growth rates in those countries with the longest experience with economic growth – the original OECD countries from Western Europe, North America, and Japan – show a sustained decline, these economists voice the concern that early-industrialized countries might soon confront the end of growth. Going back to stagnationist theories of the late 1930s, most prominently formulated by US economist Alvin Hansen, the proponents of this "new secular stagnation hypothesis" predict the demise of relevant growth rates in the coming decades. The reasons discussed for this trend range from diminished long-run growth potentials due to declining technological productivity increases to structural "headwinds" such as stagnant populations, inequality, and public debt. The term "secular stagnation" gained particular prominence through a November 2013 speech by Lawrence Summers, former President of the National Economic Council under President Obama, held at the IMF Forum, but proponents of this end of growth thesis range from Tyler Cowen, author of *The Great Stagnation*, to Robert Gordon who predicts "The Demise of U.S. Economic Growth," to such famous economists as Robert Solow, Paul Krugman, and Thomas Piketty. Even though their view does not yet form a consensus among economists, their arguments have gained considerable traction due to a continuous slack in economic output, in particular in the EU, and due to continuously low real interest rates close to or below zero (Baldwin and Teulings 2014; Cowen 2011; Gordon 2014; Piketty 2014).

In the long term, economic growth might just not develop in the form of the hockey stick currently used as visualization – being stagnant for most of human history and then speeding up very rapidly into an almost vertical rise following a J-curve. Rather, high-income economies seem to be transitioning into a development more adequately described as an S-curve, in which rapid acceleration slows down and eventually comes to a halt. At present, this only applies to those countries with the highest GDP in North America, Japan, and Western Europe, which historically industrialized first, but they seem to be showing a general trend that may eventually also apply to emerging market economies. In what may be a harbinger of upcoming transformations, China's growth rates are already declining rapidly. Thus, humanity may be at a critical juncture that can be seen as the economic version of the demographic transition.

It may, in fact, be at a larger juncture of how it can and has to define socio-economic improvement. After all, economic expansion has brought immense benefits to millions of people in many parts of the world since the early nineteenth century. According to one estimate, approximately 80 percent of people in the world in 1820 lived under material conditions roughly similar to those of the poorest 20 percent of the world population today, which means they could not afford what a US citizens could buy for $1.50 in 2014 (Ravallion 2016, 2–3). Though being poor in 1820 clearly meant something different to people in 1820 and in 2017, there is no reason to overlook the hardship that characterized the lives of average people until recently, the vast majority of whom were peasants, and for whom food security, days without work, a toilet in the building or light after sunset were beyond imagination. To be sure, the lives of many peasants could have been a lot better if the feudal rulers had seen fit to take an interest in the wellbeing of common people, but even with a perfectly even distribution of wealth there simply would not have been enough goods to ensure what, today, we would consider a comfortable life. For most of human history, the lives of most people have been characterized by scarcity, material insecurity, and poverty (cf. e.g. Pelz 2016). During industrialization, the increased energy available through fossil fuels meant that "for the first time in history, mass poverty became unnecessary" (McNeill and McNeill 2003, 232). Besides, quality of life is not defined by quantity alone. The growth of the last two centuries brought benefits qualitatively unavailable even to wealthy people of former times, such as vacation trips to foreign continents, hearing the voices of distant loved ones or having access to specialist doctors (DeLong 2000). Things considered simple today, like reading a book at night while listening to one's favourite music, were unimaginable luxuries to people anywhere even some decades ago. Economic growth has not only been about the mindless craze for more consumer items (although this has increasingly been part of it), but also about socially and culturally rich lives largely free from essential material risks.

However, in recent decades and with already improved living standards, further growth seems to be losing its ability to deliver on its two central promises: to provide for a better future for all parts of society, especially those at the bottom of the economic ladder, and to improve social equality. Both points are complex and interrelated.

To begin with, research in social history and welfare economics indicates that focusing on GDP as a measure of progress and wellbeing has literally been *Mismeasuring Our Lives* (Stiglitz et al. 2010). It has raised cogent doubts regarding the continuing positive relationship (beyond a certain threshold) between further GDP growth and welfare, equality, distribution, happiness, and employment. GDP is problematic, above all, since it is a "blind meter" – a statistical measure that "counts only output while ignoring costs and losses" – so that the deceptive logic of "more is better" leads to problematic results (Philipsen 2015, 2–3). In recent years, evidence from research both in cross-sections of countries and in longitudinal studies of individual countries, intra- and internationally has demonstrated that the welfare-benefits of GDP growth vary considerably over time and tend to diminish with increasing national wealth. Since the late 1960s or 1970s, the costs of growth in industrialized countries (such as an acceleration of life and work rhythms and a resulting increase in stress load, increasing inequality, consumerism, and destroyed environments) have been increasing faster than the benefits (such as the potential for further improvements in living standards, health, and social services), thus making GDP growth increasingly "uneconomic." Increasingly, studies also indicate that, while this may have been different in the past, in industrialized countries of today GDP growth is not indispensable for current and future human flourishing. Instead, other factors, most importantly the degree of equality, are far more important. For example, though per capita GDP in the US virtually tripled between 1950 and 1998, net economic, social, and environmental wealth (measured as the Genuine Progress Indicators or the Index of Sustainable Economic Welfare) barely increased at all in the same period and even declined after the 1980s (Offer 2006; Wilkinson and Pickett 2009).

The relationship between economic growth and socio-economic inequality has been a volatile one. Since the beginning of industrialization, economic growth and the improvement of living standards have been distributed very unevenly. In 1800, the world was not an egalitarian place. Most societies were highly unequal, consisting of a small, rich upper class and a large number of very poor people, mainly peasants. But differences between different parts of the world were small. The living standards of peasants in one part of the world did not differ dramatically from that of colleagues in other places. Industrialization ended this relative similarity of living standards and inequality between various regions surged, depending on whether they were part of the high energy development or not. Thus, the ratio in per capita income between the richest and the poorest regions of the world rose from 5:1 in 1870 to 15:1 in 1950 (Maddison 2001).

Inequality within industrialized countries decreased and remained on a relatively low level between approximately the 1930s and 1980s (Piketty 2014). For what may have been a combination of changes brought about by globalization and financialization, this tendency reversed in the 1990s, as inequalities *within* many countries increased while the rise of millions of people from poverty to various degrees of material comfort in countries like India, Brazil, and, above all, China has caused a decline of inequality *between* countries. In many ways, this is excellent news, as the world is becoming a somewhat more equal place for the first time in 200 years. However, for two reasons this development also gives grounds for concern. One is that the global gini-coefficient remains scandalously high at around 0.7 so that achieving an acceptable level of equality suggests the need for a continuation of the development of the last decades on an incomparably larger scale (Lakner and Milanovic 2013; Bourguignon 2015). This is disturbing since there can be little doubt that the improvements in material living conditions for an immense number of people in China and elsewhere have been the result of unprecedented growth rates, accompanied by large-scale environmental degradation.

The economic development in China, involving extremely high growth rates, resulted in a spectacular reduction of the poverty rate from an estimated 75.5–100 percent in 1978 to 6.7–13.2 percent in 1996 (Yao 2000) or 84.02 percent in 1981 to 13.06 percent in 2008 (Zheng and Kahn 2013). In absolute numbers, this translates into approximately 600 million people who moved out of poverty to gain various levels of material comfort within one generation. While the social value of this improvement is beyond question, it has been accompanied by massive increases in resource-demanding production and concomitant environmental degradation. China became the producer of 40 percent of global clothes; the number of private cars increased from 6.25 million in 2000 to 73.27 million in 2011 which, however, still represented a mere 18 percent of households, far below Western standards; electricity consumption more than tripled within one decade between 2000 and 2011, of which almost 80 percent were produced using coal and another 15 percent using hydropower, often involving environmentally questionable dam projects. Urban pollution increased to the point that in 2006 only 1 percent of the Chinese urban population lived in cities that met the air quality standards in particulate matter of the European Union. Though data have improved since, the air quality remains critical, while water quality has also deteriorated sharply. Rare earths mining and processing, a key component of technologies at the core of a supposedly "green economy," has created its own variety of environmental problems in the areas where they are found, notably in Inner Mongolia and Sichuan. In line with the Environmental Kuznets Curve, a combination of cleaner production processes and increasing public concern about environmental safety have initiated some improvements in fields that respond well to technological solutions and further improvement seems almost certain (Zheng and Kahn 2013). Nevertheless, in view of the limitations of technical fixes and the well-established repercussions of the rebound effect, a continuation of this development until people have reached a Western living standard in China – let alone in the world at large – is near-impossible to imagine (Jackson 2009). The problem of global inequality is thus further exacerbated by ecological crises. This becomes most obvious with regard to climate change: Those regions that have historically been least responsible for ecological destructions are being hit hardest, while those regions that have historically benefited most from industrial growth and are thus most responsible, are much less vulnerable, not least because they have acquired the resources to adapt (Bond 2012; Kenis and Lievens 2015). Some mechanism other than conventional economic growth needs to be found to solve the profound challenge of large-scale poverty and global inequality.

This challenge is highlighted by the contrasting developments at the extreme ends of global income: the very poor in the world have experienced basically no income gains, while those already extremely rich have been becoming even richer. This development has led to the absurd situation that, in 2016, 62 individuals owned as much wealth as the poorer half of the world population, pushing global inequality to a truly grotesque level. If current trends continue, it is bound to exacerbate further in the decades to come (Oxfam 2016).

Meanwhile, another disconcerting aspect of recent developments concerns industrialized countries, whose lower middle classes have also failed to receive a proportionate – or any – share of national income growth, turning them into losers in their societies' accumulation of more wealth (Lakner and Milanovic 2013; Bourguignon 2015). The result has been rising inequality within many countries in North America, Europe or in China. The repercussions are disturbing. For decades, economic growth unfolded according to an "unwritten social contract" within societies both in the capitalist and the communist world, in which poor people accepted inequality as well as economic and political repression because they could hope that they would be better off in the years to come and their children would live even better lives after them. As the material gains of economic growth accrue almost entirely to those at the very top of the income ladder, this contract no longer holds (McNeill, personal communication, June 2016; McNeill 2000, 318; McNeill 2003, 299 and 303). This change lays bare fundamentally political questions of distributional justice, which, as Stephen Macekura and Lorenzo Fioramonti make clear in their contributions to this volume, a seemingly technocratic narrative regarding an a-political economic expansion served to gloss over. This situation can be interpreted as a positive thing, since, in theory, it may force people to face essential questions about what their societies look like, what they would like them to look like and how they could get there. However, it is by no means certain that this will happen.

At the time of writing, in 2016, both Europe and the US witness a rise of populism and the emergence of a disillusioned underclass who translates socio-economic frustration into profound distrust of and hostility against the established classes in their countries (including the press) as well as against those even more vulnerable than them, notably foreign workers and immigrants, that foreshadows a serious danger to societal cohesion and to democracies in general.

Thus, it is in the interest of safeguarding the global environmental life-support system as well as democratic conditions to find a viable and convincing strategy of improving living standards and distributional justice both between and within countries. When economic growth is no longer capable of maintaining social peace and democracy, the establishment of a credible alternative, one that promises a comfortable, satisfying, and just life for the future, is taking on new urgency. In fact, it may be even more than democratic structures in a narrow sense which are at stake. If Ian Morris (2015) is right, and our moral values of egalitarianism and human rights are the result of a societal order based on fossil fuels (and economic growth as its most visible outcome), the stakes for finding an ethically acceptable alternative could hardly be higher.

This challenge is clearly intimidating, if not downright scary. So far, the spectacular improvements in living conditions of the last century have been tied to economic growth and increased resource exploitation. There is no tangible precedence to fall back and little experience to rely on when engaging in a policy of maintaining the benefits of growth without paying the social and environmental price. It is like flying blind, and understandably policy makers, economists, and citizens are reluctant – if not downright petrified – to face this ordeal or even to acknowledge that it is necessary. It is this inability to reconcile the triple goals of providing good living standards, a just distribution of wealth, and the protection of the environmental basis of human lives, which has haunted policy makers, NGOs, and generally people around the world for decades (Borowy 2016) and which forms the background for the discussions described in this volume.

Beyond growth? Historical perspectives and ongoing debates

Given the sweeping global acceptance of the pursuit of growth as a key policy goal it is easy to forget that not only the reality of economic expansion, but also the adoption of growth as a key category of economic and public discourse have been comparatively recent phenomena. This lack of historical awareness deprives the present discourse of crucial dimensions of what economic growth has or has not meant to different people at different times, both conceptually and as tangible lived experience. Without this dimension, discussants on all sides risk substituting ideology for analysis, and assumptions for critical appraisal.

Undoubtedly, economic growth remains the central goal of most policy makers and social groups, as it holds out the promise of increasing (or maintaining) employment, wellbeing, and quality of life, and never in history did so many people enjoy the benefits derived from economic growth. The global financial and economic crisis, which began in 2008, has strengthened economic growth as the corner stone and purpose of politics all around the world. At the same time, however, the vision of a world beyond economic growth is becoming more compelling. At present, advocates of growth are confronted with the strongest opposition in decades, and the dissatisfaction with growth and its problematic effects is spreading among activists, such as the indignados in Spain or the occupy movement in several countries, but increasingly also among general populations, among policy makers, and in academia (Cassiers 2015; Costanza et al. 2014; Klein 2014; Latouche 2010). Alarmed by declining growth rates in industrialized countries, climate change, and rising socio-economic inequalities, among other challenges, more and more people demand to look for alternatives beyond growth. In the political realm, these discussions are not only reflected in considerations of alternative indicators to replace GDP, but also in the creation of various governmental or parliamentary agencies focusing on sustainability, welfare, and the problems of economic growth. The Sustainable Devleopment Commission in the UK, the Stiglitz Commission in France, or the Enquete Commission of the German Bundestag are cases in point. These trends have revived more radical calls dating back to the 1970s promoting concepts of "sustainable development," "green growth," or even "post-growth" or "degrowth." While not welcoming stagnation, they call for a social-ecological transformation of industrialized societies and a fundamental shift of developmental models that overcomes the growth imperative, but disagree as to how radically to oppose GDP growth (Cassiers 2015; D'Alisa et al. 2015; Muraca 2014; Stiglitz et al. 2010).

However, so far these current debates about sustainability, post-growth, or degrowth lack a thorough historical perspective. Both proponents and opponents of growth tend to have a one-dimensional view of growth, ranging between idolizing and demonizing. At present, both the search for new statistical measures "beyond GDP" and the lively discussions about political alternatives to growth-centered development are fundamentally ahistorical in that they largely ignore and underestimate the long-term historical roots, path dependencies, and power relations of the growth paradigm. They also tend to take the negative effect of economic growth for granted without engaging in a serious debate about the real benefits it has brought to many people in various ways, for which no alternative strategy is similarly well established.

This volume seeks to address the historical background of issues that stand at the core of ongoing discussions about alternative future economic developments. The purpose is to reveal and analyze the path-dependencies underlying key elements of the existing growth-oriented socio-economic system, conceptually as well as practically. Addressing different aspects of the history of economic growth as a central and near-ubiquitous tenet of developmental strategies, the eight original chapters in this volume contribute a new perspective to these ongoing debates. The aim has been to historicize seemingly self-evident aspects of growth and to provide a critical analysis both of the conceptual evolution of the idea and of the tangible reality of growth and of the ways it has affected the lives of populations at different times and places.

The contributions follow three different avenues of enquiry: five chapters (Dale, Fressoz/Bonneuil, Westermann, Macekura, Fioramonti) take a deconstructivist approach that focuses on understanding the origins of the growth paradigm and growth-oriented policies, societies, and cultures; one chapter

(Borowy) focuses on the practical experience of growth and its real-life repercussions; and two chapters (Caradonna, Muraca/Schmelzer) study alternatives to the growth paradigm. This uneven distribution of approaches with a clear dominance of conceptual questions was not originally intended, but resulted from successes and failures in our search for authors. While we initially regretted this imbalance of focus, we have come to accept it as a sign of where the historical discourse on matters related to economic growth presently stands. In the second decade of the twenty-first century, as an increasing awareness of the unsustainability of the existing growth paradigm is competing with a continuing political commitment to growth – or an unwillingness to embrace a promising but untested and unpredictable alternative – the focus of historical research evidently lies on deconstructing this concept. By recapitulating its genesis, historians analyze what narrative structures or knowledge systems about the economy and about processes of growth were produced at different times and in different social or geographical spaces.

Gareth Dale explores the origins of the growth paradigm. Analyzing key texts of ancient civilizations, which have been suggested as early examples of growth-based thinking, he finds important building blocks, but not a fully developed growth paradigm: Bronze Age Mesopotamia, while developing agriculture and a sophisticated trade infrastructure, did not conceptualize economic growth; India's Mauryan Empire pursued a policy of increasing production, the purpose was to fill the royal household rather than to increase an abstract "economy"; and Ibn Khaldun, foremost thinker in fourteenth-century Maghreb, much like his peers in Mauryan India centuries earlier, saw social changes in wealth as an essentially cyclical process. Instead, the emergence of a coherent growth paradigm required a set of developments which took place in Northwestern Europe, notably Britain, between the sixteenth and eighteenth century. They included the spread of the mechanized clock and the concomitant change in the concept of time as an objective, quantifiable entity; the reconceptualization of land as a tradable and fillable commodity; the maritime-colonial expansion with its unleashing of new material dynamics; the scientific revolution; and, in close connection to all of the above, the rise of capitalism. The conceptual groundwork was supplied by a series of philosophers and thinkers, often with a Puritan background. Thus, Francis Bacon spread the ideas of materialism, science, and the accumulation of knowledge. Gabriel Plattes and Robert Boyle developed early forms of cornucopian thinking; and Isaac Newton and others pioneered new constructions of nature as a law-governed mechanism, thus shaping the conception of "the economy" as a law-governed mechanism later promoted by economic thinkers. Advancing knowledge in mathematics and celestial mechanics gave rise to the expectation that human behavior and social developments would similarly be determined by laws of nature and could, therefore, be understood, quantified, and predicted like clockwork. Gradually, these developments laid the groundwork for the conceptualization of an "economy" as a discrete sphere of social life, which, true to the emerging capitalist creed in accumulation and monetary return on investment, was subject to law-governed dynamics of growth.

The chapter by Jean-Baptiste Fressoz and Christoph Bonneuil continues where Dale's chapter leaves off, exploring the subsequent changes in scientific and public concepts which lead to the widespread acceptance of the growth paradigm. As key to this development, they highlight in particular the conceptual separation of the economy from its fundamental reliance on natural resources. This separation was a long process. Early economic thinkers, notably physiocrats and classical political economists, firmly rooted in an agricultural world, had taken such a connection for granted, and consequently conceputalized an organic world in which different economic sectors and actors competed for limited land, resources, and energy, especially wood. It was only by shifting to coal and thus – aided by geological experts – by tapping into age-old layers of lithosphere, that the Earth was turned from a place with a finite surface into a multidimensional, seemingly endless reservoir of fossil resources. This change allowed a subsequent shift in economics to neoclassical theory, away from a focus on factors of production to one on marginal utility, which separated economics from the material world. Prices and production functions became closed systems without connection to exogenous factors (meteorology, disasters, wars, etc.). This conceptual dematerialization of the economy continued during the Depression of the 1930s, when the end of the gold standard and Keynesianism concentrated attention on abstract money as a key economic factor, and the introduction of GDP statistics in the 1940s. These developments established the dematerialized economy as a closed and commodified system that could be conceived as growing indefinitely, unaffected by natural constraints, dependent only on the good guardianship of economic experts. The subsequent rise of the political growth paradigm obscured underlying transformations, notably the extent to which growth consisted of a "petrolization" of the world and the extent to which it relied on the development of unequal ecological exchanges on the global scale. Even the ecological critique of growth was met with visions of a dematerialized economy and with efforts to devise market instruments for environmental policy. In the process, the environment was re-introduced into economic thinking, albeit in radically transformed shape as marketable "natural capital," where limits appeared as promising investment opportunities.

Andrea Westermann analyzes a late episode in the debates regarding the relationship between economic expansion and the natural world, before a successful decoupling of the vision of sustained economic growth from material resource consumption had taken place. More particularly, she focuses on the relationship between growth and monetary metals. In the nineteenth century, most Western countries used a bimetallic standard. Mexico, China, and India used a silver standard, and only Great Britain had adopted a gold standard. Subsequent choices depended largely on mineral findings within the country's sphere of influence. Changes in mining and usage destabilized the ratio of value between the two classic monetary metals, leading to a proliferation of expert commissions, asked to study the situation and provide recommendations regarding future domestic coinage policies. Similar to the question of coal, geological expertise entered discussions about economic decision, bringing geological, planetary scales into contact with human, societal scales. Westerman focuses her case study on Eduard Suess, a professor of geology from Vienna who undertook a study which aimed at an estimate of global gold reserves. It was an ambitious project, but Suess was confident that a reasonably reliable estimate would be possible so that responsible and long-term monetary decisions would have to take these finding into account. He came to the conclusion that gold reserves, especially in Africa, would be used up in the nearer future and large reserves no longer existed, representing a natural limit to the growth of trade and economic performance. Because he predicted a decline in the future world production of gold, which would be insufficient to meet the monetary demands for global trade, he recommended a currency based on silver. However, most countries rejected his long-term, geological scale of arguing, relying instead on short-term political considerations. By the end of the nineteenth century, most countries had established the gold standard, a form of currency system which spurred free trade and cosmopolitanism. Before the First World War, the 35 national economies operating a gold standard accounted for 70 percent of world trade. However, this peak was short-lived. After the Great Depression, the countries gradually gave up the system of a mineral-based currency altogether, thus opening up the possibility of infinite monetary growth.

Lorenzo Fioramonti's chapter highlights the overwhelming dominance of GDP as a driver of political and social decisions, as demonstrated recently by austerity policies. He explains the inadequacy and, in some instances, the absurdity of GDP as a measurement of economic performance, let alone of societal wellbeing: GDP equates economic growth with market transactions regardless of social utility; it excludes household and informal work, often a substantial if not the most important component of a national economy; it measures flows, ignoring stocks and leading to unsustainable consumption of non-renewable resources and incentivizing short-term policy planning; and it disregards both the value of the natural resources consumed in the economic process and the economic costs of pollution and environmental degradation. Fioramonti demonstrates how the specific definition of GDP resulted from its historical origins in the context of the Depression of the 1930s, the prevalence of Keynesian policy interventionism, and of the Second World War. Indeed, the GDP proved a major advantage in generating revenues for the war and propelling large-scale consumption in the post-war period. Through aid policies in post-war Europe and, later, in the global South, GDP was exported to the rest of the world, soon taken up and propagated by the United Nations and the OECD. During the Cold War, the US government sought to discredit the USSR by reassessing Soviet economic performance through a GDP lens, while the Soviet Union tried, for a while, to compete with its own metric before shifting to a similar form of statistics in the 1980s. Over the years, the GDP has been severely criticized and a series of alternatives have been suggested, including the Measure of Economic Welfare, the Genuine Progress Indicator, or the Better Life Index. However, nothing has been able to dethrone GDP, which draws its persistent power from a combination of support from industry, whose pollution remains uncounted, unwillingness by policy makers to change to a metric that makes their economy look worse and reveals the political nature of wealth and income distribution, and by simple path dependency. Nevertheless, Fioramonti insists, a change in metric would be highly desirable to provide a more realistic and meaningful representation of the world, ideally a "dashboard" of indicators capable of integrating the key dimensions and human and ecological wellbeing.

Stephen Macekura connects the concepts of "economic growth" and "development" and analyzes how they co-evolved in North America and Europe in the twentieth century, changing meaning and definitions in the process. Though it is difficult to pinpoint an exact beginning of development thinking, early traces can be found in the works of David Hume and Adam Smith, it is interesting to note that the word "development" entered the English language in the mid-nineteenth century to describe colonial improvement strategies in different parts of the empire, frequently aimed at attracting and maintaining the allegiance of settlers in far-away colonies through promises of state-financed infrastructure projects. At the same time, the term gained connotations of racial and cultural superiority, as several colonial powers linked ideas of social evaluation and imperial legitimacy with hygiene, irrigation schemes, local education, and public education. By the 1920s, economists in the US, Great Britain, and other wealthy countries shifted attention from isolated factors to the entirety of "the national economy," developing the concept of GDP. Despite disagreements on what it should include, achieving high GNP growth rates quickly became a practical policy goal and powerful symbol. This number gave birth to the concept of economic growth. It was readily accepted: for governments it came with the advantage that it allowed reconstructing old conflict over distributional justice in allegedly a-political economic terms, and during a period of increasing production and consumption, the concept made perfect sense to those who experienced it and to those who wanted it. Economists in the Soviet Union developed their own measurement system, similarly predicated on the idea of growth. As leaders of countries of the global South readily endorsed the goal of GDP-growth, Western economists sought to identify the factors underlying economic growth in order to devise strategies able to trigger its "take-off" in the non-Western world. In addition, economists cooperated with social scientists to identify key aspects of life that would spur economic growth and focused on "modernization," which linked social and cultural traits with the economy and would ease "traditional" society into the "modern" world. By the 1960s, criticism of an uncritical pursuit of "development" and economic growth increased, provoked by their increasingly obvious environmental and social problems. However, as of today they proved less influential than the rise of neoliberalism in the 1980s, which shifted the development goals from governmental policies to growth based on free trade, liberalization of capital controls, privatization of state goods, and redirecting state fiscal policy from providing social security towards structuring increased market activity. As these strategies appear inadequate to meet the challenges of the twenty-first century, Macekura argues, the future of development and growth seem unclear.

Iris Borowy analyzes whether economic growth is good for health – a question, she points out, which is not only academic but has tangible policy implications. In search of evidence for the relation between economic growth and health, both proponents and opponents of growth-based policies turn to historical data, using historical findings and their interpretation as arguments for present-day policy decisions. The immediate impact of economic growth, she argues, seems to have had potentially contradictory effects: periods both of economic growth and economic recessions have at different times coincided with either improving or deteriorating health outcomes. The overall long-term effects in industrialized countries has clearly been positive. More income has provided opportunities to buy better health provisions both for individuals (better food, clothing, housing) and societies (sanitation, public health services, public education). This effect has not been automatic, but more income has provided possibilities which many societies have used. Today's populations, therefore, are the health beneficiaries of past economic growth. However, in the entanglements of global history, these benefits have come at the price of health damages suffered by people living at other times and in other places. A crucial factor for economic growth and health improvements in Europe – with Britain as its economic vanguard – was the depopulation of North America, resulting from the death of millions of Native Americans caused by old world diseases, coerced labour, forced removals, and massacres. This example of gigantic health deteriorations, stretching over a continent, proved beneficial for the health of people in Europe, where emigration reduced food and epidemiological pressure on those that remained, and by supplying "ghost acres" which European economies could incorporate. In addition, the depopulated continent provided land and slavery provided labor for sugar and cotton, which fed British workers and industrial processes. The tea, which functioned as a vehicle of intake of sugar calories feeding British workers, was bought at the price of opium addiction among people in China. Furthermore, the dependence of industrialization and unprecedented economic growth on fossil fuels means that its record also includes the health of all people today and in the future who are and will be affected by climate change. Thus, while economic growth has enabled many people to live far longer and healthier lives than earlier generations, these benefits have been achieved at the price of health damages of other people, living at other times and places, whose lives have been cut short or burdened with contingent disability and disease.

Shifting the focus to alternatives to the growth paradigm, Jeremy Caradonna provides an overview of the recent history of the concept of sustainability. The controversy whether environmental sustainability and economic growth are compatible or inherently contradictory reaches back to the beginnings of modern environmentalism. It became particularly virulent in the debates and controversies leading up to the concept of sustainable development developed in United Nation reports such as the *World Conservation Strategy* (1980), *Our Common Future* (1987), and *Agenda 21* (1992). Sustainable development is often regarded, both in politics and by scholars, as a departure from the status quo of industrial growth and as the most promising alternative to the growth paradigm. Caradonna disagrees with this interpretation. He argues that, while environmenally more sensitive, this idea was still largely shaped by neoclassical economics and conventional Westernized and GDP-oriented development thinking geared toward increasing material consumption and the integration of localized economies into monetized international markets. Although there were many people involved in sustainable development who criticized growth for depleting resources, generating pollution and destructive technologies, facilitating urbanization, unraveling traditional societies, and creating the conditions for unsustainable population growth, their voices were largely drowned out in the 1980s. This was aided by the ambivalence toward economic growth in key texts, which were based on the conviction that, given the political will, economic expansion, social justice, and ecological sustainability could be brought into harmony. While economic growth was still controversial in the milieu of 1980s-era sustainable development, by the 2010s it had developed into an adversary concept of many environmentalists, as exemplified in the degrowth movement. Characterizing the relationship between economic growth and sustainable development as an "incompatible couple," Caradonna concludes that while originally not intended as such, the norm of sustainability ended up benefitting the status quo and essentially failed to change the course of unsustainable global development.

Deepening the discussion of alternatives, in the final chapter of the volume, Barbara Muraca and Matthias Schmelzer trace the origins of what has recently been discussed as "sustainable degrowth." While discussions critical of growth reach as far back as the origins of growth thinking, they became particularly pronounced in the 1970s, which saw the emergence of the ideological precursors to current degrowth discussions. Muraca and Schmelzer highlight the importance of the various cultural contexts, which formed the backgrounds for the different evolutions of debates critical of economic growth. Degrowth can be understood as the most radical strand of a broader debate in recent years that publicly criticizes economic growth and the related processes of ecological destruction and increasing global inequalities, while at the same time proposing and demanding alternatives. Next to being an intellectual and academic position, degrowth is also a social movement, which has spread since the 2000s from Southern Europe to other industrialized regions and aims at the development of more equitable and sustainable lifestyles through the planned contraction of the current mode of economic activity, while also challenging its ideological legitimation (productivism, economism, developmentalism). While discussions critical of growth reach as far back as the origins of growth thinking, they became particularly pronounced in the 1970s in the context of the protests of 1968 and the emerging environmental movements. This was also the context of the ideological precursors to current degrowth discussions. Today's degrowth movement sees its origins in the Southern European strand of growth-related critique, as the current literature on the "sources" of degrowth shows. However, other streams of critique of and alternatives to growth have been very influential in what today can be considered an international degrowth movement. While also analyzing and discussing the Southern European sources of degrowth, in their chapter Muraca and Schmelzer enlarge the perspective by adding two other, partly overlapping variants of radical growth critique: a specific Anglo-American stream and a German-speaking one. As the chapter shows, the degrowth movement goes beyond the traditional critique of growth which addresses monetary (critique of GDP as a measure of wellbeing) and material (environmentalists' perspective on planetary boundaries and climate change) growth. Instead, its criticism addresses the structural and cultural function that growth plays for modern, capitalist societies and envisions a radical transformation of basic societal institution.

This volume presents an early contribution of the historical discipline to the question of economic development and human wellbeing of the future. However, much needs to be done and many questions can only be addressed insufficiently so far. Some of them concern the origins of growth thinking: Most existing research takes a top-down approach, focusing on philosophers, experts, governments, and organizations, suggesting that the pursuit of economic growth was a product of a ploy by the powerful. Too little is known, so far, about how the growth paradigm has resonated with existing ideas and wishes of populations in different parts of the world. A discussion of more bottom-up perspectives, including anthropological and/or psychological aspects would be helpful in this regard.

Similarly, more research attention is desirable for the unclear or ambivalent record of past economic growth. To what extent has growth, measured as GDP growth or otherwise, been beneficial or harmful and for whom (country and region, people's position in systems of domination such as class, *race*, or gender)? Again, current debates on how economic growth played out tend to disregard the bottom-up perspective by either uncritically assuming a positive effect (the classical modernization narrative) or ignoring possible positive effects (parts of the degrowth narrative). What have been short-term and long-term effects, positive and negative beyond glorification and demonization? To what extent can this experience be projected into the future? How can past reactions to limits – both external and internal – serve as a blueprint for the future? And which "past" is meant and how do lessons change when different selections of the "past" are chosen?

Finally, our understanding of historical alternatives to growth societies is underdeveloped, to say the least. Thus case studies of alternative approaches to economic wellbeing would be helpful to understand the alternatives available to us in the present and the future. Discussions would be aided by a better knowledge about the historical contexts in which alternatives emerged and how they related both to competing concepts and to lived realities of the time.

Various historical approaches could unearth historical experiences beyond growth that could inform the currently ongoing search for social structures of non-growing or degrowth societies. Are there historical examples of non-growing societies that conform to our standards of liberty and justice, and which social and institutional arrangements were important? What can we learn from historical processes of economic decline? Which historical experiments with alternative economies (i.e. the cooperative movement, bottom-up processes of economic coordination) worked well or failed and for what reasons? What were past utopias about non-growing societies that could inspire current discussions and which historical opportunities in this regard were not realized? While *History of the Future of Economic Growth* cannot answer all these questions, we hope that it will contribute to a critical discussion of these questions among scholars and in the general public.

Notes

1 While GNP measures the output generated by a country's enterprises (whether physically located domestically or abroad), GDP measures all the output produced within the borders of a country (including the output produced by foreign firms). Until the 1960s, GNP was more widely used, but GDP has since become the standard measure. Furthermore, national income differs from GDP in various ways, most importantly in so far as GDP subtracts the depreciation of capital. See also the contribution of Lorenzo Fioramonti in this volume.

2 Regarding biodiversity loss, climate change, and the nitrogen cycle, the other boundaries relating to atmospheric aerosol loading, chemical pollution, ocean acidification, stratospheric ozone depletion, the phosphorus cycle, global fresh water use, and changes in land use.

Bibliography

Baldwin, Richard and Coen Teulings, eds. 2014. *Secular Stagnation: Facts, Causes and Cures.* London: CEPR Press.

Bardi, Ugo. 2011. *The Limits to Growth Revisited.* New York: Springer.

Bond, Patrick. 2012. *Politics of Climate Justice: Paralysis Above, Movement Below.* Scottsville, South Africa: University of Kwazulu Natal Press.

Borowy, Iris. Forthcoming 2016. "Sustainable Development in Brundtland and beyond: How (Not) to Reconcile Material Wealth, Environmental Limits and Just Distribution," in: Estelita Vaz, Arnaldo Melo, and Cristina Joanaz de Melo (eds.), *Environmental History in the Making*. Springer.

Bourguignon, François. 2015. *The Globalization of Inequality.* Princeton: Princeton University Press.

Cassiers, Isabelle, ed. 2015. *Redefining Prosperity.* New York: Routledge.

Chakravarty, Debalina, Shyamasree Dasgupta and Joyashree Roy. 2013. "Rebound Effect: How Much to Worry?" *Current Opinion in Environmental Sustainanbility* 5: 216–228.

Costanza, Robert, Ida Kubiszewski, Enrico Giovannini, Hunter Lovins, Jacqueline McGlade, Kate E. Pickett, Kristín Vala Ragnarsdóttir, Debra Roberts, Roberto De Vogli, and Richard Wilkinson. 2014. "Development: Time to Leave GDP behind." *Nature* 505(7483): 283–285.

Cowen, Tyler. 2011. *The Great Stagnation: How America Ate All The Low-Hanging Fruit of Modern History, Got Sick, and Will (Eventually) Feel Better.* New York: Dutton Adult.

Crosby, Alfred. 2006. *Children of the Sun. A History of Humanity's Unappeasable Appetite for Energy.* New York: Norton.

D'Alisa, Giacomo, Federico Demaria, and Giorgos Kallis, eds. 2015. *Degrowth: A Vocabulary for a New Era.* London and New York: Routledge.

Dale, Gareth, Manu V. Mathai, and Jose Puppim De Oliveira, eds. 2016. *Green Growth: Ideology, Political Economy and the Alternatives.* London: Zed Books.

DeLong, Bradford. 2000. "Cornupcopia: The Pace of Economic Growth in the Twentieth Century." NBER Working Paper Series, Working Paper 7602: 21. Accessed November 12, 2012. http://www.nber.org/papers/w7602.pdf.

Dinda, Soumyananda. 2004. "Environmental Kuznets Curve Hypothesis: A Survey." *Ecological Economics* 49: 431–455.

Dutz, Mark and Siddharta Sharma. 2012. Green Growth, Technology and Innovation. Policy Research Working Paper 5932. Washington: World Bank.

Exner, Andreas, Peter Fleissner, and Lukas Kranzl. 2013. *Land and Resource Scarcity: Capitalism, Struggle and Well-Being in a World Without Fossil Fuels.* London: Routledge.

FAO. 2011. *Global Food Losses and Food Waste.* Rome: FAO.

Fernández-Armesto, Felipe. 2001. *Near a Thousand Tables.* New York: Simon & Schuster.

Fioramonti, Lorenzo. 2013. *Gross Domestic Problem: The Politics Behind the World's Most Powerful Number.* London: Zed Books.

Footprintnetwork. 2016. "World Footprint. " Accessed June 26, 2016. http://www.footprintnetwork.org/en/index.php/GFN/page/world_footprint.

Future Agricultures. 2011. "Land Grabbing in Africa and the New Politics of Food." Policy Brief 041, June 2011.

Gillingham, Kenneth, David Rapson, and Gernot Wagner. 2014. "The Rebound Effect and Energy Efficiency Policy." RFF Discussion Paper 14–39. Washington: Resources for the Future.

Gordon, Robert J. 2014. "The Demise of U.S. Economic Growth: Restatement, Rebuttal, and Reflections." Working Paper. National Bureau of Economic Research, February 2014. Accessed June 27, 2016. http://www.nber.org/papers/w19895.

Hirschfelder, Gunther. 2001. *Europäische Esskultur. Geschichte der Ernährung von der Steinzeit bis heute.* Frankfurt: Campus Verlag.

IPCC (International Panel on Climate Change) 2014. *Impacts, Adaptation and Vulnerability.* Cambridge: Cambridge University Press.

Jackson, Tim. 2009. *Prosperity without Growth: Economics for a Finite Planet.* London: Earthscan, 2009.

Kenis, Anneleen and Matthias Lievens. 2015. *The Limits of the Green Economy: From Re-Inventing Capitalism to Re-Politicising the Present.* New York: Routledge.

Klein, Naomi. 2014. *This Changes Everything: Capitalism vs. the Climate.* New York: Simon & Schuster.

Krausmann, Fridolin, Karl-Heinz Erb, Simone Gingrich *et al.* 2013. "Global Human Appropriation of Net Primary Production Doubled in the 20th Century." *PNAS* 110(25): 10324–10329.

Lakner, Christoph and Branko Milanovic. 2013. "Global Income Distribution: From the Fall of the Berlin Wall to the Great Recession." World Bank Policy Research Working Paper 6719.

Latouche, Serge. 2010. *Farewell to Growth*. Cambridge: Polity.

Maddison, Angus 2001. *The World Economy. A millennial perspective*. Paris: OECD.

Malm, Andreas. 2016. *Fossil Capital: The Rise of Steam Power and the Roots of Global Warming*. London: Verso.

McNeill, John R. 2000. *Something New Under the Sun: An Environmental History of the Twentieth-Century World*. New York: W.W. Norton.

McNeill, John R. 2002. "Earth, Wind, Water and Fire: Resource Exploitation in the Twentieth Century." *Global Dialogue* 4(1): 11–19.

McNeill, John R. and William McNeill. 2003. *The Human Web*. New York: W.W. Norton.

MEA (Millennium Ecosystem Assessment). 2005. *Current State & Trends*. Accessed June 28, 2016. http://millenniumassessment.org/en/Condition.html.

Montgomery, David. 2007. *Dirt*. Berkeley: University of California Press, 2007.

Morris, Ian. 2015. *Foragers, Farmers and Fossil Fuels*. Princeton: Princeton University Press.

Muraca, Barbara. 2014. *Gut leben: Eine Gesellschaft jenseits des Wachstums*. Berlin: Wagenbach.

Myers, Samuel, and Aaron Bernstein. 2011. "The Coming Health Crisis: Indirect Effects of Global Climate Change." *F1000 Biology Reports* 3(3).

OECD. 2008. *Environmental Outlook to 2030*. Paris: OECD.

Offer, Avner. 2006. *The Challenge of Affluence: Self-Control and Well-Being in the United States and Britain since 1950*. Oxford: Oxford University Press.

Oxfam. 2016. *An Economy for the 1%*. Oxford: Oxfam International.

Paech, Niko. 2012. *Liberation from Excess: The Road to a Post-Growth Economy*. München: Oekom.

Pelz, William. 2016. *A People's History of Modern Europe*. London: Pluto Press.

Peters, Glen P., Gregg Marland, Corinne Le Quéré, Thomas Boden, Josep G. Canadell, and Michael R. Raupach. 2012. "Rapid Growth in CO2 Emissions after the 2008–2009 Global Financial Crisis." *Nature Climate Change* 2(1): 2–4.

Pfister, Christian. 2010. "The '1950s Syndrome' and the Transition from a Slow-going to a Rapid Loss of Global Sustainability." In *The Turning Points of Environmental History*, edited by Frank Uekoetter, 90–118. Pittsburgh: University of Pittsburgh Press.

Philipsen, Dirk. 2015. *The Little Big Number: How GDP Came to Rule the World and What to Do about It*. Princeton: Princeton University Press.

Piketty, Thomas. 2014. *Capital in the Twenty-First Century*. Cambridge: Harvard University Press.

Polimeni, John, Kozo Mayumi, Mario Giampietro and Blake Alcott. 2009. *The Myth of Resource Efficiency*. Milton Park: Routledge.

Ravallion, Martin. 2016. *The Economics of Poverty. History, Measurement and Policy*. Oxford: Oxford University Press.

Rockström, Johan, Will Steffen, Kevin Noone, Åsa Persson, F. Stuart Chapin, Eric F. Lambin, Timothy M. Lenton, *et al.* 2009. "A Safe Operating Space for Humanity." *Nature* 461: 472–475.

Santarius, Tilman. 2015. *Der Rebound-Effekt. Ökonomische, psychische und soziale Herausforderungen der Entkopplung von Energieverbrauch und Wirtschaftswachstum*. Marburg: Metropolis.

Schade, Carleton and David Pimentel. 2010. "Population crash: prospects for famine in the twenty-first century." *Environment, Development and Sustainability* 12: 245–262

Schmelzer, Matthias. 2016. *The Hegemony of Growth. The OECD and the Making of the Economic Growth Paradigm*. Cambridge: Cambridge University Press.

Smaller, Carin and Howard Mann. 2009. *A Thirst for Distant Lands: Foreign investment in agricultural land and water*. Winnipeg: International Institute for Sustainable Development.

Smil, Vaclav. 2013. *Harvesting the Biosphere*. Cambridge, Mass.: MIT Press.

Speich-Chassé, Daniel. 2013. *Die Erfindung des Bruttosozialprodukts: Globale Ungleichheit in der Wissensgeschichte der Ökonomie*. Göttingen: Vandenhoeck & Ruprecht.

Stagl, Sigrid. 1999. "Delinking economic growth from environmental degradation? A literature survey on the environmental Kuznets curve hypothesis." Working Paper No.6, Series of the Research Focus Growth and Employment in Europe: Sustainability and Competitiveness. Wien: Wirtschaftsuniversität Wien.

Steffen, Will, Paul Crutzen, and John McNeill. 2007. "The Anthropocene: Are Humans now Overwhelming the Great Forces of Nature?" *Ambio: A Journal of the Human Environment* 36(8): 614–621.

Steffen, Will, Wendy Broadgate, Lisa Deutsch, Owen Gaffney, and Cornelia Ludwig. 2015. "The Trajectory of the Anthropocene: The Great Acceleration." *The Anthropocene Review* January 16: 1–18.

Stern, Nicholas. 2007. *The Economics of Climate Change: The Stern Review*. Cambridge: Cambridge University Press.

Stiglitz, Joseph, Amartya Sen, and Jean-Paul Fitoussi. 2010. *Mismeasuring Our Lives: Why GDP Doesn't Add Up*. New York: New Press.

Sorrell, Steve. 2009. "Jevons' Paradox revisited: The evidence for backfire from improved energy efficiency." *Energy Policy* 37(4): 1456–1469.

UKERC (UK Energy Research Centre). 2008. The Macroeconomic Rebound Effect and the UK Economy. UKERC/WP/ESM/2008/001. London: UKERC.

UNEP Global Environmental Alert Service 2014 Sand: Rarer than One Thinks, March 2014. Accessed October 14, 2016. http://www.unep.org/pdf/UNEP_GEAS_March_2014.pdf.

Vitousek, Peter M., Paul R. Ehrlich, Anne H. Ehrlich, and Pamela Matson. 1986. "Human Appropriation of the Products of Photosynthesis." *Bioscience* 36: 368–373.

Wilkinson, Richard and Kate Pickett. 2009. *The Spirit Level: Why Equality is Better for Everyone*. London: Allen Lane.

World Bank. 1992. *World Development Report*. New York: Oxford University Press.

World Bank. 2014. *Turn down the Heat*. Washington: World Bank Group.

WWF. 2014. *Living Planet Report*. Gland: WWF International.

Yao, Shujie. 2000. "Economic Development and Poverty Reduction in China over 20 Years of Reforms." *Economic Development and Cultural Change* 48(3): 447–474.

Zheng, Siqi and Matthew Kahn. 2013. "Understanding China's Urban Pollution Dynamics." *Journal of Economic Literature* 51(3): 731–772.

1 Seventeenth-century origins of the growth paradigm

Gareth Dale

The growth paradigm, as I understand the term, refers to the idea that 'the economy' exists as an identifiable sphere of society, that it possesses an inherent tendency to grow, that its growth is imperative, continuous (even, essentially, limitless), and that growth is an acknowledged social goal and a fundamental social good – even indeed the principal remedy for a catalogue of social ills.[1] One may question one or the other element of this formulation but there is little doubt that a set of ideas of this type has been profoundly influential, across the world and for a long time. This invites the question: how long? When did the growth paradigm come into being? Out of what materials was it fashioned and by whom?

These are the questions explored in this chapter. It begins by surveying a sample of civilizations, including ancient Mesopotamia, India's Mauryan Empire, Tang-dynasty China, and fourteenth-century Maghreb, in each case parsing documents and other evidence that provide insight into behavioral and ideological phenomena that, *prima facie*, resemble the modern growth paradigm. In each case, it is suggested, the differences outweigh similarities. The chapter then moves on to propose that, in close connection with the rise of capitalism and Europe's colonial land grab, a set of socio-economic, cultural, and ideological changes conducive to the growth paradigm arose during the middle of the last millennium – roughly speaking, the sixteenth through eighteenth centuries. It charts the advent of a new conception of time: abstract, infinite, and uniform, locked to the metronome of capital investment and increasingly connected to a social concern with quantification. It then examines the interconnections between three major developments that were unfolding in seventeenth-century western Europe – maritime-colonial expansion, the scientific revolution, and the rise of capitalism (including, crucially, the ascendancy of the 'market paradigm' in economic thought) – and explores their relationship to early scientific economics and to the 'Eden project': the crusade to create paradise on Earth by means of 'improvement' and colonial plantation. These processes put wind in the sails of the idea of Progress and, simultaneously, facilitated the discursive construction of 'the economy' as an entity subject to law-governed dynamics of growth. Clearly, in this short chapter I cannot analyze these transformations in detail. Instead, I shall attempt to sketch them in broad brush strokes.

From Mesopotamia to the Maghreb

If one searches for evidence of the growth paradigm in documents from the ancient civilizations one comes away empty-handed. Consider for example Bronze Age Mesopotamia. One could be forgiven for thinking that all ingredients were present necessary for the emergence of something that would at least bear a resemblance to the growth paradigm. There were rulers who drove their subjects to work harder, as immortalized in the Epic of Gilgamesh (Sedlacek 2011, 21). There were markets and trading, acquisitively minded individuals and the ability to amass wealth and to pass it on to one's heirs. There were sophisticated accounting techniques and a form of money, enabling different types of wealth to be rendered commensurable and their dimensions measured. Technological and scientific genius were evidently not in short supply. The Mesopotamians are credited with inventing agriculture, animal domestication and the seeder plough, glass, and of course the wheel (for pottery, later for chariots), as well as complex writing and arithmetic (to keep inventories of the secular and religious elite's possessions). They came up with the concept of zero, and the minute. They were, arguably, the first to construct towns, not to mention countless inventions and innovations in irrigation and sanitation techniques, in architecture (the arch, column, and dome), and in politics (the state, including two of its basic forms: the city state and the empire). This was in many respects a bustling and innovative society – but of the growth paradigm? No sign.

Skip forward to what the philosopher Karl Jaspers designated the Axial Age, the period from 800 to 200 BC that witnessed, more or less simultaneously in China, India, Greece, and Persia, a flourishing of philosophical thought – broadly defined as the application of principles of systematic reasoned inquiry to the great questions of existence. What was it that occasioned this momentous eruption of critical inquiry? Greater literacy was one factor. Another, argues Richard Seaford (2013), was the spread of coinage (in India, China, and Greece), and markets. These developments, David Graeber conjectures (2011, 237–239), fostered a "habit of rational calculation, of measuring inputs and outputs, means and ends" which found an echo in a "new spirit of rational inquiry."

Something of this spirit can be seen for example in documents from Greece and India in the fifth century BC. In India, the age of Buddha saw thriving urban economies, with merchant classes trading the agricultural and artisanal surplus, and the rise of the Mauryan Empire, initially under the leadership of Chandragupta Maurya. The Mauryan monarchy maintained a colossal standing army and a vast bureaucracy that enabled it to sponsor a major expansionary drive, constructing irrigation projects, founding new settlements, and encouraging *sudras* to settle as farmers on state-granted land (Thapar 1987; Harman 1999, 49–50). Chandragupta's advisor and minister, Kautilya, is thought to be the main author of a remarkable text, the *Arthashastra*.[2] Although normally translated as "manual of statecraft," in that it consists of advice to rulers, a more literal translation would be "the royal road to wealth." "Artha" means worldly success in terms of power and wealth, and the *Arthashastra* is restricted to a special aspect of it: the enhancement of royal power and revenue (Habib and Jha 2004, 46). Much of it is devoted to spelling out the techniques of maintaining the royal household (such as revenue collection, and accounting), and certain passages have an arrestingly modern resonance. Kautilya (1962, 76) advises that the ruler should "facilitate mining operations," "encourage manufactures," promote the "exploitation of forest wealth, [...] construct highways both on land and on water, ... and plan markets." In agriculture, he should confiscate lands that are left uncultivated and should "give to cultivators only such farms and concessions as will replenish the treasury and avoid denuding it" (Kautilya 1962, 75). Some passages are concerned with productivity. In mineral extraction, the ruler is advised that the best mines are those that "can be exploited with least expenditure of resources, yielding valuable products and commanding easy communications" (Kautilya 1962, 130). Other passages offer a guide as to which activities bring prosperity to the exchequer and which represent a drain. The former category includes "reward for enterprise, suppression of crimes, economy in administration, prosperity of harvest, growth of trade, conquest of adversity and crisis, reduction of tax-remissions, inflow of precious metals." The latter includes defalcation and individual trading with state funds, "investment," and "extravagance" (Kautilya 1962, 86).

One should think twice before taking the *Arthashastra* at face value. It is not always easy to ascertain which passages are descriptive and which are normative or strategic. Some were added by later authors, and translations from the Sanskrit may have introduced a modern gloss. Is it nonetheless a ground-breaking text? Certainly, its recommendation of the single-minded pursuit of "artha" broke dramatically with traditional Brahminic codes (Habib and Jha 2004, 46, 156). But it is not an exemplar of the growth paradigm. That investment is categorized as a drain on the exchequer, next to the misappropriation of funds, is perhaps a hint of this, and so too is Kautilya's suspicion of merchants and his vehement opposition to permitting prices to rise and fall in line with supply and demand (Boesche 2002, 99). These are not in themselves necessarily antithetical to the growth paradigm but they are symptomatic of a fundamental point: the acquisitive projects that *Arthashastra* describes belong strictly to the royal household (not to "the economy" in general), and its purpose is specific: to ensure the royal treasury is full to the brim. Neither did *Arthashastra* advocate a theory of progress, or anything remotely resembling one. Instead, Kautilya's theory of history is cyclical. Kingdoms come and kingdoms go; they undulate continuously and ceaselessly through three phases – decline, stability, advance – and so on *ad infinitum* (Boesche 2002).

Following the passing of its most celebrated leader, Ashoka, the Mauryan Empire entered terminal decline. Ashoka had elevated Buddhism to a state religion and sponsored its missionary outreach. In China under the Tang dynasty (seventh to ninth centuries AD), Buddhist monasteries established themselves as dynamic centers of economic activity. A striking instance was the "Three Levels" movement. Its monasteries presided over a remarkable process of accumulation, in so-called *Inexhaustible Storehouses.* Their "inexhaustible" wealth, the sinologist Jacques Gernet explains (1995, 169), referred to that portion of the monastery's assets that was dedicated to the provision of credit at interest. The historical records tell of astonishing scenes, as devotees vied over who could donate the most to the Inexhaustible Storehouses. From across the empire they streamed to the central headquarters in Chang'an (Xi'an) – then the biggest city in the world – at the gates of which they would deposit cartloads of silks and silver (Hubbard 2001, 154, 198). The fortune was disbursed in the form of alms, harvest loans, and investment in the monastery's religious infrastructure and commercial enterprises.

Buddhist communities, with the Three Levels sect to the fore, "introduced a form of modern capitalism into China," Gernet argues (1995, 228), with "consecrated property, constituted by an accumulation of offerings and commercial revenues." Graeber (2011, 264–268) makes a similar claim, linking it directly to the growth paradigm. The Inexhaustible Storehouses, he argues, manifested "the quintessential capitalist imperative of continual growth; the Treasuries had to expand, since according to Mahayana doctrine, genuine liberation would not be possible until the whole world embraced the Dharma." This was "something very much like capitalism," in that it embodied "the need for constant expansion. Everything – even charity – was an opportunity to proselytize; the Dharma had to grow, ultimately, to encompass everyone and everything, in order to effect the salvation of all living beings." But how comparable to the capitalist growth imperative is the commitment, however fervent, to the growth of dharma? It is worth recalling that the bulk of the wealth contained in the Inexhaustible Storehouses consisted of offerings of the faithful (Gernet 1995, 211). Their gifts were a monetary form of confession: giving absolved the karmic debts one incurs in this life and in previous lives (Hubbard 2001). The term *inexhaustible*, writes Gernet (1995, 214), "far from signifying an endless accumulation of interests, refers to the psychological mechanism that motivates the gifts. A gift invites a gift in return, and giving is contagious." This was the secret of the sect's success. Charitable disbursements "constituted a form of investment that was highly advantageous" because they elicited "new offerings in turn" (Gernet 1995, 217). Quite unlike a capitalist economy geared to infinite accumulation and the imperative of continuous growth, this was an economy of gift-giving based on the principle of tithing (Hubbard 2001, 153). (Tithes are used by churches for the pursuit of religious goals, including self-preservation and propagation.) Thus, the function of the Inexhaustible Storehouses was to gather together small donations into a common treasury, the better to redistribute the goods received by channeling them into charitable works, liturgical services and above all the infrastructure of religious establishments themselves: stupas, temples, and sanctuaries, the casting of bells and statues, and so on (Gernet 1995, 214). Whereas the modern growth paradigm holds that accumulation proceeds "inexhaustibly" on the basis of continuous increases in productive capacity and corresponding increases in consumption, the inexhaustibility of the storehouses consisted in something else: first and foremost in their ability to persuade followers to part with goods, and secondarily in revenues from interest payments. It was, Gernet concedes (1995, 93), concerned more with returns on loans, and with acquisitions, "than with production." Its purpose was not the "accumulation of goods" but principally "their redistribution and circulation." It sought to expand not profits but expenditure – expenditure geared above all to ensuring the continuity and prosperity of the storehouses and the sect itself (Gernet 1995, 217).

The economic efflorescence of Tang China resumed under the Song. The Song dynasty's celebrated culture of invention and innovation contributed to surges in productivity growth in agriculture and manufacturing. This same period, from the seventh to the thirteenth century, also saw significant economic growth in the Arab and Islamic world. Not unlike China, the Abbasid caliphate unified a vast sweep of relatively rich territories, from Persia to the Maghreb (Harris 2003, 28). The caliphates of the southern Mediterranean presided over intensive commercial and martial activity, with organized slave raiding deep into sub-Saharan Africa, luxury trade routes stretching eastward to China and Japan, and a sophisticated financial sector. A succession of dynastic regimes in the Maghreb – the Fatimids and Almoravids, the Almohad caliphate and the Marinids – gained economic and cultural dynamism from their crossroads location: between mountain tribes and lowland towns, between Andalusia and the Atlas, the Sahara and the sea. It was into this world that a pioneer of economic growth theory, Ibn Khaldun (1332–1406), was born.

Ibn Khaldun's *Muqaddimah*, his *Prolegomena* to the history of the world, includes a sophisticated analysis of growth dynamics. Prosperity, he argues (1950, 84), rests on "the intensity of human efforts and the search for gain," as well as an increase in population, which affords greater scope for cooperative labor and specialization. Rising prosperity generates a virtuous circle, based upon private and public consumption creating a stimulus that feeds into the wider economy through multiplier effects. The development of new wants leads to "the creation of new industries and services," and the rising level of demand and incomes contributes to "a rise in the income and expenditure of the whole community" (Ibn Khaldun 1950, 93–95). Together, these stimuli give rise to further increases in prosperity and economic activity, in a self-reinforcing process.

In his theorization of growth, Ibn Khaldun forms an exception to the thought of his age, but it is one that proves the rule. For one thing, his ideas on growth did not become hegemonic. For another, they were embedded in a cyclical theory of development, in which population and commercial expansion synergize with benevolent rule and minimal taxation to yield an upward curve, following which, "at the end of two generations, the dynasty approaches the limit of its natural life. At that time, civilization has reached the limit of its abundance and growth" (Ibn Khaldun 1950, 33). With prosperity comes a demanding citizenry, and luxury, which saps the martial spirit. Together, these put upward pressure on taxation, which suppresses trade. As living standards rise and former fighters "begin to enjoy more than the bare necessities, the effect will be to breed in them a desire for repose and tranquility" (Ibn Khaldun 1950, 87, 117–118). Ibn Khaldun's thesis on growth is equally a thesis on decline, and is nested within a historical-sociological account of the movement from agriculture to industry, which, in turn, rests upon a Platonic philosophy of civilizational rise and fall. As an analysis of growth dynamics it is strikingly sophisticated for its times, but nowhere does it exhibit the sense of linear historical progression that was essential to the growth paradigm as it gained shape in the following centuries.

Clockwork rhythms

In sifting the ingredients from which the growth paradigm came to be constituted, one could do worse than begin with the transformation in the social construction of time and space. The middle of the second millennium witnessed a tendential shift from 'enchanted' time and territory to measurable, linear, gridded conceptions. A potent early lever of the transformation of time was the invention (by a Buddhist monk in Tang China) and diffusion (in fourteenth-century urban Europe) of the mechanical clock. To Europeans of the early modern period the presence and sophistication of church and town clocks came to symbolize the level of a country's mechanical capacity and material well-being (Heller 1996). Striking equal hours, they facilitated the measurement and quantification of time, and its re-conception in linear and abstract terms. In the words of Lewis Mumford (in Gimpel 1976, 169), mechanical clocks "brought a new regularity into the life of the workman and the merchant. The bells of the clock tower almost defined urban existence. Time-keeping passed into time-saving and time-accounting and time-rationing." When one thinks of time, he continues (in Mathai 2013, 23), "not as a sequence of experiences, but as a collection of hours, minutes and seconds," it can be added, rationed, and accounted, enabling it to assume the character "of an enclosed space: it could be divided, it could be filled up, it could even be expanded by the invention of labor-saving instruments." Time slipped, so to speak, from the numinous to the numerical.

As with time, so with space. In the sixteenth to eighteenth centuries the development of the sciences of geometry and cartography, which were experiencing a renaissance courtesy of the European "voyages of discovery" and associated colonial ventures, encouraged the tendency to see territory as emptiable and fillable, and space as abstract, infinite, and apprehendable in the form of quantitative data. Roman law had conjured the possibility of absolute property and thus the imposition of hard spatial demarcations, a grammar of territoriality that was radically deepened and universalized by the revolutions of commerce and capital (Sack 1986, 63). With land defined as an alienable and commodity-like substance, a revised conception of nature, as existing principally to serve the purposes of landowners and as ontologically external to human beings, lay at hand. Landed property became fully exchangeable with, and even substitutable for, money. In seventeenth-century England, observes Moses Finley (1953, 268), when Lord Nottingham "ruled that 'The principal right of the mortgagee is to the money, and his right to the land is only as security for the money,'" the idea of collateral came to prominence. "Implicit in that transformation was a conception of property whereby everything is readily translated into money." This paralleled a re-evaluation of productivity, summarized by Jason Moore (2014, 204), as a shift from a characteristically feudal orientation to the productivity of land to an emphasis on labor productivity.

The more that economic life came to be geared to value expansion, the more its processes and elements (living standards, for instance) became subject to a regime of quantification. Of course, in previous civilizations, labor, society, and nature had been subordinated in certain respects to the calculations and quantitative measures of the ruling institutions, but none exhibited this to anything like the degree found in capitalist society. Modern accounting – the measurement of business activity utilizing double-entry book-keeping in a codified and systematic form – gave greater definition to the abstraction of profit and therewith the concept of capital, and at the same time, in its separation of enterprise and capitalist, contributed to the rationalization and depersonalization of business activity (Nussbaum 2002, 160). Accounting formed a vital element in the process of apprehending labor as a commodity. It formed part of the mechanism whereby, as Catchpowle, Cooper, and Wright put it (2004, 1041–1042),

> the various heterogeneous forms of human labour are turned into quanta of value; in which concrete labour is dominated by "abstract labour" in Marx's terms, and in which the production of various useful things to satisfy various specific human needs is dominated not by the satisfaction of those needs but becomes a means to the pursuit of the accumulation of capital.

When land, labor-power, and raw materials are, as a rule, subject to sale and purchase, the same authors continue, "the subjection of the labour process to complete calculability" becomes possible, and competition enforces the subordination of "all aspects of the labour process to calculation, with the aim of profit, of capital accumulation." Accountancy, in short, pervades the capitalist realm, for it is in accounting that

> the penetration of the calculating, quantifying intrusions of those intent on extracting a surplus, reaches its fullest extent. It seeps, through the process of ever deepening commodification, into the heart of social life; insidiously, not without irrepressible opposition, but profoundly and systematically.

In similar idiom, Moore (2014, 204) has described the sixteenth-century construction of regimes of abstract social labor and what he terms "abstract social nature" (a set of spatio-temporal processes that simplify, standardize, and map the world "in service to the quantitative expansion of abstract labor"). The regimes of abstract social labor and abstract social nature nourished and were sustained by the scientific revolution, by advances in cartography and "processes of standardization, quantification [and] mathematicization," in the absence of which, value simply could not exist (2014, 200). Capitalism, he concludes (2014, 235), was remaking reality "in its own image and according to its own rhythms."

The conceptualization of time as an abstract, infinite continuum was a prerequisite for the supplanting of pre-existing conceptions of economic affairs by a new imaginary of economic life, as existing in a state of "continuous growth and cultivation" (Düppe, 2011, 88–89). The systematic measurement of abstract objectified time, moreover, was a necessary (albeit not sufficient) factor enabling the emergence of economic growth as a systemic social goal – for growth can only be rigorously expressed as units of value. "Only if output can be unambiguously ranked along the ordinal value index can there seriously be said to be more of anything," Philip Mirowski (1985, 93) points out. In the England of 1600 the growth paradigm could hardly have existed, for, as Paul Slack observes (2015, 2), no one knew the nation's territory, population or income. But by 1700,

> all these had been calculated within acceptable margins of error and were widely known; they could be related to one another, so that average incomes per head and the distribution of population and taxable wealth could be determined; and they could be compared with data from other countries and from the past, where they were available. New information enabled England's improvement, its material progress, to be measured.

The generalization of value relations and monetary calculation, with correlative codes of abstract space and time and of quantification, measurement, and standardization, exerted a profound impact within mid-second millennium West European thought upon the conceptualization of rational behavior and helps to explain its tendencies to scientific thinking, abstraction, and self-reflexivity (Sack 1986). In the early-modern period some of the ideological clothing of these transformations was provided by Protestantism; in particular Puritanism, with its moral imperatives of dutiful labor and accumulation and its miserly calendar. As early as 1597, the Puritan English clergyman William Perkins (in Münch 1993, 55) bracketed Catholics together with rogues, beggars, and vagabonds on the grounds that they added 52 saints' days to the 52 Sabbaths appointed to God and thereby condemned the flock to spend over a quarter of the year "in rest and idleness." Puritan time was mechanical and constant and relentlessly reified. Time is currency, wrote the Presbyterian preacher Richard Baxter in *A Christian Directory*, with an audience of merchants and agrarian improvers in his mind's eye, "so use every minute of it as a most precious thing, and spend it wholly in the way of duty." Remember, he admonished (in Thompson 1967, 87), "how gainful the Redeeming of Time is [...] in Merchandize, or any trading; in husbandry or any gaining course, we use to say of a man that hath grown rich by it, that he hath made use of his Time." "Time is money," chimed Ben Franklin, setting the seal on the transition from the old perception of time as a divine offering to the new view: time set to the metronome of capital investment.

The diffusion of the mechanical clock, the conception of abstract time and space, and modern science marched in lockstep. Carolyn Merchant (1980, 42, 288) contrasts Western Europe in 1500 – its economic life largely subsistence oriented, and governed by seasonal cycles; the cosmos imagined organically, as geocentric, finite, and cyclical; bodies assumed not to move "unless activated, either by an inherent organic mover or a 'contrary to nature' superimposed 'force'" – with the same region two centuries later when those realities and their accompanying conceptions had been turned upside down. The economies of the Netherlands and Britain were pulsing to the accumulation of capital; Copernicus and Galileo had shown the universe to be heliocentric and potentially infinite; Galileo and Newton had revealed nature to be a law-governed mechanism, with bodies assumed to move like clockwork: uniformly unless hindered.

Gardening Eden, planting Empire

In the Middle Ages, ideas of social and scientific progress, a culture of agricultural improvement, and the spirit of inventiveness, of knowledge seeking, and a searching, empiricist approach to knowledge acquisition, were not unknown. In Renaissance Europe, interest in social change, in skeptical systematic inquiry and humanistic values blossomed. Nonetheless, ideas of scientific progress, and especially of *social* progress, remained weakly developed until the sixteenth and seventeenth centuries. That juncture witnessed a growing confidence in the propensity of human thought to progressively develop its understanding of the cosmos. In England, Francis Bacon championed materialism and experimental science, together with the notion that knowledge advances progressively. His writings are noteworthy for their use of the term 'growth' equally in relation to flora and knowledge. In the Netherlands, René Descartes presented the accumulation of knowledge as the logical result of the application of rational thought (Friedman 2006, 25). By the time of Bacon and Descartes, beliefs in the progressiveness of science and the propensity of the stock of knowledge to continually grow were beginning to become commonsensical.

The context within which this occurred was formed by Europe's maritime-colonial expansion, the rise of capitalism, and the scientific revolution. At a general level, the voyages in space accelerated the sense that the times were changing. As described in *History of the East and West Indies* by Diderot and his fellow *philosophes*, the first major history of the European assault on the world:

> There has never been any event which has had more impact on the human race in general and for Europeans in particular as that of the discovery of the new world, and the passage to the Indies around the Cape of Good Hope. It was then that a commercial revolution began, a revolution in the balance of power, and in the customs, the industries and the government of every nation. It was through this event that men in the most distant lands were linked by new relationships and new needs. The produce of equatorial regions was consumed in polar climes. The industrial products of the north were transported to the south; the textiles of the Orient became the luxuries of Westerners; and everywhere men mutually exchanged their opinions, their laws, their customs, their illnesses and their medicines, their virtues and their vices. Everything changed, *and will go on changing*
>
> (in Outram 1995, 57, emphasis added).

The question of what to make of the peoples encountered in the New World, and what implications followed from their property arrangements, stimulated a new conceptualization of the human story as a history of social progress. From the vantage point of the colonialists, if "they" were at the primitive stage, had "we" once occupied it too? If so, how did "we" get from there to here? In the imagination of philosophers such as Thomas Hobbes and John Locke, imbued with a capitalist attitude to "improvement" and an imperialist attitude to other peoples, "America" figured as postlapsarian Nature, its "savage" inhabitants exhibiting the rudimentary form taken by human society within a state of nature. With the original stage of humanity envisioned as primitive and contemptible, the conceptual environment was created for the liberal-imperialist "four stages" model of progress to emerge, one that fused formal universalism with the assumption of European command and control. It is no accident that the European voyages of discovery were hailed by Bernard de Fontenelle (in 1686) as proof of Europe's technical genius. Fontenelle has been hailed as the first to have decisively broken with the idea of historical development as cyclical and to have posited instead the doctrine that human knowledge and wisdom progresses historically, as if by natural law, in an ongoing and unlimited way, evidenced by events documented in the past and observable in the present (Nisbet 2009). His *The Origin of Fables* sketched the rudiments of a stadial progress theory. In the first ages of the world, human beings must have been plunged in the same depths of ignorance and barbarism as "the Kaffirs, the Lapps, or the Iroquois today," but just as, say, the Greeks had evolved into rational beings, so too, given time and tutelage, will the Native Americans (Meek 1976, 27).

Colonization of the New World not only spurred European philosophers to elaborate a racialized Progress narrative, it also unleashed material dynamics.

The flow of silver plundered from the Americas provided the specie for Europe's trade with the East, helping Dutch and English colonial corporations to monopoly positions in the trade with India. In the West, the American colonies enabled European capital to benefit from an "extraordinary ecological bounty," and their plantation slave complexes were used as laboratories of capitalist experimentation (Pomeranz 1997, 113; Anievas and Nisancioglu 2013). Slave labor was the foundation of the Atlantic colonial trade, providing England's economy with an injection of demand that was at times indispensable – for instance after 1650 when intra-European commerce was in the doldrums (Anievas and Nisancioglu 2015, chapter 5). As Marx put it (in Miéville 2006, 199),

> the great revolutions that took place in trade in the sixteenth and seventeen centuries, along with the geographical discoveries of that epoch, and which rapidly advanced the development of commercial capital, were a major moment in promoting the transition from the feudal to the capitalist mode of production. The sudden expansion of the world-market, the multiplication of commodities in circulation, the competition among the European nations for the seizure of Asiatic products and American treasures, the colonial system, all made a fundamental contribution towards shattering the feudal barriers to production.

As feudal relations began to buckle in England and the Netherlands, peasants increasingly produced for the market. A prolonged process of rural social differentiation saw the emergence of the triadic class structure of landlord, tenant farmer (yeoman), and laborer. Direct control of agricultural production was increasingly in the hands of yeomen whose engagement in competitive struggle to produce for the market encouraged them to specialize and invest profits in new leases and productivity improvement (Wood 1984). In France too, capitalist forces were making themselves felt already by the sixteenth century: the Wars of Religion expedited processes of primitive accumulation, with poorer peasants uprooted from the land, resulting in large-scale proletarianization and the revaluation of land as capital (Heller 1996).

Where capitalist relations took root, a heightened consciousness of material progress and the language of 'improvement' could be discerned. Across north-western Europe ancient texts on husbandry were rediscovered and new scientific works were published – an outpouring of "how to" manuals by (often Puritan) agronomical reformers. In mid-sixteenth century France, "writers were stressing the virtues of diligence and industry which enabled agriculture to flourish and the need to encourage commerce, provided it did not lead to an outflow of treasure" (Slack 2015, 2). In Elizabethan and Cromwellian England the language of improvement gained ubiquity, and the deployment of new methods of production and the availability of new products made the connections between the advancement of science and changes in everyday life plain to see. It was here, and now, that the idea of improvement – applied to a bundle of processes, including land enclosures, technological inventions and innovations, and rises in living standards – first "became a fundamental part of the national culture" (Slack 2015, 1). Manuals for agricultural improvement multiplied: between 1600 and 1660 their rate of output doubled, a rate of increase rivalled only by publications on mathematics (McNally 1988, 39). The dates are significant. For it was in bourgeois-revolutionary times that the most bourgeois-evolutionary of injunctions, that to improve the condition of the nation requires gradual and piecemeal change based on material wealth and the well-being that it engenders, first flowered. What one historian calls the "revolutionary moment" of improvement was England in the 1640s and 1650s, "when 'inventions and improvements' became a catchphrase summarizing what useful knowledge and economic advance could be expected to achieve" (Slack 2015, 7). An emblematic example was the publication of *The English Improver*, written in 1649 by Walter Blith, a Parliamentary soldier, and its later edition, *The English Improver Improved.* It promised its dedicatee, Oliver Cromwell, that by means of enclosure and technical progress all lands can be improved: some by two or three times, others by as much as five or six, "and many under a Tennfould, yea Some under a Twentyfould Improvement." The title page of the 1652 edition graphically illustrates the nexus of improvement, imperialism, and science. It depicts the swords of the New Model Army being turned into the ploughshares of Providential abundance, and the English Republican turned into the surveyor and improver of the world. Science, alloyed to private property and Puritan diligence, would make the Earth abundant once more (Drayton 2000, 52).

In multiple ways, colonial and capitalist improvement was bound up with transformations in science and technology. Agrarian improvement was fueled by scientific discoveries. These, in turn, were stimulated by the navigational and martial demands of explorers, freebooters, and conquerors. European settlers in the New World not only exterminated and subjugated "new" peoples but turned to objectifying and cataloguing them, drawing comparisons with their own kind and "improving" them. Early in the process, some English settlers were hesitant to take pride in technological advantage, seeing in it a form of idolatry, but this quickly changed. Colonists came to emphasize the differences between their culture and customs, in particular their cultivation of abstract sciences such as chemistry, and those of indigenous peoples. The latter were apprehended as objects of improvement, a paternal intervention that would, it was assumed, redound to their good as well as that of the colonizers. Thus, by the middle of the seventeenth century, "the English had constructed an image of the Indian that fits the modern stereotype: the native as pre-scientific and technologically deficient" (Chaplin 2001, 38, 322). Defining their American exploits as "improvement," English settlers were linking their colonial handiwork to the same process in the mother country.

The sharpest minds of the seventeenth century were alive to the connections between overseas exploration, the accumulation of knowledge, the invention of technology, and the promise of a new Eden – the myth of a paradise that, interweaving European, Arabic, and Indian philosophical traditions with the Middle Eastern idea of the botanical garden, had become central to Christian eschatology. Again, Bacon is the exemplar. According to Christopher Hill (1972, 164),

> he shared the hope of alchemists and magical writers, that the abundance of Eden might be recreated on earth, in Bacon's case by experiment, mechanical skill, and intense cooperative effort. Sin for him was largely the product of ignorance and poverty. Labour, the curse of fallen man, might be the means whereby he would rise again.

Before the English revolution of the 1640s, Bacon was virtually unknown, but in its aftermath his popularity soared in intellectual circles. He has been fairly described as "the most important philosophical and scientific authority of the Puritan Revolution," and Baconianism as "the official philosophy of the Revolution" (McNally 1988, 36). His ideas informed a new image of human progress, one which, although divinely ordained, nevertheless "operates within the world of natural forces, *including human agency*" (Friedman 2006, 34).

Bacon felt that the voyages of "discovery" were opening up new possibilities, and a new agenda, for natural philosophy. Certainly, his *New Organon* (2000 [1620]), a paean to what he called "the growth of science" (and elsewhere in the same pamphlet the "growth of the sciences," the "growth of natural philosophy," etc.) posited a causal relationship between the discovery of new territories and the progressive accumulation of knowledge. Knowledge, being spread far and wide, should be "sought out and gathered in (as if by agents and merchants) from all sides" (Bacon, in Langman 2011, 63). Once gathered, scientific procedure requires data to be "numbered, weighed, measured and defined" (Bacon, in McNally 1988, 37–38). In *New Atlantis*, he presented this epistemology – knowledge conceived as a colossal sum of items of natural-historical information, to be collected by "agents" and accumulated at metropolitan hubs – in the form of literary utopia. The novel follows a group of voyaging Europeans who chance upon a technologically superior culture, Bensalem. The Bensalemian mission is to accumulate natural-scientific knowledge in order to improve human livelihood – or, as one Bensalemite informs the European tyros, to acquire "knowledge of causes, and secret motions of things; and the enlarging of the bounds of human empire, to the effecting of all things possible" (Bacon 1627, 31).

In several respects, Bacon's thinking meshed with emergent bourgeois norms and attitudes. One was his preference for the empirical experience of the scientist and artisan over the dogmatic authority of the priest and university teacher, and, relatedly, his contempt for the economic role of the nobility (McNally 1988, 38). Another was his mechanistic philosophy, on which more below. A third was his vision of conquering nature through empire and *vice versa.* To claim that the idea of dominating nature began with Bacon would be hyperbole. But he and his followers (such as Samuel Hartlib, Robert Boyle, Locke), more overtly than anyone hitherto, injected imperial strains into the ideal of subduing the earth. Colonization, Sarah Irving has shown (2008, 1), was central to their project of restoring "man's empire over nature." They saw the colonies as "a repository of information about the natural world," with America as a potential new Garden of Eden. For them, recovering knowledge of nature was a religious mission. Acting on behalf of God and mankind, English farmers and planters would make the earth fruitful again. (Indeed, "plantation" evolved in its usage in a way that simultaneously denoted the mastery of nature and of empire. It had previously referred to the "act of planting," with "planting" a synonym of husbandry. In the sixteenth century it came to mean colonial settlement, before migrating to its eighteenth-century meaning: a large estate, typically in regions of colonial settlement, dedicated to the cultivation of cash crops.)

Bacon established a justification for plantations in terms of their "improving," "civilizing" thrust. He cleared a path for the likes of Hartlib, Boyle, Locke and William Petty, all of whom turned the concern to improve domestic "waste land" in the interest of enhancing agricultural and royal revenue into a justification for settling and improving the colonial "waste lands." But they faced a new political context: the English Civil War. It was triggered by events in Ireland – the anti-colonial rebellion of 1641 – and it also ended there, as Cromwell's armies invaded, channeling revolutionary fervor into an exceptionally brutal conquest. Cromwell's colonization of Ireland sealed the success of the English revolution, blocking the path to feudal-absolutist reaction, but in the process it infused England's existing imperial disposition with the revolutionary energy and Puritan zeal of the victorious Parliamentary party.

Whereas Bacon died before the Commonwealth, Hartlib was closely associated with it, and with Cromwell. He carried forward the Baconian project to record and accumulate natural-scientific knowledge, with its Puritan tendency to focus upon *useful* (and hence *economic*) knowledge. He was an impresario of projects and ideas for social and educational reform, agrarian improvement, and colonial plantation. To these ends, he corresponded indefatigably with a roster of largely English and German intellectuals, almost all of whom were Puritan by creed or inclination – including his friends Blith, Boyle, Petty, and Gabriel Plattes. Hartlib's famous 'Circle' of correspondents evolved into the 'Invisible College' and later (*sans* Hartlib) into the Royal Society, England's academy of science. Members of the Circle shared a belief that humankind, in the Fall, had lost agricultural knowledge and technique and that their restoration is a prerequisite for the recreation of our Edenic dominion over nature.

As the Hartlibian project of reestablishing Eden advanced, two of its march routes are relevant to my argument. One led from improvement via plenitude to free trade, the other to empire. The first of these begins with the idea that the universe is essentially fecund and cornucopian. It was common to a number of philosophers discussed in this chapter (Descartes, for example) but was held especially fervently by members of the Hartlib Circle, notably Plattes and

Boyle. They were emphatic that cornucopia had to be unlocked by industry. (In their argot: Eden requires Adam.) In 1639, Plattes published *A Discovery of Infinite Treasure* which aimed to prove that the earth is "capable of producing an infinite amount of agricultural goods if husbandry were properly improved" (Finkelstein 2000, 213). The case rested upon the beliefs that improvements in agricultural technique are key to ending "povertie and beggerie," and that the soil can be endlessly regenerated thanks to the infinite and inexhaustible supply of fertilizing substances such as "limestone and chalke" (Plattes 1974). Deploying the metaphor of the hive – as Bacon had before him – Plattes argued that people, like bees, should work diligently and for the good of society, and that when as a result their population increases, "so by their industry their food may increase, even as twenty Hives of Bees being all industrious do live as well, as if there were but one in the same garden." For Boyle, similarly, the Earth is a storehouse stocked for the benefit of man. Nature's "grand business," he wrote (in Wood 1984, 58), is to constitute and manage man's "Productions, as to furnish him with Necessaries, Accommodations, and Pleasures," but man has to play his part in the grand cornucopian scheme, and to this end God has furnished him with "a multiplicity of desires" in order that he be industrious enough to complete the conquest of nature (in the sense of knowing it as well as profiting from it).

Cornucopian thinking of the Plattes–Boyle variety provided inspiration to proto-liberal economists, too. Nicholas Barbon, for example, is noteworthy for his theorization of the infinite potential of supply and social demand. The wealth of a country, he maintained, is "perpetual, and never to be consumed" (cited in Finkelstein 2000, 212). For the "Beasts of the Earth, Fowls of the Air, and Fishes of the Sea, Naturally Increase: There is Every Year a New Spring and Autumn, which produceth a New Stock of Plants and Fruits. And the Minerals of the Earth are Unexhaustable." Labor, Barbon was asserting, can create infinite wealth from the limited but renewable – and in this sense infinite – resources of the earth. Given the infinitude of supply, trade is vital in order to carry away the surplus production, and if it does not, the "Labour and Industry of the People" will grind to a halt – for trade is "like the blood through the heart, which by its motion giveth life and growth to the rest of the Body" (in Finkelstein 2000, 207). In this way, Barbon's cosmology of plenitude underwrote a precociously liberal theory of free trade – the links between an embryonic growth paradigm and market paradigm were coming into view.

The Eden Project's other route was toward empire. According to Irving (2008, 49–52), Hartlib et al. "brought together the idea of Adam's dominion over nature with colonization." Having earlier focused on a utopian drive for social reform, the quest to improve nature now sallied forth under the flag of empire and state-building. It was hitched to the colonial project, with scientific advance pursued under Anglo-Protestant colors, and the goals of knowledge accumulation linked to those of imperial expansion. No one was clearer about the program than Boyle. A leading colonialist of the day, his family had been awarded vast tracts of expropriated Irish lands, the revenues from which helped to establish the Royal Society (Linebaugh and Rediker 2012, 123), and it was he who "first put forward a programmatic suggestion for the way in which man's dominion over nature could be restored by fostering a relationship between naturalists and the English colonies" (Irving 2008, 21). In his prospectus, England would function as the world's Bensalem, accumulating natural data drawn from its colonies and applying it to technological development. Nature *was* America. The Earth and the colonies were storehouses for the benefit of England and Europe, with improvement and science pointing the way to prosperity and colonial expansion. But how did these ingredients combine together to bring forth the growth paradigm? In this, I suggest in the next section, the theses and contradictions of scientific economics played a crucial role.

Homo economicus imperiali

As discussed in the previous section, agrarian-capitalist "improvement" and its theologically intoxicated transplantation to colonial locations generated new data and new demands for detailed knowledge. (How profitable is this tract of land? How can it be made more profitable?) It was a mission that demanded a new type of natural philosophy, one that could appear to be "exact, quantifiable and objective" (Irving 2008, 66). Just such a philosophy was coming into being in the seventeenth century, thanks to the likes of Bacon, Hobbes, Galileo, Newton, Boyle, and Descartes. Unlike an ontology – prevalent for example during the Renaissance – that postulates the world as a living macrocosm pervaded by active forces, these thinkers modeled the world as a mechanism: an ordered system composed of modular components connected in a causal nexus in which motion, originally supplied by God, is transmitted in regular temporal sequences from part to part, and as such is accessible to deductive reasoning and mathematical computation (Merchant 1980; Leiss 1994).

The recourse, by Bacon and company, to mechanistic metaphors in their explanations of society and nature arguably relates to their social environment, as an age of manufacture, captivated by the mechanisms of clocks and other devices, met with a new economic system based on abstract labor and exchange-value, with money rendering individual acts commensurable and homogenous and with the rational calculation of profit and loss occupying increased prominence. With reference to these developments, Franz Borkenau (1971) speculates, the new vision was of the human being as a mechanically functioning creature, a cog in the machine. And if Bacon et al. were preoccupied with laws of motion, this, plausibly, related to their location in a world of increasing motion (and commotion), of flux and transition, of discovery, exploration and revolution, and of the supplanting of land by mobile wealth (capital) as the dominant form of wealth for the first time in history. Surely, too, the commercial and accounting revolutions played a part. After all, as Mirowski observes (1989, 119), "the major innovations in the theory of motion follow the changing center of gravity of the major trading axis of early modern Europe, stretching from northern Italy through the low countries and terminating in southeastern Britain" – and this is the same vector along which modern accounting techniques diffused.

The rise of accounting and the scientific revolution stimulated the application of mathematics to human behavior. If this was not altogether novel, it did assume a qualitatively new dimension in the seventeenth century. Baruch Spinoza, Gottfried Leibnitz, Descartes, Newton, Hobbes, and others, "began to build a universal quantitative science, *Pantometrika* or *Mathesis universae*, with its branches of *Psychometrika, Ethicometrika,* and *Sociometrika* designed for investigating psychosocial phenomena along the lines of geometry and physical mechanics" (Sorokin 1956, 103). In England the high priests of the cult of measurement and quantification congregated at the Royal Society, where they presided over the first great age of positivist natural *and social* science. As if by osmosis, motifs, metaphors, and theories from the natural sciences percolated into the imaginations of economists. For example, Hobbes drew attention to the parallels between the circulation of blood in the human body and that of money within the body politic (Caffentzis 2003, 206). Increasingly, the modeling of nature as a law-governed mechanism such that bodies tend to move like clockwork, as pioneered by Newton and others in the seventeenth century, influenced the conception of 'the economy' as a law-governed mechanism that appeared later in the same century in the work of economic thinkers such as Barbon and Dudley North.

Advances in mathematics and celestial mechanics nourished the hope, most obvious in the work of Hobbes, that human action, just like falling bodies and planetary orbits, may be determined by uniform laws of motion (Hirschman 1997, 13). Hobbes, who was amanuensis to Bacon during his last five years, sought to apply Baconian scientific rules to the "science" of the social. He construed the mind as a special kind of machine, with the faculty of reason seen as "nothing but 'reckoning,' that is adding and subtracting, of the consequences of general names agreed upon for the 'marking' and 'signifying' of our thoughts" (Merchant 1980). In mechanizing the human mind and body he pioneered the utilitarian understanding of behavior, as driven by the desire to achieve pleasure and the need to avert pain. "Life it selfe is but Motion, and can never be without Desire," he proposed, and felicity is the "Continual successe in obtaining those things which a man from time to time desireth, that is to say continuall prospering" (in Feldman 2001, 7). The human core, then, is *homo economicus,* whose orientation to material prosperity is sufficiently uniform and predictable that its behavior can be modeled.

In its essentials, this method was adopted by economists, notably William Petty. He devised the first statistically rigorous accounting of the wealth of a country, with the state conceived as a household, and national income accounting as household bookkeeping (Fioramonti 2013). Petty developed it as an exercise in what Foucault terms "governmentality" – statistical practices deployed by early modern states to manage populations – but with a colonial-ideological twist: to produce a cadastral survey of Ireland that would assess its economic potential for purposes of plunder (including by Petty himself) and "improvement," in a manner that could be presented as scientific – through quantification and the reduction of goods to numbers – and hence as "objective." For Petty, the imperative to render economic affairs scientific requires the reduction of all economically relevant phenomena to "number, weight and measure." The phrase crops up repeatedly – a mantra – in his writings, but his interest in numbers was only secondarily as a statistician. More important was their political and ideological function: numbers enabled the claim of scientific authority to be made, and in this respect the vital element was not their precision or accuracy but the "formal procedure" through which they are produced. It was this, Till Düppe has argued (2011, 118), that enabled Petty to claim objectivity "not in the sense of referring to the existence of particulars, but in the sense of appearing to work beyond his own interest in claiming something particular." The moral stance of disinterestedness was flourishing in a society that was busy re-imagining itself as a congeries of competing interests that lacked an institution capable of negotiating them. It was part and parcel of the new perception of the economy as an institution designed to negotiate interests, and therewith of a discipline, economics, that presents itself as unbiased and scientific. In short, Petty made a seminal contribution both to the arts of economic administration (statistics) and to the conceptualization of "the economy" as a distinct field subject to scientific study and accurate measurement. He secured a place for quantification at the heart of the emergent discipline of scientific economics, customized to the purposes of English empire and deployed ideologically, in particular by making the most of the sheen of objectivity with which economic statistics ("political arithmetic," in Petty's lexicon) comes coated. The policy consequence was that legislators should not seek to overturn natural law ("market forces," in today's lexicon). "Nature must and will have its course," Petty intoned (in Ullmer 2011); to decree "Civil Positive Laws against the Laws of Nature" would be "vain and fruitless" – not unlike decreeing a law to reverse Jupiter's solar orbit.

In this, Petty exemplified a general phenomenon of seventeenth-century English economic thought whereby mercantilists, in teasing out some of the contradictions within their positions, prepared the ground for liberal political economy – with its (to us moderns) recognizable approach to growth. One contradiction was between the mercantilists' export boosterism and a long-established moral economy that sees trade as a hazard to virtue – for it encourages luxury, and, in turn, "avarice." But were avarice and luxury evils? Moralists had traditionally regarded them as inevitable but regrettable vices, condemning all consumption as "luxury" by dint of its tendency to focus attention upon the body and the senses, rather than the soul and the spirit (Cruise 1999). But by the early seventeenth century the thirst for money on the part of monarchs, gentry, and burghers was becoming a secular religion, luxury was gaining legitimacy, and pamphleteers identified "private gain" as the compass by which "men generally saile" (Appleby 1978). The end of the century saw post-mercantilist economists develop prototypes of the doctrines that trade and accumulation follow natural laws and that legislative obstacles should not be placed in the path of commerce. This cultural transformation received its blessing from religious institutions. Puritanism, in particular, issued its convoluted stamp of approval for material success and "improvement," legitimizing the drive to accumulate wealth – previously regarded as the prerogative of monarchs, monks, and merchants – for the multitude.

A second contradiction concerned the understanding of trade as a zero-sum game. Mercantilists viewed *international* trade in these terms, but they simultaneously held the expectation that *within* a nation the growth of commerce yields all-round beneficial effects. When trade flourishes, wrote Edward Misselden, "the income to the crown is augmented, lands and rents are improved, navigation increases and the poor people find work. If trade declines, all these decline with it" (in Rubin 1979, 37). "Trade if it be well managed," wrote Edward Coke in 1670 (in Cruise 1999, 76), adumbrating a demand-side theory of growth, "no where thrives better than where men spend above the ordinary means of living." Josiah Child (in Viner 1948) declared that "it is evident that this Kingdom is wonderfully fitted by the bounty of God Almighty for *a great progression in wealth and power*; and that the only means to arrive at both, or either of them, is to improve and advance trade." Child also used the term "growth" not only in its traditional sense, to denote that which "grows" in a country, its natural produce, but also to refer to more abstract phenomena: the "growth of population," the "growth and increase" of the plantations in Virginia and Barbados, and the "growth of trade," referring to general indicators such as numbers of individuals in a colony, the volume of goods produced and shipped, and the frequency of journeys undertaken (Child 1751, ix, 139). In this respect he is at the hinge, at which the connotations of 'growth' in economic literature shift from natural and concrete to general and abstract. The modern form of the growth paradigm was edging into view.

A third contradiction in mercantilist thought pertained to questions of free trade. This might sound puzzling. Was not mercantilism a dirigiste dragon that laid waste to polite civilization before Adam Smith arrived to slay it? And yet one finds, at least among post-Restoration mercantilists, unambiguous statements in favor of free trade, exemplified by Charles Davenant's contention (in Hont 2005 216) that nations that "thrive by Traffick" are those which have "few Laws relating to Trade." Child (1751, 10–11) believed that the laws of money, with their "foundation in nature," ensure a downward trend to interest rates and a correlative upward trend to economic growth – in which respect he quotes Petty: "nature must and will have its course." That mercantilist economists such as Petty, Child, Locke, North, and Barbon were early champions of the "automatic" operation of the price mechanism and free trade is not only counterintuitive but paradoxical. They all were penning theses on the "natural laws" of trade with one hand while, with the other, they made their fortunes from palm-greasing, bribery, slavery, imperial conquest, and war, and the establishment and administration of chartered monopoly-colonial corporations.

The moral authorization of the profit motive as an economic incentive, and the theorization of *laissez faire*, the laws of free trade, and the conceptualization of equilibrium advanced by Child, Locke and especially North and Barbon in England, and Pierre le Pesant (alias Boisguilbert) in France, combined to move economic theory out of the mercantilist framework and onto liberal terrain. The vindication of the profit motive suggested an identity between private economic and social interests, such that the economic acts of individuals promote prosperity and general welfare (Tieben 2012, 101). In this way, and in contrast to traditional autocratic justifications of social order and even to Hobbes' positing of the necessity of an absolute sovereign, North, Barbon et al. laid the foundations of a new model of social order. It arises unintentionally and automatically from the aggregate actions of myriad individuals seeking to improve their lives, actions that manifest as the forces of supply and demand. These, in turn, ensure that the tendency of some to gain at the expense of others is checked not by absolute rule but by market competition. If earlier political-economic thought had construed its subject as an extension of the royal household, this new model posited an interconnected market field that functioned essentially outside the state. In turn, the idea of the economy as a self-regulating mechanism shone a new light upon the question of what arrangements would facilitate sustained economic growth. This new way of seeing moved to center stage in the age of Adam Smith and the industrial revolution – an era that witnessed a lurch forward in the evolution of the growth paradigm but which lies outside the scope of this chapter.

Conclusion

If economic growth, envisaged as the increase in year-on-year per-capita output, has since the eighteenth century been sustained and rapid, before then it was sporadic, modest, or absent. The growth paradigm was largely absent too, as argued in the first section above. Before the eighteenth century little sense existed of "the economy" as a discrete sphere of social life, still less one that could be measured such that its growth could be estimated. Nor was there a perceived compulsion to growth, nor an ideology of secular, linear progress. The story of the modern growth paradigm is too lengthy and complex to be treated in full in this chapter. (I sketch some aspects in Dale 2012 and 2015). What I have developed instead is a thesis on the social and ideational context in which the growth paradigm was born. I argue that northwestern Europe in the seventeenth-century – a century of explosive bourgeois ambition, creativity, and cruelty – marked a watershed. Before, capitalist social relations, behavior, and morality had established themselves, even in England, only sporadically. After, they rapidly gained sway. Before, mathematics and the methods of natural philosophy were the preserve of monks, magi, and mavericks. After, they provided the key to understanding the cosmos as well as practical problems of everyday life, not only for philosophers and scientists but for wide sections of society, from improving farmers to enlightened monarchs, from merchants to economists. Natural philosophy – "science" – came to be identified with control of the natural world and with the associated payoffs for citizens' welfare and military might; and when "economics" began to precipitate out of natural philosophy its form and purpose were similar. The cosmos, and by analogy the market economy, came to be envisaged as a rule-governed realm, the divinely authored natural laws of which could be understood – and put to good use ("improvement") – by rational men.

In tandem with these developments arose a new doctrine of historical change. Cyclical concepts remained influential but a unilinear alternative came to prevail. The early narratives of progress focused on the accumulation of knowledge, in some cases infused with a millenarian faith in divine providence. Over time, the narrative secularized, and its scope broadened out from the cumulative progress of scientific knowledge and the general fate of humanity to include human conduct in all its major dimensions: morality and the institutions of government and economy (Wagner 2016). Irrigated by maritime expansion and colonialism, by the scientific revolution and its commitment to cumulatively expand humanity's knowledge of the natural world, by the spirit of rational calculation and quantification and by the conviction that technological arts and scientific knowledge can be applied to the steady improvement of the material conditions of existence, the doctrine of progress flourished. By the early eighteenth century, the idea that a nation, or even humanity as a whole, has developed from primitive beginnings and would continue to grow in cultivation and sophistication was widely held. In some accounts, such as Vico's, the doctrine incorporated cyclical elements. In others, notably that of Britain's Whigs, progress was envisaged as uniform and unilinear. Adam Smith and his ilk were convinced that 'material progress' was central to civilizational development, that reaching the "commercial stage" of economic life was essential, and that, once achieved, further growth was desirable. In rural areas the idea of 'improvement' gained ground, while in the towns, the values of the 'new men' – the merchants and manufacturers, mine owners, and bankers, and the technicians, doctors, and clerks – underpinned the idea of progress (Pollard 1968, 17). All, whether improving farmers or urban merchants, inhabited a society that exhibited an increasingly chrematistical pulse – one that contrasted starkly with the pre-capitalist world. In contrast to the political economy of antiquity (think for example of Aristotle's view on chrematistics as a threat to the polis, an essentially cancerous process of the self-reproduction of useless, even dangerous, cells within the body politic), for the political economy of seventeenth-century England and France, from North, Barbon and Boisguilbert onward, the chrematistical pulse represented an opportunity, even a necessity: the principle of circulation through the arteries and veins of the body economic, pumped by the insatiability of the human appetite for material improvement. Even now, the doctrine of Progress was not automatically linked to the advocacy of year-on-year economic growth. That connection would crystallize later. But the foundations of the modern growth paradigm had been laid.

Notes

1 The research for this chapter was funded by a British Academy Mid-Career Fellowship (2013–14, project title "Economic growth as ideology: Origins, evolution and dilemmas of the 'growth paradigm'").

2 According to Thapar (1997, Appendix 1) the *Arthasastra* was written by Kautilya but was edited in later centuries. According to Habib and Jha, most of it was written between BC 500 and 200. See also Habib and Jha (2004).

References

Anievas, Alex and Kerem Nisancioglu. 2013. "What's at Stake in the Transition Debate? Rethinking the Origins of Capitalism and the 'Rise of the West.'" *Millennium: Journal of International Studies* 42(1): 78–102.

Anievas, Alex and Kerem Nisancioglu. 2015. *How the West Came to Rule: The Geopolitical Origins of Capitalism*. London: Pluto.

Appleby, Joyce. 1978. *Economic Thought and Ideology in Seventeenth-Century England.* Princeton: Princeton University Press.

Bacon, Francis. 2000 [1620]. *The New Organon*. Cambridge: Cambridge University Press.

Bacon, Francis. 1627. *New Atlantis*, www2.hn.psu.edu/faculty/jmanis/bacon/atlantis.pdf.

Blith, Walter. 1652. "The English Improver Improved, or the Survey of Husbandry Surveyed." Accessed July 27, 2016. www.tu-chemnitz.de/phil/english/chairs/linguist/real/independent/lampeter/pdf/ecb1653.pdf.

Boesche, Roger. 2002. *The First Great Political Realist: Kautilya and his Arthashastra*. Lanham: Lexington Books.

Borkenau, Franz. 1971 [1934]. *Der Übergang vom feudalen zum bürgerlichen Weltbild: Studien zur Geschichte der Philosophie der Manufakturperiode.* Wissenschaftliche Buchgesellschaft.

Caffentzis, George. 2003. "Medical Metaphors and Monetary Strategies in the Political Economy of Locke and Berkeley." *History of Political Economy* 35 (suppl.): 204–233.

Catchpowle, Lesley, Christine Cooper and Andrew Wright. 2004. "Capitalism, States and Accounting." *Critical Perspectives on Accounting* 15: 1037–1055.

Chaplin, Joyce. 2001. *Subject Matter: Technology, the Body, and Science on the Anglo-American Frontier, 1500–1676*. Cambridge: Harvard University Press.

Child, Josiah. 1751 [1668/1690]. *A new Discourse of Trade.* Glasgow: Robert and Andrew Foulis.

Cruise, James. 1999. *Governing Consumption: Needs and Wants, Suspended Characters, and the 'Origins' of Eighteenth-Century English Novels.* Plainsboro: Associated University Presses.

Dale, Gareth. 2012. "The Growth Paradigm: A Critique." *International Socialism* 134: 55–88.

Dale, Gareth. 2015. "Origins and Delusions of Green Growth." *International Socialist Review* 97.

Drayton, Richard. 2000. *Nature's Government: Science, Imperial Britain, and the 'Improvement' of the World.* New Haven: Yale University Press.

Düppe, Till. 2011. *The Making of the Economy: A Phenomenology of Economic Science.* Lanham: Lexington.

Feldman, Leslie Dale. 2001. *Freedom as Motion*. New York: University Press of America.

Finkelstein, Andrea. 2000. *Harmony and the Balance: An intellectual history of seventeenth-century English economic thought*. Ann Arbor: The University of Michigan Press.

Finley, Moses. 1953. "Land, Debt, and the Man of Property in Classical Athens." *Political Science Quarterly* 68 (2): 249–268.

Fioramonti, Lorenzo. 2013. *Gross Domestic Problem: The Politics Behind the World's Most Powerful Number*. London: Zed Books

Friedman, Benjamin. 2006. *The Moral Consequences of Economic Growth*. New York: Vintage.

Gernet, Jacques. 1995. *Buddhism in Chinese Society: An Economic History from the Fifth to the Tenth Centuries*. New York: Columbia University Press.

Gimpel, Jean. 1976. *The Medieval Machine: The Industrial Revolution of the Middle Ages*. London: Gollancz.

Graeber, David. 2011. *Debt: The first 5,000 years*. New York: Melville House.

Grove, Richard. 1995. *Green Imperialism: Colonial expansion, tropical island Edens and the origins of environmentalism, 1600–1860*. Cambridge: Cambridge University Press.

Habib, Irfan and Vivekanand Jha. 2004. *Mauryan India*. New Delhi: Tulika Books.

Harman, Chris. 1999. *A People's History of the World*. London: Bookmarks.

Harris, Nigel. 2003. *The Return of Cosmopolitan Capital: Globalization, the State and War*, London: I.B. Tauris.

Heller, Henry. 1996. *Labour, Science and Technology in France*. Cambridge: Cambridge University Press.

Hill, Christopher. 1972. *The World Turned Upside Down: Radical ideas During the English Revolution*. New York: Penguin.

Hirschman, Albert. 1997 [1977]. *The Passions and the Interests: Political Arguments for Capitalism before Its Triumph*. Princeton: Princeton University Press.

Hont, Istvan. 2005. *Jealousy of Trade: International Competition and the Nation-state in Historical Perspective*. Cambridge: Harvard University Press.

Hubbard, Jamie. 2001. *Absolute Delusion, Perfect Buddhahood: The Rise and Fall of a Chinese Heresy*. Honululu: University of Hawai'i Press.

Ibn Khaldun, Abu Zaid 'Abdel Rahman. 1950 [1377–1406]. *Selections from the Prolegomena*, edited by Charles Issawi. London: John Murray.

Irving, Sarah. 2008. *Natural Science and the Origins of the British Empire*. London: Pickering & Chatto.

Kautilya. 1962 [BC 500–200]. *Essentials of Indian Statecraft*, edited by T. Ramaswamy. New Dehli: Munshiram Manoharlal Publishers.

Langman, Pete. 2011. "'I Giue Thee Leave to Publish': New Atlantis and Francis Bacon's Republic of Knowledge." In *Centres and Cycles of Accumulation in and Around the Netherlands During the Early Modern Period*, edited by Lissa Roberts. Münster: Lit Verlag.

Leiss, William. 1994. *The Domination of Nature*. Montreal: McGill-Queen's University Press.

Linebaugh, Peter and Marcus Rediker. 2012. *The Many-Headed Hydra: The Hidden History of the Revolutionary Atlantic*. London: Verso.

Marx, Karl and Friedrich Engels. 1845. *The Holy Family*. Accessed July 27, 2016. www.marxists.org/archive/marx/works/1845/holy-family/ch06_3_d.htm.

Mathai, Manu. 2013. *Nuclear Power, Economic Development Discourse and the Environment: The Case of India*. London: Routledge.

McNally, David. 1988. *Political Economy and the Rise of Capitalism: A Reinterpretation*. Berkeley: University of California Press.

Meek, Ronald. 1976. *Social Science and the Ignoble Savage*. Cambridge: Cambridge University Press.

Merchant, Carolyn. 1980. *The Death of Nature: Women, Ecology and the Scientific Revolution*. New York: HarperCollins.

Miéville, China. 2006. *Between Equal Rights: A Marxist Theory of International Law*. London: Haymarket Books.

Mirowski, Philip. 1985. *The Birth of the Business Cycle*. New York: Garland Publishing.

Mirowski, Philip. 1989. *More Heat Than Light. Economics as Social Physics: Physics as Nature's Economics*. Cambridge: Cambridge University Press.

Moore, Jason. 2014. *Capitalism in the Web of Life: Ecology and the Accumulation of Capital*. London: Verso.

Münch, Paul. 1993. "The Thesis Before Weber: An Archaeology." In *Weber's Protestant Ethic: Origins, Evidence, Contexts*, edited by Hartmut Lehmann and Guenther Roth. Cambridge: Cambridge University Press.

Nisbet, Robert. 2009 [1969]. *Metaphor and History: The Western Idea of Social Development*. New Jersey: Transaction Publishers.

Nussbaum, Frederick. 2002 [1933]. *An Early History of the Economic Institutions of Europe*. Washington, D.C.: Beard Books.

Outram, Dorinda. 1995. *The Enlightenment*. Cambridge: Cambridge University Press.

Plattes, Gabriel. 1974. *A Discovery of Infinite Treasure Hidden Since the Worlds Beginning*. Amsterdam: Theatrum Orbis Terrarum.

Pollard, Sidney. 1968. *The Idea of Progress*. London: Watts & Co.

Pomeranz, Kenneth. 1997. *The Great Divergence: China, Europe, and the Making of the Modern World Economy*. Princeton: Princeton University Press.

Rubin, Isaac Ilyich. 1979 [1929]. *A History of Economic Thought*. London: Ink Links.

Sack, R. D. 1986. *Human Territoriality*. Cambridge: Cambridge University Press.

Seaford, Richard. 2013. "Influence between India and Greece?" Accessed July 27, 2016. http://atmanandpsyche.exeter.ac.uk/2013/09

Sedlacek, Tomas. 2011. *Economics of Good and Evil: The Quest for Economic Meaning from Gilgamesh to Wall Street*. Oxford: Oxford University Press.

Slack, Paul. 2015. *The Invention of Improvement: Information and Material Progress in Seventeenth-Century England*. Oxford: Oxford University Press.

Sorokin, Pitirim. 1956. *Fads and Foibles in Modern Sociology and Related Sciences*. Chicago: Henry Regnery Company.

Thapar, Romila. 1987. *The Mauryas Revisited*. Calcutta: KP Bagchi & Company.

Thapar, Romila 1997. *Aśoka and the Decline of the Mauryas*. Oxford: Oxford University Press.

Thompson, E. P. 1967. "Time, Work-Discipline and Industrial Capitalism." *Past and Present* 38: 56–97.

Tieben, Bert. 2012. *The Concept of Equilibrium in Different Economic Traditions: An Historical Investigation*. Cheltenham: Edward Elgar.

Ullmer, James. 2011. "The scientific method of Sir William Petty." *Erasmus Journal for Philosophy and Economics* 4(2): 1–19.

Viner, Jacob. 1948. "Power and Plenty as Objectives of Foreign Policy in the Seventeenth and Eighteenth Centuries." *World Politics* 1(1): 1–29.

Wagner, Peter. 2016. *Progress: A Reconstruction*. Cambridge: Polity.

Wood, Neal. 1984. *John Locke and Agrarian Capitalism*. Berkeley: University of California Press.

2 Growth unlimited

The idea of infinite growth from fossil capitalism to green capitalism

Jean-Baptiste Fressoz and Christophe Bonneuil

This chapter describes the adjustments to the world picture which discredited the finitude of the Earth and legitimized the idea of infinite economic growth during the nineteenth and twentieth centuries. It focuses on two disciplines, geology in the nineteenth century and economics in the twentieth, which played a crucial role in the redefinition of nature as well as of ideas regarding its influence on human societies, its capacity to reproduce itself, and the wealth it offered to industry.

Geology, at the beginning of the nineteenth century, demonstrated the immensity of the age of the Earth and thus justified the shift from an organic to a mineral economy. Geology mitigated the anxieties linked to coal exhaustion: thanks to its antiquity, the Earth, despite the obvious finitude of its surface, became an endless reservoir of fossil resources.

In classical economics, the idea of growth was bound up with a process of material expansion: it was a question of increasing the production of a particular material, or of opening up new resources or new territories to trade. With the advent of neoclassical economics focused on marginal utility calculations, with the rise of Keynesianism, and finally with the institutionalization of GDP, economics unburdened itself of nature and further naturalized the idea of infinite growth. In the second part of the twentieth century, the tools and ontologies of economics have been projected back onto a nature that it had so potently externalized. Environmental economics reconstructed environmental problems and the whole Earth, from climate to ecosystems, as an ensemble of financial assets, which could be subjected to economic optimization. From this perspective, even limits to growth became opportunities for growth.

The limits of the organic economy

In 1754, the satirist Edward Moore depicted a young mathematician who had after long calculations discovered "that the profusion of man consumes faster than the Earth produces. Vast fleets, and enormous buildings have wasted almost all our oak [...] What shall we do when the coal, iron and lead mines are exhausted?" (Moore 1755, 262). In the second half of the eighteenth century, many voices complained about the depletion of nature. Many depicted the forests as "exhausted". Complaints about the scarcity of wood multiplied. According to Buffon, "wood which used to be very abundant in France, is now hardly sufficient for the most indispensable uses and we are under the threat of an absolute want of wood in the future" (quoted in Buridant 2008, 22). This alarm was widespread. For fishermen collectively managing their resources, for villagers collecting wood in local forests, or even for miners, resource exhaustion was an obvious concern that oriented and circumscribed their action.

Until the second half of the nineteenth century, European elites were still largely agricultural, and the aristocracy was suspicious of industrialization. They preferred the economic and social stability of the rural world to an uncontrolled industrial and urban growth. In England, until the 1850s, the dominant Tory ideology was deeply pervaded by an Evangelical Protestant idea of economics, conceiving poverty, trade crises, and bankruptcies as dispensations of Providence. The economy was seen as static and cyclical. The market was more a place of moral retribution, penitence, and gratification than an instrument of growth (Hilton 1997).

The question of limits was also fundamental in the political economy of the time. For the Physiocrats, Thomas Malthus, and also for classical political economists such as David Ricardo the economic theory of the early industrial period ruled out the idea of infinite growth. The law of diminishing returns, for instance, reflected the perception of an asymptotic limit to agricultural resources. Europe, like the rest of the world, lived in an organic economy, in which the limits of agricultural land and forests formed a strong constraint on growth (Wrigley 2004). The economy based on solar, wind, and hydraulic energy flows was embedded in a very constrained energy budget: four hectares of forest, for example, were needed to produce a ton of iron, two hectares of pasture to feed a horse, etc. Every development of one kind of production had a negative effect on the growth capacity of others. The rise of forges and glassworks as new consumers of wood came into conflict with the needs of village and urban communities for firewood, threatening the productivity and docility of the labor force. After more than two centuries of shrinking forests, Western Europe thus experienced a serious forestry crisis at the turn of the nineteenth century, the source of social tensions and fears of global climatic disturbance (Fressoz and Locher 2012). The price of wood doubled in France between 1770 and 1790 (Buridant 2008). In 1788, the *intendant* of Brittany predicted that "within twenty years all the present manufactures will fail for want of wood to fuel them" (quoted in Sée 1924, 362). The survival of the people, the maintenance of manufactures, and the rank of the nation all seemed to depend on the future of the forests.

The initial response to this sense of permanent limitation was to introduce "rational" forestry. By imposing organized cuttings with rotation of up to two centuries (for the masts of warships), it was supposedly possible to guarantee to the monarch and his army a stable and predictable supply of wood at the same time as an increased income for the forest proprietors. This "rational forest management" approach, the forerunner of the contemporary idea of sustainable development, was founded on an iterative conception of nature, which reproduced itself uniformly and whose future could be securely predicted. Developed within the German cameral science of the early eighteenth century, rational forestry conquered Europe at the start of the nineteenth, followed by the colonial territories in the second half of the century (Lowood 1990; Barton 2004). In the 1850s, however, foresters noted the extreme fragility of the ecosystems they had created. Forests of uniform age and species were very vulnerable to parasites, storms, and meteorological accidents. The introduction of the word *Waldsterben* (forest death) in Germany in the late nineteenth century attests to the gravity of the situation (Scott 1998, 11–22). The result was the development of a new forest hygiene, which aimed to recreate the soil and the symbioses that existed before the introduction of forest monoculture. Despite its negative ecological effects and the social conflicts it aroused, the mathematical management of the forest was a promise, a scientific guarantee of the future, making it possible to circumvent the fears bound up with the scarcity of wood that were so forcibly expressed in the late eighteenth century.

The infinite planet of the geologist

In fact, the main factor that relieved the energy constraint and the shrinkage of forests was the exploitation of coal. This was even presented as what we might retrospectively call "green energy" by such forest champions and experts as François Antoine Rauch in France, who called for a "generalized use of these fuels" in order to spare "our depopulated forests" (Rauch 1802, 51–52). Yet coal also aroused sharp fears concerning the risk of its rapid exhaustion. At its beginnings, it seemed only a temporary solution to relax the pressure on forests. In 1792, a French deputy explained that the conservation of the forests was important, since coal mines "are not as common as is thought. It is noticeable that those of the Auvergne are becoming exhausted, and the investigations that have proliferated around the capital have not been successful."[1] In 1819, on the subject of gas lighting, Chaptal estimated French coal resources as too low to be wasted for illumination: better to reserve them for the production of iron, which was far more useful for national defense (Fressoz 2012, 209). In the same vein, at the start of the railway age, the engineer Pierre-Simon Girard argued against steam engines and for animal traction, estimating that the price of coal was bound to increase as mines were gradually exhausted (Girard 1827, cxxv). In Great Britain, at the same time, the exhaustion of certain mines, combined with parliamentary debates on the taxation and export of coal, led the House of Lords to set up commissions on this subject in 1829 (Sieferle 2001, 187).

The rise of geology played a major anxiolytic role. In the 1800s, William Smith, an English surveyor working in the construction of mines and canals, used fossils as markers of geological strata, and showed that the study of their succession made it possible to predict the presence of coal in a given subsoil. By indicating probable deposits, guiding the digging of pits and avoiding useless work, geologists made investment in the mining sector less risky and more lucrative. Geological maps (of which Smith's surveys were a precursor) encouraged the owners of land situated in favorable zones to undertake probes, thereby increasing proven reserves (Torrens 2002). In a general sense, geology constructed the image of a subsoil organized according to vast mineral strata that were hidden but continuous (Rudwick 2005, 431–445). By moving from the sporadic viewpoint of the mine exploiters to a larger and continuous view of the subsoil, it created reassuring concepts such as "potential discovery" or "probable reserves," allowing far more optimistic estimates than mine practitioners.

As a fossil fuel from a world long since disappeared, coal transformed the perception of time in many respects. Above all, it conferred on the capitalist the freedom to store energy and mobilize it at the desired moment and in the degree needed. Sadi Carnot, writing at the dawn of its use, had perfectly glimpsed the temporal power of the steam engine: "it has the invaluable advantage of being employable at any time and in any place, and of never suffering an interruption in its work" (Carnot 1824, 2). The steam engine made it possible to homogenize space, to ignore watercourses and gradients, and above all to relocate production where the balance of power was more favorable to capitalists than workers (Malm 2016). While fluctuations of horses, wind, and water required adjustments in accordance with a nature in flux, coal formed an energy store that could be accumulated and made it possible to smooth out production, to linearize time, and subject it to market imperatives. The continuous time of industrial capitalism, imposed on recalcitrant workers, was then projected onto cultural representations of the future, conceived as a continuous progress unfurling to the rhythm of productivity gains.

This linear time was likewise projected onto nature by way of the rise of gradualism in geology. This theory, according to which the terrestrial globe was shaped by present causes acting over a very long time (rather than by catastrophic events), was anchored in European culture at the same time as the new centrality of coal. According to James Hutton, the fact that coal was found in different qualities, corresponding to the intermediary stages of its formation, supported the gradualist thesis and indicated that the process was still under way (Hutton 1788, 33). In fact, the Earth had to be given an antiquity sufficient to leave the relics of past vegetation time to accumulate in thick layers, providing for centuries of industrial need.

The discordance postulated between the time of the Earth and the time of history, as well as the switch from an organic surface energy to an underground fossil energy, favored a sense of externality in relation to a nature that was infinitely old and thus immensely rich. From the dawn of time, wrote Sadi Carnot (1824, 1), nature had prepared the "immense reservoir" from which industry could prosper in the future. Jean-Baptiste Say (1840, 262) went even further: "happily, nature placed in reserve long before the formation of man immense provisions of fuel in coal mines, as it foresaw that man, once in possession of his domain, would destroy more combustible materials than it could reproduce." The geologist and theologian William Buckland (1837, 403) saw the providential hand of God in the depth of the coal seams: "however remote may have been the periods, at which these materials of future beneficial dispensations were laid up in store, we may fairly assume, that… an ulterior prospective view to the future uses of Man, formed part of the design." Thanks to its antiquity, the Earth, despite the evident finitude of its surface, became an endless reservoir of resources. In his *Statistical Account of the British Empire*, John McCulloch demonstrated the unchallengeable superiority of Great Britain and the unshakeable stability of its domination. By lengthy tables, the bourgeois Victorian was relieved to discover fabulous amounts of resources. Coal in particular was described as inexhaustible: "the coal fields of Durham and Northumberland are adequate to furnish the present annual supply for more than 1,340 years." The precision of this figure, and the vague expression "more than," opened the perspective of an almost infinite quantity (Freedgood 2000, 18–28). In a few decades, geology had thus transformed Malthus's "dismal science" into a reassuring argument for limitless growth.

In the second half of the nineteenth century, the globalization of geological prospecting further shored up the confidence of the imperial powers as to the material bases of their domination. In 1860, in the House of Commons, Disraeli, opposing the free-trade treaty with France (the Cobden–Chevalier treaty), maintained that, since English reserves would cover no more than three or four centuries of national consumption, it was imperative for the long-term survival of the empire that exports should be taxed. Gladstone, on the other hand, a champion of free trade, mentioned other geological studies that estimated reserves at 2,000 years of consumption. A scarcity foreseeable in three centuries seemed to justify a course of action that was economically damaging in the present. The long term of English politicians managing their empire, instilled with classical references and quoting Gibbon, was in the order of millennia.[2] Jevons's well-known treatise on *The Coal Question* (1865) takes place in this debate about free trade and the material foundation of empire. The fact that his views were seen as pessimistic although he predicted a dominant position for the British economy during the following 300 years provides a telling example of Great Britain's imperial self-confidence at the time.

The main effect of Jevons's *Coal Question* was to intensify the activity of the British Geological Survey across the Empire (Stafford 1989). In the same way, international geological conferences (starting in 1877) established a global inventory of energy and metal resources. The 1913 conference, held in Toronto, was devoted to coal and led to the first quantification of global reserves. A certain vagueness in the definition of "likely reserves" and the extension of the limit of economically exploitable coal to 4,000 feet (instead of the previous 2,200) allowed a massive overestimate – in any case a figure six times higher than contemporary estimates (Madureira 2012). By the late nineteenth century, worries about the exhaustion of the mineral world had been circumvented by this global construction of resources by the science of geology.

The dematerialization of the economic discipline

It was only in the second half of the nineteenth century that theorists began to view the economy as an object distinct from natural and material processes and subject above all, if not uniquely, to human laws and conventions. Jevons initiated the marginalist, neoclassical revolution in economic theory, which turned away from the study of factors of production (labor, capital, and land) and focused on the subjective states of consumers and producers seeking to maximize their individual utility (Breslau 2003). Goods were envisaged according to their psychological effects, as purveyors of utility, rather than according to their material characteristics. In the same way, capital was not conceived as a concrete set of productive mechanisms, but rather as assets generating financial flows. The economy no longer shared an object with the natural sciences (the production of material wealth), but its mathematical tools only: the economists trained in neoclassical economics transposed equations taken from physics so as to create the illusion of a second nature as coherent as the first one, but external to it (Mirowski 1991). Natural resources now occupied only a very marginal place in economic theory. Between 1870 and 1970, their study formed only a small subdivision of the discipline, the economics of conservation, which took its ontology and mathematical tools from neoclassical theory. A dynamic approach to the economy, which envisaged long-term evolution in a context of increasing scarcity (with Jevons for example), was replaced by a microeconomic context and a static approach. Thus in 1931, in a fundamental article on the economics of natural resources, Hotelling analyzed the situation of a mine owner in a competitive situation who sought to maximize his real income. The problem was no longer that of the long-term future of a national economy, but more modestly how a mine owner could find the optimal path for extracting an exhaustible resource so as to maximize its financial value. The mine became an abstract entity, disconnected from the rest of the productive system (despite fueling it), simply a reserve of value that obeyed the same type of calculation as a stock portfolio (Pottier 2016, 112–122).

In the 1890s, econometric tools made it possible to study the systemic relationships between different prices. Instead of correlating them with exogenous factors (meteorology, disasters, wars, etc.), the price system transformed the economy into a homogeneous, closed system. "External" causes, whether natural or political, were no more than secondary disturbances. The economy became an autonomous object on which scientific action was possible.

On the macroeconomic side, neoclassical tools such as the production function proposed by Cobb and Douglas in 1928 and the growth theories of Robert Solow did not allow any place for nature (and its limits). At best, they viewed it as a factor that could be substituted by an increase in capital or by technological innovation. According to Solow, "if it is very easy to substitute other factors [e.g., labor or capital] for natural resources, then there is, in principle, no 'problem.' The world can, in effect, get along without natural resources" (Solow 1974, 11).

In the same way, mainstream Marxists, by focusing on the labor theory of value and the distribution of the product between two classes, workers and capitalists, essentially saw only two factors of production: capital and labor. Marx and Engels did address the metabolic rupture between earth and society that capitalism had produced, and certain Marxists such as Podolinsky sought to refound the labor theory on energy. But until the recent emergence of a fruitful eco-Marxism, Marxist economic science abolished the role of metabolism and energy, rejecting as "Malthusian" (and thus conservative) any idea of limits to the planet's resources (Georgescu-Roegen 1975).

Paradoxically, the economic crisis further naturalized the idea of growth. The overproduction crisis of the 1930s, Keynesianism, and then the development of systems of national accounting completed the process of dematerialization of the economy. The abandonment of the gold standard in that decade (i.e., the end of the idea that banknotes represented gold) was a key turning-point (see also the contribution by Andrea Westermann in this volume). Keynes, in a famous passage of his *General Theory*, explained that the end of coal would be unimportant, what mattered was the correct circulation of money: it would be enough, therefore, for the British Treasury to bury banknotes and ask miners to hunt for them, in order to ensure employment and economic prosperity (Mitchell 2011, 123–124). Growth was reconceived not in material terms but as the intensification of the totality of monetary relations. By means of this dematerialization, the economy could at last be conceived as growing indefinitely, outside any natural determinisms and without coming up against physical limits, thanks to the good guardianship of economic experts.

Growth was also naturalized by new statistical measurements and the institutionalization of a new political keyword: Gross National Product (GNP) (see the contribution by Lorenzo Fioramonti in this volume). National income, which had long been estimated by economists or journalists concerned with studying the distribution of wealth between wages and profits, was now calculated by national official bureaus. In the United States in 1936, the economist Simon Kuznets, a Harvard academic appointed to the National Bureau of Economic Research, established rules for calculating GNP, which would be taken up across the world. First envisaged as a tool for monitoring the economy during the Depression, the calculation of GNP would serve above all during the Second World War as a means to optimize the American military effort without compromising economic growth. In 1900, only eight countries had published data on their national income, a figure that grew to 39 in 1946 and to 80 some 10 years later (Tooze 2001, 8).

The change was also qualitative: the new mode of calculation, which originated from corporate accounting, was based on an equation between expenditure and income. This had two major consequences: first of all, the calculation of GNP (and later the similar GDP) naturalized the idea of the economy as a closed circuit, a circular flow of value between production and consumption cut off from its natural moorings; and second, by measuring it with just one figure, national accounting reified the economy and made it possible to erect it into an entity separate from society, politics, and nature.

National accounting rested, finally, on the hypothesis of a completely commodified economy. Housework and "free" services (including those rendered by nature) were absent from the calculation. In 1949, a fascinating debate took place among the early promoters of GDP: Simon Kuznets, Colin Clark, François Perroux, George Shirras among others (Clark et al. 1949). We find here the earliest and most radical critique of national accounting. According to its own progenitors, GDP was narrowly correlated with military expenditure and could not simply be used for peacetime conditions. Nor could it be used for less developed countries, as the non-market sphere plays too important a role here, falsifying international comparison. Second, GDP had to be reduced by the "costs of civilization," which included among other things pollution, traffic jams, police, judges, freeways, advertising "that stimulated artificial needs," not to mention "the work of insurers, trade associations, lawyers, bankers and statisticians." Third and above all, mining activity had to be counted negatively, since the exhaustion of resources impoverished the nation. In the end, none of these proposals were taken on board, opening an endless discussion on the "new indicators" of wealth and well-being. But this would have been simple enough: GNP, which already adjusted for the amortization and physical erosion of capital, could also have adjusted for the wear and tear of natural capital. This solution was not accepted on the pretext that it did not take the discovery of new mines into consideration. Had the inventors of GNP won this debate, this adjusted GNP would have given a rather different view of Western economic development. Indeed, according to an "alternative" calculation of GDP, if we deduct the value of annual oil exploitation from GDP in the US, it would have been in decline from the 1970s onwards (see also the Genuine Progress Indicator, which also takes account among other things of the costs of pollution, road accidents, and the loss of wetlands: Anielski and Rowe 1999).

The unequal ecology of the "Growth Paradigm"

After the Second World War, two new objects of thinking and government became globalized: "the economy" with a definite article, understood as the totality of economic transactions on a given territory, and "growth" as the ultimate goal of Cold War governments (Mitchell 1998). In the immediate postwar years, the United States government was concerned to create conditions favorable to the expansion of its economy, and to the growth of the Western camp in general. It was in this context that a new international economic regime was established, based on free trade and growth: the Bretton Woods agreements of 1944 established the dollar as world currency, the General Agreement on Tariffs and Trade liberalized trade in 1947, coupled with the Marshall Plan and the Point Four Program of the Truman Administration, which created the concept of "development aid." This world order made it possible to find outlets for the United States' gigantic industrial and agribusiness production and ensured full employment and social pacification after the great strikes of 1946. It also aimed at the social stabilization of the Western world by drawing it into growth. The Fordist and consumerist social compromise was viewed as the best protection against communism (Linnér 2003). Growth and mass consumption were presented as an alternative to communism: the United States would beat the Soviet Union at its own game by destroying the traditional barriers of class society. It was also the goal to "develop" the Third World so as to avoid its turn to communism, while ensuring cheap raw materials for the US and its industrialized allies. Fordism at home, reconstruction in Western Europe, "development" in Africa and Asia, growth everywhere. The OECD (heir to the OEEC, which had been created to implement the Marshall Plan) constituted the strategic arm of the Western camp's growth policies (Schmelzer 2016). At the same time, a gigantic exploitation of natural and human resources enabled the Eastern bloc to engage in its own policy of growth in the arms race, in space, in production, and even in consumption, which was by no means the least important terrain of Cold War confrontation.

The growth paradigm obscured a series of fundamental transformations taking place in the metabolism of the world economy after the Second World War. First, "economic growth" was in fact just another name for the petrolization of the world. Suburbanization and motorization explained a great part of the growth of the US GDP. In 1965, car production in the United States reached a historic peak of 11.1 million cars. One job in six was related to automobile construction. Provided with an abundance of cheap oil, the energy efficiency of many Western economies actually decreased, a rare exception in the long-term history of the relationship between energy and growth. The growth paradigm reflected the globalization of a switch from an organic economy to a fossil one, which also represented a loss of matter and energy efficiency on the part of the world economy. Whereas in the first half of the twentieth century an annual increase of 1.7 percent in the use of fossil fuel was required for an economic growth rate of 2.13 percent, between 1945 and 1973 an annual rise of 4.48 percent in fossil fuels (not to mention uranium) corresponded to an economic growth rate of 4.18 percent.[3]

Second, the growth paradigm relied on the development of unequal ecological exchanges on the global scale. Whereas the rise of the West during the industrial revolution was based mainly on local resources (coal, iron, etc.) and Western industrial countries were still almost self-sufficient (at least from a quantitative point of view), in the first half of the twentieth century their imports of materials rose abruptly from 299 billion tonnes in 1950 to 1,282 billion in 1970.[4]

This colossal extraction of resources from the peripheral regions of the world-system was the object of a deliberate strategic attention effort on the part of the US political leaders. Continuing the wartime logic of supply, access to

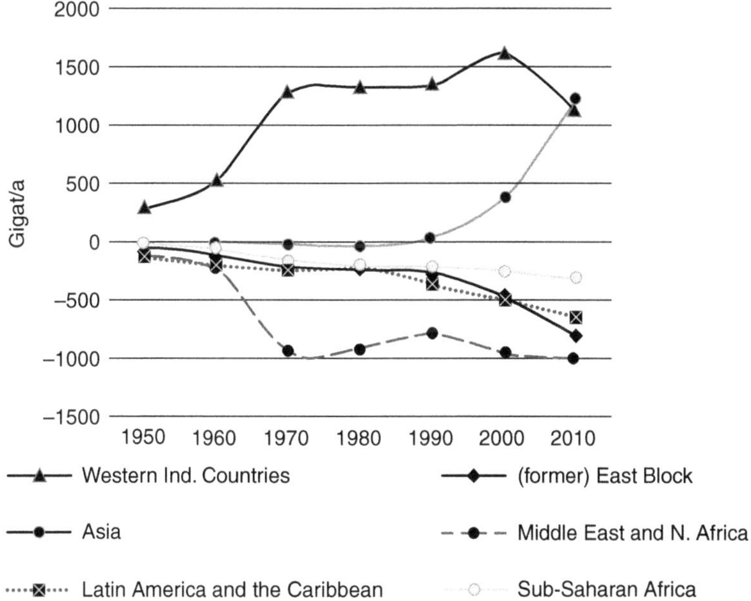

Figure 2.1 International Physical Trade Balance since 1950
Source: Bonneuil and Fressoz (2016, 247), based on data from Schaffartzik et al. (2014).

such crucial resources as uranium, rubber, and aluminum (as the key ingredient for modern aircraft) now became a strategic imperative, with policies implemented to secure energy and access to resources, from Venezuelan and Middle Eastern oil to Indian manganese and Congolese uranium. While the US rise in economic power between 1870 and 1940 had largely been based on the intensive use of its own domestic resources (wood, coal, oil, iron, copper, water, etc.), after the War the United States moved from the position of net exporter of raw materials and energy to one of net importer: congressional reports and commissions (the Paley Commission of 1951–1952), backed up by private think-tanks (Resources for the Future), now proposed the mobilization of world resources to secure the West while preserving American resources for the future (Linnér 2003; Bonneuil and Fressoz 2016, 247–248).

The United States supported the movement of decolonization as a means for securing its supplies by direct access to resources without the mediation of the European colonial powers. It initiated the UN Scientific Conference on the Conservation and Utilization of Natural Resources (UN 1950). At this event, representatives of 49 countries called for the inventory and "rational use" of the planet's natural resources that were as yet unexplored or underutilized for lack of adequate technologies, or (in rare cases) deemed overexploited for want of scientific knowledge. The United States and the UN's Western experts thus set themselves up as masters of world resources and guardians of their "right use" (Robertson 2008; Mahrane and Bonneuil 2014).

The economicization of the world

In this context, the case of the management of fish stocks is a case in point. After the Second World War, Mexico and countries in South America, Peru in particular, sought to forbid the activity of US trawlers in their territorial waters. In a similar way, South Korea complained of the incursions of Japanese and Russian vessels. In order to preserve the principle of freedom of the seas, essential for its commercial and military power, the United States imposed on international fishery law a new principle, that of "maximum sustainable yield," according to which fishing had to be authorized as long as the ratio of catch to effort had not yet reached a maximum. In order to apply the optimization principle, the model neglected both relationships between species and between marine environments. It conceived fishery resources after the model of a field which would be stimulated by increased catches (since young fish grow more quickly). Natural processes were conceived as linear and reversible. If the fishing effort declined, the resource would automatically increase. The mode of reasoning of neoclassical economics, based on the ideas of optimum and equilibrium as well as on market instruments, became central in the definition of the proper uses of the world. Under this regime of supposedly sustainable fishing, catches rose dramatically from 20 million tons in 1950 to 80 million tons in 1970, leading to a generalized decline in stocks (Finley 2011).

From the 1970s onwards, the notions of sustainability and durability became a stake in the fundamental ideological battle to circumvent mounting criticisms of the Western growth model. The year 1972 saw the publication of the famous report to the Club of Rome on *The Limits to Growth* (Meadows 1972). This report, which followed in the wake of major work by Kenneth Boulding, Herman Daly, and Nicolas Georgescu-Roegen, should have forced economics to come down to earth, but it led, on the contrary, to new constructions of the world which aimed to discredit any idea of a limit to growth (Vieille Blanchard 2011).

First of all, orthodox economists accused the report of neglecting technological innovations that enabled the replacement of "natural" capital by economic capital, or even the invention of new resources (synthetic rubber replacing natural rubber, for example). In economic theory this idea was reinforced by the famous Environmental Kuznets Curve, according to which, from a certain point onwards, growth is increasingly less harmful to the environment. The environment is degraded in order to escape from poverty, but the rise in GDP then permits better conservation. The prospectivist movement, very active in the 1970s, strengthened the hope of a growth that was dematerialized thanks to innovation. The physicist Herman Kahn (who inspired the character of Dr. Strangelove in Kubrick's film) explained that within a few decades innovations would make it possible to feed billions of human beings (through transgenic cereals capable of fixing atmospheric nitrogen), propelling them into space, etc. (Kahn 1976). Another futurologist, Alvin Toffler, author of the bestseller *The Third Wave*, likewise depicted a dematerialized high-tech future, realizing the "post-industrial society" envisioned by Daniel Bell (Toffler 1980). In France, the Groupe des Dix, Joël de Rosnay's book *Le Macroscope* (1975 [1979]) that glorified "green biotechnologies," or again the Nora–Minc report on *L'informatisation de la société* (1978), developed similar perspectives: the next industrial revolution, it was argued, would introduce a bio-optimized and dematerialized service economy, enabling the fearless pursuit of economic growth while resolving environmental problems. It was in this vein that biotechnologies were promoted in the 1970s as alternatives to chemical fertilizers, and new digital technologies as the vector of dematerialization of the economy (meanwhile, the consumption of rare earths and the energy used by the global digital infrastructure have become colossal). At present, it is geoengineering and synthetic biology, which are promoted as new technological solutions to deal with global warming and the erosion of biodiversity.

Second, a new intellectual construction of nature is asserting itself, aligned to the frameworks of neoclassical economics. In this perspective, environmental problems are framed as "market failures" that can be corrected by setting a price on nature. In the social-democratic version of economization, this price can be obtained by the state through payment of a tax that enables environment and growth to be reconciled.

From the 1970s onwards, however, a "free-market environmentalism" has come to prevail, based on the theory of Ronald Coase that it is economically optimal to attribute marketable rights to pollute and leave actors to negotiate among themselves. In various guises, the "law and economics school," the "new resource economics" or "green economics," "solutions" were promoted that depended on market instruments: markets in emissions rights for sulphur dioxide and CO_2, markets in fishing quotas or the extraction of ground water, even markets in "ecosystemic services" for biodiversity. These markets stimulated a global movement of appropriation of land for the purpose of activities rewarded by the sale of "carbon credits," "biodiversity credits," etc., further dispossessing rural and indigenous populations from their commons (Heynen et al. 2007; Bonneuil 2015a).

Through instruments such as these, the whole Earth was subjected to an economic calculation of optimization. Economists thus reconsidered the atmosphere and its ecosystems according to the model of an economic resource, whose present net value could be maximized, for example by defining optimal paths for CO_2 emissions. Global climate change was translated into a problem of maximizing economic growth under climate constraint. In the last 15 years, negotiations under the aegis of the UN Climate Convention remained trapped in what Stefan Aykut and Amy Dahan call a "reality schism," with a façade of global governance and virtuous official targets quite removed from a "world reality, that of the globalization of markets and the frenetic exploitation of resources" causing greenhouse gases annual emission to boom (Aykut and Dahan 2014, 399–401). Carbon credits, for their part, collapsed, then revived, and will most likely continue to whirl without sufficient examination of their material references, among other factors because the environmental auditors who assess the CO_2 emissions reductions of "clean development projects" have no interest in appearing too strict. At all events, their very existence and exchange are enough to create the promise of an economy at last ecologized (Stephan and Lane 2015).

What view of nature underlies these new mechanisms for governing the biosphere and atmosphere? It is claimed, on the one hand, that the best way of conserving the planetary environment is to set a price on it, to serve as a signal and enable the market, deemed cognitively superior to public action, to internalize the value of nature. On the other hand, since Gareth Hardin's famous article on "The Tragedy of the Commons," it is believed that only private property makes possible the proper management of nature, and that the ideal for certain economists is thus to "securitize the biosphere" (Chichilinsky and Heal 2000), i.e., attribute property rights to all the different elements and ecological functions of the Earth system. With nature assimilated to a "natural capital," it becomes fungible with finance capital. All the "services" rendered by the Earth system (carbon capture, pollination, water purification, aesthetic or religious services, etc.) can be valued in dollars and made the object of environmental service markets, rewarding the proprietors of the corresponding spaces who would then maintain them as good managers. The old distinction between (natural) wealth and (social) value gives way to a fetishism of nature as "the biggest business in the world" (in the expression popularized by the IUCN in 2009), as itself the producer of an economic value, already existing independent of any human labor or relation of production (Bonneuil 2015b).

In this perspective, there is no longer a limit to economic growth: the preservation of the environment, the environmental crisis, and the scarcity of resources are actually presented as economic opportunities for a "green" growth harnessing "ecosystems services" and sustaining "natural capital." As the company *Advanced Conservation Strategies* predicts: as "we enter a new era of scarcity, environmental markets are exploding."[5] In 1997, the scientific journal *Nature* published a preliminary calculation of the monetary value of services rendered annually by nature on the planetary level, which were estimated at between $16 trillion and $54 trillion dollars, or the same order of magnitude as global GDP. The annual loss of biodiversity was estimated at $4,400 billion and the same *Advanced Conservation Strategies* has no hesitation in promising that "by 2030, carbon will be the most important commodity exchanged in the world."

Conclusion

At the start of the nineteenth century, industrial modernity constructed the idea of a nature as a resources stock that was mobilizable, external to the economy, and constituting an inexhaustible storehouse. By the late twentieth century, it seemed that a new phase of capitalism – financial, postmodern, flexible, and network-based – was challenging certain ontologies of early modernity: now it was a question of giving value to diversity as well as standardizing production, commodifying flows more than tapping into stocks, services as much as material production, relationships as much as entities. The film *Avatar*, counterposing the terrestrial capitalist firm hunting for mineral ore to the "connected" nature of the Navi, is emblematic of this "network" turn of Western representations of nature. The "invisibilization" of the limits of Earth is no longer just a result of an externalization (as a great outside that humans can draw from and jettison into without problem), but on the contrary of a radical internalization of earthly entities and processes into the realm of financial markets. This internalization is expressed in the efforts to measure ecosystemic functions in terms of financial flows, conceptually creating a nature that is liquid and capitalizable even in its most intimate processes. Internalization into the market also resonates with the ontological dissolution of nature by constructivist philosophies that deny its alterity in relation to humans, and with the geo-constructivist engineering project of all aspects of the Earth system, from the genome to the biosphere (Danowski and Viveiros de Castro 2014; Neyrat 2016).

Notes

1 *Archives parlementaires de 1787 à 1860*, Paris: Paul Dupont, 1892, vol. 39, 292.

2 See House of Commons Parliamentary Papers, Hansard, 3rd Series, vol. 157, pp. 216–330.

3 Sources: for GDP and population, the Maddison series, www.ggcc.net/maddison; for consumption of materials and energy, data from the Institute of Social Ecology: http://www.uni-klu.ac.at/socec/downloads/Online_data_global_flows_update_2011.xls.

4 Nonetheless, South America, Africa, and Asia did provide key raw materials, especially for the second industrial revolution such as rubber, copper, or tin.

5 See www.advancedconservationstrategies.org (accessed March 15, 2013). The page containing this quote has since been deleted.

References

Anielski, Mark and Rowe, Jonathan. 1999. *The Genuine Progress Indicator – 1998 Update*. San Francisco: Redefining Progress.

Aykut, Stefan and Dahan, Amy. 2014. *Gouverner le climat? 20 ans de négociations internationals*. Paris: Presses de Sciences Po.

Barton, Gregory. 2004. *Empire Forestry and the Origins of Environmentalism*. Cambridge: Cambrdige University Press.

Bonneuil, Christophe. 2015a. "Tell Me Where You Come From, I Will Tell You Who You Are: A Genealogy of Biodiversity Offsetting Mechanisms in Historical Context." *Conservation Biology* 192: 485–491.

Bonneuil, Christophe. 2015b. "Une nature liquide? Les discours de la biodiversité dans le nouvel esprit du capitalisme." In *Le pouvoir de la biodiversité. Néolibéralisation de la nature dans les pays émergents*, edited by F. Thomas and V. Boisvert, 193–213. Paris: IRD éd.-Quae.

Bonneuil, Christophe and Fressoz Jean-Baptiste. 2016. *The Shock of the Anthropocene. The Earth, History and us*. London: Verso Books.

Breslau, Daniel. 2003. "Economics Invents the Economy: Mathematics, Statistics, and Models in the Work of Irving Fisher and Wesley Mitchell." *Theory and Society* 32(3): 379–411.

Buckland, William. 1837. *Geology and Mineralogy Considered with Reference to Natural Theology*, vol. 1. Philadelphia: Carey.

Buridant, Jérôme. 2008. *Le premier choc énergétique. La crise forestière dans le nord bassin parisien, début XVIIIe-début XIXe siècles.* Ph.D. thesis Paris IV.

Carnot, Sadi. 1824. *Réflexions sur la puissance motrice du feu*. Paris: Bachelier.

Chichilinsky, Graciela and Geoffrey Heal. 2000. "Securitizing the biosphere." In *Environmental Markets, Equity and Efficiency*, edited by Graciela Chichilinsky and Geoggrey Heal, 169–179. New York: Columbia University Press.

Clark, Colin *et al.* 1949. "The Measurement of National Wealth: Discussion." *Econometrica* 17: 255–272.

Danowski, Deborah and Eduardo Viveiros de Castro. 2014. "L'arrêt de monde." In *De l'univers clos au monde infini*, edited by Émilie Hache, 221–339. Paris: Dehors.

De Rosnay, Joel. 1979. *The Macroscope: A New World Scientific System*. Harper & Row [1975 1st French ed.].

Finley, Carmel. 2011. *All the Fish in the Sea: Maximum Sustainable Yield and the Failure of Fisheries Management*. Chicago: Chicago University Press.

Freedgood, Elaine. 2000. *Victorian Writing About Risk*. Cambridge: Cambridge University Press.

Fressoz, Jean-Baptiste. 2012. *L'Apocalypse joyeuse. Une histoire du risque technologique.* Paris: Le Seuil.

Fressoz, Jean-Baptiste and Locher, Fabien. 2012. "Modernity's Frail Climate. A Climate History of Environmental Reflexivity." *Critical Inquiry* 38: 579–598.

Georgescu-Roegen, Nicholas. 1975. "Energy and Economic Myths." *Southern Economic Journal* 41(3): 347–381.

Girard, Pierre Simon. 1827. *Mémoire sur les grandes routes, les chemins de fer et le canaux de navigation*. Paris: Bachelier.

Heynen, N., McCarthy, J., Scott, P., and Robbins, P. (eds). 2007. *Neoliberal Environments: False Promises and Unnatural Consequences.* London: Routledge.

Hilton, Boyd. 1997. *The Age of Atonement: The Influence of Evangelicalism on Social and Economic Thought, 1785–1865*, Oxford: Oxford University Press.

Hutton, James. 1788. "Theory of the Earth." *Transactions of the Royal Society of Edinburgh*, 1, 209–304.

Kahn, Herman *et al.* 1976. *The Next 200 Years: A Scenario for America and the World.* New York: Morrow.

de La Roche, Tiphaigne. 1760. *Essai Œconomique sur les mers occidentales.* Paris: Bauche.

Linnér, Björn-Ola. 2003. *The Return of Malthus: Environmentalism and Post-war Population-Resource Crises.* Isle of Harris, UK: The White Horse Press.

Lowood, Henry E. 1990. "The Calculating Forester". In *The Quantifying Spirit in the Eighteenth Century.* Berkeley: University of California Press.

Madureira, Nuno Luis. 2012. "The Anxiety of Abundance: William Stanley Jevons and Coal Scarcity in the Nineteenth Century." *Environment and History* 18: 395–421.

Mahrane, Yannick and Bonneuil, Christophe. 2014. "Gouverner la biosphère: de l'environnement de la guerre froide à l'environnement néoliberal" In *Le Gouvernement des technosciences. Gouverner le progrès et ses dégâts depuis 1945*, edited by Dominique Pestre, 133–169. Paris: La Découverte.

Malm, Andreas. 2016. *Fossil Capital. The Rise of Steam Power and the Roots of Global Warming*. London: Verso Books.

Martinez-Alier, Juan and Schlupmann, Klaus. 1993. *Ecological Economics: Energy, Environment, Society*. Oxford: Blackwell.

Meadows, Donella H., Meadows, Dennis L., Randers, Jørgen, and Behrens III, William W. 1972. *The Limits to Growth*. New York: Universe Books.

Mirowski, Philip. 1991. *More Heat than Light: Economics as Social Physics, Physics as Nature's Economics*, Cambridge: Cambridge University Press.

Mitchell, Tim. 1998. "Fixing the Economy." *Cultural Studies* 12(1): 82–101.

Mitchell, Timothy. 2011. *Carbon Democracy: Political Power in the Age of Oil*. London: Verso.

Moore, Edward. 1755. *The World*, vol. 3. London: Dodsley.

Neyrat, Frédéric. 2016. *La part inconstructible de la Terre. Critique du géo-constructivisme*. Paris: Seuil.

Nora, Simon and Minc, Alain. 1978. *L'informatisation de la Société*, Paris: La Documentation française.

Pottier, Antonin. 2016. *Comment les économistes réchauffent la planète?* Paris: Seuil.

Rauch, François Antoine. 1802. *Harmonie hydro-végétale et météorologique*. Paris: Frères Levrault.

Robertson, Thomas. 2008. "This is the American Earth: American Empire, the Cold War, and American Environmentalism." *Diplomatic History* 32(4): 561–584.

Rudwick, Martin. 2005. *Bursting the Limits of Time*. Chicago: Chicago University Press.

Say, Jean-Baptiste, 1840. *Cours complet d'économie politique pratique*, vol. 1. Paris: Guillaumin.

Schaffartzik, Anke, Mayer, A., Gingrich, S., Eisenmenger, N., Loy, C., and Krausmann, F. 2014. "The Global Metabolic Transition: Regional Patterns and Trends of Global Material Flows, 1950–2010." *Global Environmental Change* 26: 87–97.

Schmelzer, Matthias. 2016. *The Hegemony of Growth. The OECD and the Making of the Economic Growth Paradigm*. Cambridge: Cambridge University Press.

Scott, James C. 1998. *Seeing Like a State*. New Haven: Yale University Press.

Sée, Henri. 1924. "Les forêts et la question du déboisement en Bretagne à la fin de l'Ancien Régime." *Annales de Bretagne* 36: 355–379.

Sieferle, Rolf Peter. 2001. *The Subterranean Forest: Energy Systems and the Industrial Revolution*. Cambridge: The White Horse Press.

Solow, Robert. 1974. "The Economics of Resources or the Resources of Economics." *American Economic Review* 64(2):1–14.

Stafford, Robert A. 1989. *Scientist of Empire: Sir Roderick Murchison, Scientific Exploration, and Victorian Imperialism*. Cambridge: Cambridge University Press.

Stephan, Benjamin and Lane, Richard (eds). 2015. *The Politics of Carbon Trading*. London: Routledge.

Toffler, Alvin. 1980. *The Third Wave*. New York: Bantam Books.

Tooze, Adam. 2001. *Statistics and the German State, 1900–1945*. Cambridge: Cambridge University Press.

Torrens, Hugh. 2002. *The Practice of British Geology, 1750–1850*. Aldershot: Ashgate.

UN (United Nations). 1950. *Proceedings of the United Nations Scientific Conference on the Conservation and Utilization of Resources, 17 August–6 September 1949, Lake Success, New York*. New York: United Nations, 6 vol.

Vieille Blanchard, Élodie. 2011. Les Limites à la croissance dans un modèle global – Modèles mathématiques, prospectives, réfutations. Doctoral thesis, EHESS.

Wrigley, Tony. 2004. "Two Kinds of Capitalism, Two Kinds of Growth." In *Poverty, Progress and Population*, 68–86. Cambridge: Cambridge University Press.

3 The end of gold?

Monetary metals studied at the planetary and human scale during the classical gold standard era

Andrea Westermann

In 1877, Eduard Suess, a professor of geology from Vienna published *The Future of Gold* (*Die Zukunft des Goldes*). In 1892, the year the Austrian Government convened an expert commission to discuss its Empire's transition from a 40-year period of inconvertible paper money to a gold coinage standard, he published his update *The Future of Silver* (*Die Zukunft des Silbers*). Suess's studies are very early examples of mineral resource estimates undertaken on a global scale. Suess was a pioneer of global tectonics. He coined many planetary concepts still in use today such as hydrosphere, lithosphere, and biosphere, argued for Gondwana, the former supercontinent in the Southern hemisphere, and introduced "Eurasia" as a structural unit on a continental scale. With his estimates of the world gold reserves, Suess not only contributed to creating yet another globe-spanning entity or abstraction, he also intended to ward off the trend for an internationally adopted gold standard. The Austrian geologist predicted a probable decline in the future world production of gold, and that in the long run, the supply of monetary gold would not be sufficient to meet the demands of rapidly expanding world trade. The global production of silver, in contrast, would increase at a more regular rate. According to Suess, the money of the future was silver.

Not everyone agreed with his assessment. Frank William Taussig, an American economist objected: "Whatever geological time may bring, there is nothing to indicate that in the historical future, silver will succeed in displacing gold as the money of the civilized world" (Taussig 1893a, 366). Carl Menger, Vienna's star professor of political economy and monetary theory, alluded in one of his statements before the Austrian currency reform commission (*Währungs-Enquete-Kommission*) to Eduard Suess's famous words that "the planet may be measured by man, but not according to man" (Suess 1904, 17). He turned upside down Suess's appeal to overcome the deeply entrenched restrictions of human imagination for the sake of advancing geological research, by making it a statement of sober pragmatism in governmental affairs: "I say that we should act according to human judgment ('nach menschlichem Ermessen'), because we do not have any other" (Menger 1970, 277).

What motivated Suess to encompass geological and monetary notions of gold stocks in one and the same study? Why did he think the former would bear on the latter in a politically meaningful way? And how did Suess's opponents respond to the geologist's attempt to link the planetary and the societal scale and discuss global mineral resource consumption and predicted scarcity amid growth-oriented international monetary politics? This chapter explores these questions.

Problems of scaling and commensuration in the earth sciences have been troubling environmental historians and historians of science alike for a while now. Scholars are turning to the history of geology to study how people simultaneously cope with the planetary scale and the human scale or, for that matter, their reluctance to do so. In view of global environmental change, they aim to spur our current scalar practices, highlighting climate science and history. Michael Northcott, in his *A Political Theology of Climate Change*, reminds us of scale shifts associated with religious and cultural ideas about "the influence human beings believed they had over the climate, and nature, before the Copernican revolution" (Northcott 2013, 2). Naomi Oreskes examines "how earth science became social science" (Oreskes 2015). Matthias Heymann and Dania Achermann call for "reinventing the human scale" to better face global ecological crises (see Call for Papers for an open session at the Annual Meeting of the Society for the History of Technology SHOT, 22–26 June 2016 in Singapore, January 18, 2016). Deborah Coen (2016) looks into plural forms of commensuration in science and society of the nineteenth century. And Jean-Baptiste Fressoz (2016) critically examines the aesthetic category of the sublime underlying our ambitious projects of geoengineering the global climate, arguing that the emotional power of the sublime precisely stems from juxtaposing, not bridging the experience of divergent, incommensurate scales.

The business of global mineral resource estimation is yet another field where the planetary and the societal scale meet in order to become commensurate. In mineral resource estimates, economic and geological notions of mineral stocks or mineral depots/deposits are offset against each other. Mineral resource appraisals started out as local or regional endeavors. Geologists examined the underground assets of a particular mine in order to predict the size, quality, and duration of its commodity production or determine the selling price of the operation at a given time (Westermann 2014, 23). From a national perspective, the numbers of individual mines and regional mining districts could be added to the state level; by 1900, national numbers were selectively put in an international comparative perspective (Westermann 2015). In a collective effort, the international community of geologists presented a first world-spanning survey of iron ore resources, the powerhouse of the machine age, at the 11th International Geological Congress held in Stockholm in 1910 (The General Secretary of the Congress 1910).

Suess neither inventoried the iron ore nor the energy resources fueling the industrial revolution.[1] By investigating the stock of "monetary substance" available to a world busy expanding its markets, he still focused on what was regarded a necessary material investment for economic growth:[2] Thriving economies absorbed an ever-growing supply of money.[3] Considering that the alchemical ambition of generating never-ending wealth by making "noble" or precious metals out of base metals had stopped informing the practice of governance some time ago, a possible exhaustion of the natural gold stocks was important news.[4] Suess's works were widely read and "spread general alarm."[5] The direction of the US Senate Committee on Finance had the book on silver translated by a member of the Geological Survey (Suess 1893). Although not part of the Vienna committee, Suess was invited to report to the German Silver Commission, convened in Berlin in 1894.

I argue that the combination of geological, cameralistic, and cosmopolitical reasoning and routines motivated Suess to intervene in gold standard issues. Yet ultimately, the Vienna geologist could not persuade his contemporaries to adjust their reactions to the predicted end of monetary gold. By the end of the century, after lengthy discussions on monetary metals in almost every country, all the Western nation states had established the gold standard. Facing highly aggregated numbers indicating orders of magnitude at best, people opted for suspending Suess's absolute definitions of world gold and silver reserves or his forecast of peak gold, sticking instead to the temporal logics of politics. As Emil Russell, a bank director who sat on the Berlin silver committee put it:

> Professor Suess argues that, in very general terms, geologists are able to delineate what can be expected. These rough predictions unfold their meaning within historical periods of two, three, or four hundred years. I think that such long-term prospects should not be a part of our current monetary discussions. If the end of gold was expected within the next five or ten years, well, then we would have every reason to address the problem of scarcity. Yet when confronted with a time span of 50, 100, or 150 years, I advise: *reproducator* (resubmission) after 100 years.[6]

Moreover, economists did not believe that the past and future of the metal money rose or fell in lockstep as Suess suggested. While all the experts embraced monetary politics as a tool for growth economies, the idea of precious metals being the defining feature of "good" or "ideal" money started to lose ground. Economists began to disassemble and institutionally redistribute the monetary functions that theories of money had long based on its metal content: a standardized measure of value, a medium of exchange, and a reliable store of wealth.

Global cameralistics: Suess intervenes in international gold standard debates

Monetary politics escaped historians' attention as an early context that would initiate global mineral resource appraisals. Yet fiscal questions and monetary metals were not far-fetched issues for a geologist like Suess whose discipline had formed part of, and took its modern shape among, the state or cameral sciences. The word comes from the German "Kammer" meaning "royal treasure chamber," i.e. "a specialized collegial body dedicated to administering the sovereign finances" in German-speaking countries of the late seventeenth and eighteenth centuries (Wakefield 2014, 134; Westermann 2011). The human scale – supporting societal concerns – had thus been at the core of geology from the beginning. Entrusted with managing a state's territory and its human and natural resources, the cameral sciences maintained the idea of economically organized nature lending itself readily to the service of society (Lindenfeld 1997, 28–29; Reith 2010). While agriculture and forestry were subject to the "quantifying spirit" from the mid-eighteenth century onwards (Frängsmyr 1990; Lindenfeld 1997, 30), geological mapping and local or regional mineral appraisal followed suit. In 1791, Saxony led the way when Abraham Gottlob Werner was commissioned to make the first comprehensive mineral survey.[7] A better understanding of nature's "mineral economy" ("oeconomia mineralium," Reuss 1777, 11) and the genesis of fossil fuel and ore deposits promised to increase the output of royal mines and hence the gains from mining concessions, an important source of state revenue. The accumulation of precious metal stocks above ground as a steady source of princely wealth – part of the extracted precious metals, usually 10 percent, went directly to the treasury – was another reason for studying the mineral stocks underground (Bartels 2013, 117). Precious metals often took the form of money (on the costs and gains of coinage see Rössner 2012, 333–388).

Suess was a modern cameralist, if I may use this somewhat paradoxical characterization. Besides being a geologist, he was a member of Vienna's city council from 1863 to 1873 and again from 1882 to 1886; he sat in the *Niederösterreichischer Landtag* (State Parliament of Lower Austria) from 1869 to 1896; and on the *Reichsrat* (Imperial Council, the Empire's legislative body) from 1874 to 1897 as a liberal party member. He planned and managed the city's new drinking water supply: Vienna got its famous mountain spring water supply line built from 1861 to 1873. He was also the leading expert on the Danube correction works (1870–1875) (Hamann 1983).[8] Suess believed in the value and longevity of science-based infrastructure and decision-making (Suess 1902, 8). This attitude explains his intervention in international monetary politics – and was not entirely out of place considering both his urban infrastructural projects are still functioning today. He argued: "A century is a short time span in the development of world traffic, communication and commerce ('Weltverkehr'). The suggestion to demonetize silver should not be a measure that needed revision after one or two centuries; it should rather be, as far as one can tell, a permanent change in how to use both metals as media of exchange." (Suess 1877, 76)

Extending the cameral sciences beyond narrow definitions of state territory was yet another rather natural move for Suess, given both his interest in global tectonics and the continental expanse of Imperial Austria (Coen 2012).[9] The gold standard debate struck a third chord: Underlying the debates on international currency standardization were the gospels of free trade and cosmopolitanism. Aiming for a global gold standard testified to a "cosmopolitan tendency," Suess noted approvingly (Suess 1877, 31). Born in London into a merchant family with kin ties to Saxony, Vienna, and Prague, Suess was a cosmopolitan himself (Hamann 1983). Free traders voted for a unified currency, and rightly so – in principle: A single currency standard would reduce transaction costs and price reductions would ultimately benefit everyone (Suess 1877, 361; see Meissner 2002, 2). Yet, this attitude demanded, as Suess saw it, "desisting from any local and provisionary circumstances and assessing the world demand and production of metals from the most comprehensive perspective" (Suess 1877, 32). As will become clear, Suess's cosmopolitics of scaling monetary matters up to the largest, "most comprehensive level" went beyond the political and economic realm. It also included epistemic and cultural questions of how to understand the globe in both its worldly and earthly dimensions (I am indebted here to Tresch 2014).

No government had assigned Suess the task of appraising the global inventory of monetary metals. Still, his books on the future of gold and silver contributed to the wider debate in the second half of the nineteenth century, on how newly opened large gold and silver deposits coming on stream impacted on currency reforms and monetary politics. Large-scale overseas mining and the advances in metal refining not only dramatically changed the raw metal production outlook (Leith 1970. repr. of 1931, 34). The more abstract realm of monetary standards was also affected.

Most Western states at the time operated with commodity money and on a bimetallic standard. Their currencies were based both on silver and gold, with the face value of the coins matching the value of their metal content. Mexico, China, and India were on a silver standard. Only Great Britain had shifted to a gold-based currency in the 1820s. From 1848 onwards, large gold finds from California, and shortly afterwards Australia, came to the international markets, while the production of silver stagnated. This made silver more expensive in relation to gold, a development that allured people to gamble. Massive amounts of silver coins were sold on the world market because their commodity value had become higher than their nominal value stamped on them. In response, governments on a silver or bimetallic standard started to demonetize their silver coins. Between 1860 and 1880, the discovery and mining of rich silver deposits in Nevada brought in turn a huge flow of silver to the markets. Consequently, the ratio of value between the two classic monetary metals, which had been reasonably stable for several decades, began to totter. Everywhere national expert committees were commissioned to report on the recent developments in the monetary situation and perhaps suggest reforms to domestic coinage politics (see Wagner 1880 and 1881; Lexis 1890; Soetbeer 1892 for contemporary reviews of the torrent of publications). International monetary conferences were held; monetary unions were created, similar to the Latin Monetary Union founded in 1865 to defend bimetallic currencies (de Cecco 1992, 58–67).

In the last three decades of the nineteenth century, the drift was toward gold. Imperial Germany turned to gold after 1871. It seized the opportunity and switched by acquiring gold bullion and specie through war indemnities imposed on France. In the rest of Europe, Germany's shift had both a signaling effect and palpable consequences for domestic monetary politics because Germany started to demonetize its silver coins, thus causing further deterioration in prices for the silver commodity. Before the First World War, the 35 national economies operating a gold standard accounted for 70 per cent of the world trade (Mitchener 2012, 88; for another good overview see Officer 2008).

Peak gold: framing the earth socially

Suess imagined the future of gold, many decades before geologists convened for a first collective effort to assess the "gold resources of the world" and the business of mineral resource estimation was gradually becoming professionalized in the early and mid-twentieth century.[10] In 1892, Suess claimed that the insights, empirical as well as theoretical, which geologists had collectively gained over the decades were such that "the data given by nature" enabled us "to establish a prognosis for perfectly definite economic questions" (Suess 1893, 101). Following on from this, the limits "nature has set to the wealth of its gifts" needed to be taken into account: "Man's control of his planet has reached a point where these limits must never be lost from view" (Suess 1893, 61).

As I will show in this section, Suess tried hard to convey to his readers a sense of earth matters – mineral resources that were very large, but of restricted access to man and finite nonetheless – and make these insights bear on national and international life. The earth's inner layers were difficult to approach, much more so in the nineteenth century when geophysical remote sensing was in its infancy. Suess explained to his audience that "physical man is very small when compared to the globe" ("Erdball"): "Proud to dig a tunnel reaching down 1000 meters, he readily forgets that the radius of the earth measures 6.5 million meters" (Suess 1877, 88). In 1875, the Austrian government had celebrated the 1,000 m mark reached in one silver mine in Pribram, Bohemia, in a week-long festivity with international guests and, of course, a commemorative coin. At the time, the reference to Pribram's "unique feat" was prominent among geologists (Deutsche Silberkommission 1894b, 35).

While mines were important complements to natural outcrops such as mountain ranges or coastlines, inventorying the whole earth's crust remained an ambitious goal. Small wonder that estimating the world's mineral resources would turn out to be a notoriously provisional undertaking. Producing only snapshots in time, global mineral resource appraisals are repeated recurrently, are undertaken for specific reasons and metals or fuels, and, in hindsight, almost always prove to be erroneous. Yet global mineral resource estimates and those who assign, produce, and use them embrace what Alain Desrosières has called the "realism of aggregates." Aggregates are both a reality and a convention. They depict important features of the world and, at the same time, help "to establish the reality they describe" (Desrosières 1998, 3 and 1). In so doing, global mineral appraisal efforts combine natural and social scientific knowledge. They not only seek to make an inventory of the mineral content of the earth's crust in absolute terms and determine, for instance, how much gold there is in the earth's upper crust that has not yet been mined or dug up. They also investigate the consumption side and estimate how long the known global mineral reserves will last.

In mining, the physical (earth-bound) and economic (society-bound) availability of minerals has converged at the most basic level from early on. In the geological and mining vernacular, the notion "ore" is a dynamic intersect: It only includes those metallic mineral resources which are within technological reach and will be mined at a profit in the present or near future (Westermann 2015, 154). On the one hand, the definition is a great example of making the planetary and societal scale commensurate considering that Wendy Espeland and Mitchell Stevens take commensuration as "the transformation of different qualities into a common metric" (Espeland and Stevens 1998, 314).

On the other hand, mineral resource appraisals rest on a range of geological, political, and historical reasoning and assumptions that do not always translate into neat aggregate numbers but take the form of trends or magnitudes instead, i.e. of aggregates still exposing their qualitative and narrative character (Westermann 2014, 33). Suess's ideas about the metallogenesis of gold are a case in point of such creative numerical reasoning. He assessed the mineral content of the earth's crust by extrapolating ore genesis and concentration in theoretical terms from a bulk of empirical data. Suess introduced his readers to a mainstay of the geology discipline, that the entire mass of the planet Earth was much denser than its outmost layers of rock strata, "hence the conclusion that the heaviest elements tend to be located towards the inner core" (Suess 1877, 354). He argued that heavy metals – heavy compared to the same volume of water, a metric not in use anymore – were created deeper in the earth's crust and consequently more seldom found at the earth's surface than light metals (Suess 1877, 77; Petzholdt 1845, 492). With a specific weight of 19'253, gold was at the lower end in the group of heavy metals; silver (10'474) and lead (11'352) did not count as heavy metals at all, occurring abundantly in the earth's upper crust. To underscore his transforming a material's different qualities, i.e. its depth-owed rarity and ensuing societal value into a common metric, the measurement of density, Suess also drew on recent spectral analyses of the sunlight lending themselves to suggestive analogies. While earthly elements such as magnesium, aluminum, calcium, iron, cobalt, nickel, copper, or zinc had been identified as burning solar matter, precious metals did not show up as yet, perhaps because, Suess gladly assumed in accordance with the notion of earth's heavy metals, they were simply not to be found anywhere near the sun's surface (Suess 1877, 80–82).

Suess resorted to other forms of scaling while making his case for global mineral resource estimates. Reading Suess's 389-page book on gold is not unlike reading environmental journalist Elizabeth Kolbert's essays on climate change (such as her piece on the rising sea level in Miami Beach, for instance,

Kolbert 2015). Just like Kolbert, Suess mastered the juxtaposition of distinct narrative scales as a rhetorical device for relating earth history and societal history. Knowledgeably, he linked earth history (chap. 4), recent history of coinage politics (chap. 1), and investigation of the lost geography of fabulously rich Ophir, the biblical gold land (314–315 and 317–318). He added inventories of the world's mineral districts, which in themselves combined precious metal production data and histories of mining with political, archaeological or art historical sources (chap. 6–13). The book is full of details on gold mining's work organization adapted to different geological environments (chap. 3), stories of gold rushes changing lives for thousands of men who flocked to California only to move further up to British Columbia's Fraser River in 1858, and parables of the last big bonanzas. In his 1892 update on the political economy of monetary metals, Suess inserted a chapter on the sudden rise and fall of Comstock Lode in Nevada to connect his readers with the eternal drama of the glitter of gold buried behind the numbers:

> The dead figures in statistical tables do not speak of the vicissitudes under which the exploitation of great treasures is often accomplished and yet every estimate is one-sided if it does not take these vicissitudes into account. As an example we will select Comstock Lode in Nevada. This lode was the greatest accumulation of precious metal that man ever laid hands on. Gold and silver were found united. Hundreds of millions of dollars, almost half in gold, were poured into human commerce, and here we can learn how through the great richness of the ores, and the consequent inflaming of the passions, a great lode mine may become as short-lived as the treasures of the alluvial land.
>
> (Suess 1893, 37)

He also told the story of Californian hydraulic mining, a process inextricably linking nature, earth, large-scale infrastructure, and human labor. While the use of jets of water directed under high pressure through hoses and nozzles at alluvial placer gold deposits to wash out the metal was utterly devastating for the environment, hydraulic mining also depended on the "weather, just like farming" when it came to collecting the yield. People would talk about the collection of gold in terms of harvesting wheat or barley. "It will rain," he cited an issue of the US *Engineering and Mining Journal*, "a good harvest of gold is expected" (Suess 1877, 69).

Yet the drama of gold not only unfolded on the rough edges of culture. It also shook the very heart of urban life. On behalf of his readers, Suess browsed the *Mining Journal* published in London, where between 1880 and 1913, more than 8,400 mining companies procured capital or transacted part of their business at the newly opened London Metal Exchange (Westermann 2014, 23). The journal regularly reported on gold mining undertakings without any return on investment for those who staked their fortunes. This was the main reason why mineral resource estimation was becoming professionalized bottom up: Referring to the millions German investors had lost on mining projects in Africa in 1913, a German chemical and smelting engineer pointed out what made the "difference between mining as an industry or as mere speculation": the specific risk of the business, i.e. the "size of the ore reserves" had to be assessed seriously.[11]

Suess concluded that whatever the capital, environmental and labor investment raised or lost: People around the globe were attracted to the same mineral object of desire, sold and bought at a world price (Suess 1877, 71). By highlighting the emotional stakes in world gold production and recreating them at a textual level, he was offering his readers a "sense of planet" (Heise 2008) of a special kind. In his books, Suess identified gold as the highest value and market good in a world subject to the universal metric of pricing.[12] Putting the work of mineral resource appraisal in its appropriate context, he aptly described the omnipresent processes of monetary quantification. By underlining the flipside of the market world, i.e. the losses, damages, depletions, or no-finds related to gold mining, he evoked the universal experience of failure, drama, and overwhelming limits set by nature. Taken together, the narratives called for connecting with the notion of world gold reserves in a "history of mentalities" way, a perspective that stressed the weight of continuity and persistence and undergirded Suess's long-term view on the subject of monetary metals.

When gold, as Suess explained, had originally formed deep in the inner layers of the earth's crust, how then did it come within man's technological reach in the first place? Suess distinguished two types of gold finds. Alluvial placer gold ("Wasch"- or "Seifengold") was one, often and rather easily found as ready-to-use pebbles, nuggets or lumps in recent rock sediments, having been weathered out over geological time from deep below and deposited in and near current or former riverbeds, and mountainsides. From antiquity until the late nineteenth century, Suess agreed with many geologists and historians studying gold, most of the gold produced had come from alluvial sources. Over the previous 15 years, the alluvial sources' share of total gold production numbers was steadily decreasing (Suess 1877, 356; Suess 1893, 47; del Mar 1880, VII). In his view, the recent boom and bust history of gold rushes since 1848 only substantiated the trend of depleting alluvial gold reserves.

The second type of gold deposits was lodes ("Erzgänge"). Including the geology of the South American Atlantic coast and California, Suess explained that gold lodes routinely accompanied volcanic and seismic activities. He described lodes as faults and fractures produced by tectonic quakes and filled with metallic matter by geochemical and hydrological processes. Lodes could be seen as "the fossilized source of an earthquake" as he put it suggestively (Suess 1877, 95 and 101). Taking into account the existence of rich but local bonanzas and gossans ("Adelsvorschub" and "Eiserner Hut"), Suess assumed their gold content was declining rather dramatically with increasing depth (Suess 1877, 108). Moreover, the picture of fissure suggested no widespread occurrence – all in all bad news for ongoing sustainable production. As a rule, the richer gold lode deposits were found to lie in older strata, tectonically uplifted to the surface, rather than in younger, conformably lying geological formations. Arguing that most of these formations had been located already, Suess made a peak gold prognosis *avant la lettre*: "If we survey, on the globe, these regions leaving aside the sea floor, the younger surface strata [...] and those patches of the earth's crust veiled by polar ice, and compare them to the older surface strata already exploited more or less completely in the course of the millennia since Ramses II had a well dug in the gold land of Akita, we see that much more than half of the gold deposits available to man until now have been extracted" (Suess 1877, 337–338).[13] Accounting for the accelerating rates of gold production he had witnessed over the last 15 years alone, Suess firmly restated in 1892 that, "presumably, in a few centuries, the production of gold will diminish permanently and to an extraordinary degree" (Suess 1893, 49).

Suess still ignored the soon to be discovered deposits of a new type in South Africa when forecasting peak gold in 1877. Gold also existed as strata of gold-bearing conglomerates lying in the oldest geological units on the African continent.[14] The massive influx, since the mid-1880s, of gold from the Transvaal to the London market eased international liquidity problems by facilitating an expansion of the gold base and money supplies without the dangers of inflation induced by printing non-backed paper money (Van-Helten 1982, 533; de Cecco 1992, 55–58; Grewe 2013). The material experience arguably strengthened the idea of a gold currency as the world standard. Although Suess forecast a bright near future of South African gold mining in his 1892 book (Suess 1893, 4, 45, 47), much of the controversy about his predictions focused on the unexpectedness and apparent uniqueness of these gold finds as well as their actual size and probable lifetime.

Suess's global mineral appraisals under scrutiny: the history and future of gold mining

With the US Congress repealing the Sherman Silver Purchase Act and Britain closing the Indian Mints for silver in 1893, two major actors demonetized silver provoking yet another decline in its commodity price. In February 1894, the German Reich chancellor Graf von Caprivi appointed a committee to discuss a potential German contribution to the appreciation and stabilization of the silver currencies (Deutsche Silberkommission 1894a). While no decision-making was planned for the committee and Imperial Germany would not repeal its gold standard, it considered signing international contracts fixing the ratio of value between gold and silver.

Four geologists sat on the committee.[15] In addition, Wilhelm Lexis, mathematician and political economist from Göttingen, part of a small number of international experts on precious metal statistics, had been drafted.[16] Since the development of precious metal mining was considered a decisive factor in determining the ratio of value between the two monetary metals, the silver committee had agreed to meet, for its 17th to 20th sessions, in an altered constituency as a "production of precious metals committee." This subcommittee was to address Suess's appraisals of the world gold reserves. Although reluctant to give such importance to the matter of allegedly dwindling world gold reserves, the gold standard proponents on the silver committee thought it tactically unwise and potentially damaging for any recommendation they might make if they did not consider the geological expert who had lobbied most outspokenly against a gold standard. This would suggest, they maintained, "that Suess was such a dangerous man that his report would overthrow the whole gold standard … He would never succeed in doing so, even if he used all his powers of persuasion" (Deutsche Silberkommission 1894a, 43–44). Two other geologists were invited to critically examine Suess's prognostications: Alfred Wilhelm Stelzner, professor of geology at the Mining Academy in Freiberg and Karl Schmeisser who had just surveyed the gold fields of the Transvaal on behalf of the Prussian Ministry of Commerce (Schmeisser 1894). Schmeisser's report and a 67-page report "on the present situation of the precious metal production of the world" written by Wilhelm Hauchecorne, committee member and Berlin geologist, had been assigned reading for the special committee.

The discussion centered on the future productivity of the Witwatersrand minerals district and, consequently, on the appropriate analogies for imagining and assessing the size and richness of this new type of gold conglomerate deposit. In an information search routinely used for compiling his multivolume synthesis of global tectonics, *The Face of the Earth*, he was writing at the same time, Suess had asked local experts in the Transvaal to send him both their geological interpretations as well as anything of value for remote opinion-forming: maps, drilling protocols, production statistics, rock specimens, and the like. Suess's mineralogy colleague in Vienna, Anton Pelikan, examined the received specimens chemically and under the microscope, hoping to find clues that would explain the conditions of their sedimentation. Pelikan reported back that, in his opinion, the gold grains and flitters had originated as lodes embedded in quartz rock, undergone smashing by tectonic mechanisms and been transported away to accumulate as the conglomerate strata in question (Pelikan 1894, 424). Suess compared the setting to alluvial placer gold deposits. Given their old age, he characterized the gold-bearing conglomerate as a "fossil placer deposit" (Deutsche Silberkommission, 1894b, 14–15).

In contrast, Hauchecorne and Schmeisser compared the stratigraphy of the gold fields to the conglomerate horizons as known in the German mining districts: the conglomerates accompanying the coalbeds in Westphalia and Saarbrücken or the seams of copper in Mansfeld. Both analogies came with their own rules of geoeconomic extrapolation and mineral resource assessment. According to Suess, the patterns of discovery and rapid depletion of alluvial gold placers had remained the same "since the dawn of human history" no matter the exact quantities (ibid., 50). Schmeisser and Hauchecorne thought that the conglomerate seams had precipitated in an ocean environment, were therefore fairly consistent in their mineral composition, extended conformably over many kilometers, and reached great depths. Other than the "complete randomness" (ibid. 33) of gold lodes and different from alluvial gold, the Witwatersrand picture suggested sustainable production numbers over a very long time – once the technical feasibility of mining beyond the magical landmark of deeper than 1,000 m had become commonplace (ibid., 30, 78–79).

There was general agreement among the group to talk about trends, magnitudes, and decades of the production of gold since "no exact numbers could be given" (ibid., 54; see also 18, 19, 46, 55, 59). Yet the committee members had different assumptions about how well the tectonics and stratigraphy of the earth's crust were already known. Suess pictured the planet's surface layer as a confined space whose structure and mineral content had already been roughly clarified by earth scientific research. Africa was the last place on the map waiting for geoeconomic exploration. "Later there will come a time when Africa is also at an end and large reserves no longer exist because the entire earth has been opened up" (ibid., 51). He believed there would be a huge passing wave of gold production and then it would be over, "never again another Africa" (ibid., 20). Theodor Hertzka, a member of the Austrian *Währungs-Enquete-Kommission* and the economics journalist for Vienna's major liberal newspaper *Neue Freie Presse* had already identified Suess's "Malthusianism."[17] In contrast, Alfred Wilhelm Stelzner shared his German colleagues' optimism not only regarding the extraordinary finds in South Africa (Deutsche Silberkommission 1894b, 87). He also underscored the provisionary character of current global mineral resource knowledge recommending not to draw any hasty definite conclusions.

Suess did not, however, easily give up the ambition to convince people about his long-term forecast against gold. He claimed there was a big difference between the end of new gold findings and the end of gold-backed currencies. "The end of the world production of gold will be preceded by a long, long period of its increasing value" with prohibitive consequences for its monetary use (ibid., 55). Growing industrial demands would lead to a steady rise in gold's commodity price and hence further hamper its monetary work. According to Suess, gold was already steadily leaking out of monetary circulation, a situation that prefigured the future dry-out. For his 1892 publication, he assessed how much gold was currently produced per year; and to which commercial sectors the gold had gone. In this calculation, the 168,000 kg of gold produced worldwide in 1890 (Suess 1892, 88–89) counteracted a global consumption of gold for industrial, arts and crafts, and hoarding purposes of well over 120,000 kg, more probably some 150,000 kg (Suess 1892, 102). Suess concluded that the watch and jewelry industry had recurrently used up almost all the newly produced gold, while also feeding itself on existing monetary gold. In a reply to his own "scattered" but, as he asserted, indicative inquiry into gold consumption trends, Geneva's largest gold refinery noted that it had recycled 1,200 kg of gold coins for its 1889 production of 6,800 kg of gold. From a monetary point of view, Suess even defined gold as a non-renewable resource and polemically engaged in the geologist's penchant for a *longue durée* perspective: "Where is the great stock of gold which humanity is said to have accumulated from generation to generation throughout millennia? If the sum of the total bank reserves and active circulation in gold is not even equal to the production of the last forty years, but falls almost one-third below it, where then is the remainder of our former riches?"[18]

Commodity money: shifting values of materiality

When predicting the disappearance of global monetary gold, Suess anticipated the logics of some early mineral resource economists. Harold Hotelling, for instance, would claim that intergenerational optimal depletion of non-renewable resources could be achieved through pricing mechanisms. He suggested that mine owners impose scarcity rents on non-renewable resources, which would increase when approaching depletion of the resource in question (Hotelling 1931). The underlying idea was that long before actual depletion became an acute problem, less expensive alternative resources or solutions – material and organizational – would be established. Just like Hotelling, Suess assumed rising prices for increasingly scarcer monetary gold reserves. This trend would at some early point lure away all monetary gold to industrial production because the ratio between mint parity, i.e. the officially determined price of gold in terms of domestic currency, and gold's market price, would diverge even more sharply. Suess's stance stopped short at an important point though: Hotelling expected societies to deal creatively with rising costs by severing the link between mineral consumption and economic growth.

His work contributed to a fairly brief period in the making, the period of unfettered attempts at "denaturalizing" the economy (Schabas 2005; see Haller et al. 2014, 11–12 for the geopolitical turn of the time counteracting the idea of a denaturalized economy). Once the economy was detached from the world of earth matters, economists argued in the early and mid-twentieth century, it also lent itself "to human control" (Schabas 2005, 158). Suess did not seek to free the world from its mineral base but wanted to make better use of the metallic substrate of money, just as his infrastructural projects for Vienna did not bypass nature but improved and deepened its entwining with the urban environment. All the credit instruments of war finance and long-distance trade or culturally complex public and individual debt relations notwithstanding, European money had derived its value from the purchasing power of the metal commodity on which it was based (Rössner 2015, 452; Wennerlind 2014, 82; Schabas and Wennerlind 2011, 219; Bryan 2010, 15–56; Muldrew 2001, 83). Against the backdrop of the long history of precious metals mining and metallic currencies, Suess aimed to perfect – not loosen – the interdependence between earth matters and monetary politics.

If Suess clung, in cameralistic affinity perhaps, to substantialist notions of money, his position was not a minority vote. The encyclopedia *Meyers Konversations-Lexikon*, while registering a retreat of metal money in the late 1880s, did not predict its end any time soon: "Decreasing demand from the mints for gold is not expected for the time being, as long as the credit institutions do not substitute the use of metal money on an even greater scale than today" (Entry: Gold 1885–1892, 482). Still, some monetary experts began to question the mineral determinism of monetary regimes.

In several reviews of Suess's books, Taussig, the Harvard expert on international trade, opposed the assumed material limits to growth in monetary politics. Contrary to Suess's suggestions, face-value coins became rarer in everyday transactions, and were substituted with banknotes, silver non-face value coins or forms of noncash payment, he argued. "The fact is that in modern communities, gold is used, but to an insignificant extent as medium of exchange. The great bulk of the exchanges are effected by credit substitutes of various sorts" (Taussig 1893b, 151). Suess was incorrect on a second point as well, Taussig argued. Admittedly, "an ever-increasing volume of credit is based on a relatively smaller foundation of specie" (Taussig 1893c, 583). But to broaden the metallic "substructure" and make silver the international standard, as Suess advocated, thus having a stronger "foundation for the high towers of credit papers" in terms of plentiful global mineral resources, would bring only momentary relief ("Grundmauerung," Suess 1892, 113). Soon, politics would enlarge the quantities of money or the volumes of credit accordingly, and the problem would return. Rather than assuming that banks cover their liabilities and the paper money in circulation with ever growing stocks of gold, monetary politics should aim to make gold reserves stronger institutionally to keep gold working as a metric of worth, "something in terms of which the values of commodities are expressed." Taussig did not argue for a radical break with metal or commodity money; gold would still be the last resort standard value. Yet he described money as an artifact, a sociotechnical phenomenon; and he claimed that a shift in emphasis as to the material dimension of this artifact was on the way, if tentatively. Taussig suggested storing gold reserves in the bank vaults of only a small number of central banks and making those the privileged actors who would decide in matters of international monetary politics; hence back monetary gold with trust in institutions' arrangements.

Not only in theory but also in practice did the international gold standard signal the end of the long history of commodity money. As commodity money, foreign silver currencies of the pre-gold standard era had been circulating alongside domestically issued currencies without regard to national distinctions (Bryan 2010, 34; Flandreau 2004). Silver commodity money, primarily Mexican and Spanish currency, had formed the bulk of the domestic coinage up until the 1850s in the United States. Foreign silver coins had also been widely used in Latin America and East Asia, in the Middle East, and the Ottoman Empire (Helleiner 2003, 21–23). Suess indulged in the global reach of the Mexican Dollar and the Austrian Maria Theresia Thaler (Suess 1877, 342–343; Tschoegl 2001; Piatt 1904). Fueled by global tectonic research and the history and practice of cameralism, Suess's cosmopolitics held the monetary work of silver in great esteem for its "centrifugal, civilizing" power around the world: “It may well be said that to the zone of silver in all these states falls the greatest work; that is to say, with silver the greatest number of purchases and obligations are discharged” (Suess 1893, 54). Gold, so the history of money had taught, was “far too immobile to be able to enter into the finer arteries of commerce” (Suess 1893, 54). It rather moved centripetally towards the international hubs of high commerce. In a spirit of solidary cosmopolitanism embracing “the rise of the lower classes” around the globe, silver – and for that matter copper – should not stop being the money of a globalized world (Suess 1893, 54). Notice that the physical terms “arteries” or “veins” were readily used in both economic fields, commerce and mining. Silver was known to ramify most delicately within the earth’s crust: the finely branched pure silver wire specimens, mainly extracted from the Freiberg silver mine *Himmelsfürst Fundgrube*, were firmly fixed in European geologists’ imagination.[19]

The proper mix of large and small denomination coins as well as their patterns and velocity of circulation – what was known as the “big problem of small change” – had always been a topic of debate (Sargent and Velde 2002; Rössner 2015; Desan 2010). And not only Suess but also late nineteenth-century governments monitored the circulation of their coins (for example *La composition de la Circulation Monétaire de la France* 1891). In a way, they followed Suess’s suggestions regarding the choice of monetary metals. Eric Helleiner pointed out in his *The Making of National Money* that the international gold standard had a strong national component: It linked newly established national currencies. The emerging nation states of the nineteenth century established the massive use of silver- and copper-based divisional coins as low denomination money with stable relations to higher denominations. Yet other than commodity money coins, these could only be used, just like the newly issued bank notes, as legal tender within state territory boundaries. In so doing, governments prioritized the creation of vertically integrated national markets: they pursued a domestic strategy of economic growth targeting the inclusion of their entire population and ending the tradition that “different classes used different money” (Helleiner 2003, 62).

Conclusion

Throughout the twentieth century, the potential scarcity of industrial metals and fossil fuels was regularly debated and analyzed; yet ultimately it has not been interpreted as a predicament. Absolute limits to growth in terms of raw material exhaustion were regularly contested and are empirically hard to prove. When Hotelling’s allegedly rising prices found no empirical support, resource economists concluded that technological change had offset ongoing resource depletion, explaining the drop in prices (Barnett and Morse 1963). Moreover, organizational innovations stepped in, changing the picture and, in some cases, contributing to the denaturalization trend in economic affairs mentioned above. The dependency on gold for monetary politics serving economic growth was undone in the course of the twentieth century. My case study hence points to a major collective experience: the successful decoupling of the vision of sustained economic growth on the one hand, and monetary metals consumption on the other.

My endeavor to historicize contemporary discourses on the planetary limits to growth may portray an illusionary triumph over nature's restrictions, given that our main fears today are the climate-bound limits of societal life on earth. We do not worry so much about the amount of fossil fuel left in the earth's crust, but rather about how to leave the bulk of what remains where it is – underground. It is worthwhile though to study how and why people were not only invited to embrace the geological scale of earth matters, but also agreed to consider new pictures of the earth and the world, and eventually decided to discard overtly pessimistic resource forecasts in anticipation of short- and mid-term societal change. Admittedly, Suess operated at a planetary scale when assessing the gold resources unevenly created and distributed in the earth's crust over deep time. Yet he was framing the earth socially – down-scaling from geological to historical time – when he predicted the end of monetary gold in a few centuries. What we see is utterly familiar to us: No invocation of geological time was needed for people to refrain from letting longer-term prognostications guide their political decision-making. Thinking in the societal long term of "a few centuries only" already proved to be unworkable politically. Contrary to what Suess might have wished by recalling the long European and global history of metal currencies, projecting the historical *longue durée* into the future is a collective endeavor requiring robust cosmological and institutional corroboration, and one that is seldom achieved. This was true even for the late nineteenth century, which the conceptual historian Lucian Hölscher (1989) has described, for the European context, as an important time for future thinking in his *Weltgericht oder Revolution. Protestantische und sozialistische Zukunftsvorstellungen im deutschen Kaiserreich.*

I would like to conclude on a third note: I think the notoriously overambitious practice of global mineral resource appraisal that Suess initiated and promoted among economists and politicians finds its legitimization not so much in demarcating absolute limits to economic growth. For twentieth-century governments, it turned out to be more a tool of geopolitical calculation in the broader sense of shaping and managing international affairs. Inadvertently perhaps, global mineral resource appraisals also unearth the culturally laden aspects of geopolitics: raw materials are much less "raw" in the sense of Claude Lévi-Strauss and a good deal more "cooked" than their name suggests. Gold is a prime example.

Notes

1 For the history of Britain's early and mid nineteenth-century national and imperial estimates of coal resources preceding Jevons (1865), see Jonsson (2014, 160–164 in particular); for the future of coal in Prussia and beyond, see Nasse (1893).

2 "Geldstoff," see Entry: Edelmetalle (1885–1887, 307).

3 Suess (1893, 57); see Mitchener (2012, 89–90) for the quantity theory of money and its assumed self-regulating money supply underlying the gold standard politics.

4 See Smith (1994, 173–227), for the early modern relationship between alchemy, gold, treasury, and commerce.

5 "Entry: Soetbeer, Adolph" (1915, 441); see also the report by the political economist from Halle and editor of the *Jahrbücher für Nationalökonomie und Statistik*, Johannes Conrad (1893, 31–32).

6 Verhandlungen der deutschen Silberkommission, vol. 2 (1894, 53); the protocol recorded "Laughter; Shout: only 50 years!" For a similar case, see Jonsson (2011, manuscript pp. 8–9).

7 Twenty years later, in 1811, Werner submitted his *Relation über die aus sämtlichen bisherigen geognostischen Untersuchungen im sächsischen Lande sich ergebenden Ergebnisse in Hinsicht auf das Vorkommen nützlicher, besonders brennbarer Fossilien und deren zweckmäßigste Nutzung*.

8 Suess served as a founding member and president of the *Donau-Verein zur Hebung der Fluss- und Kanalschiffahrt in Österreich* (1879–1885); was founding member of the *Verein zur Abwehr des Antisemitismus* in 1891; the president of the University of Vienna (1888–1889), and the president of the Imperial Academy of Science (1898–1911).

9 And one that further blurs the boundaries between production-oriented cameralism and trade-oriented mercantilism, a historiographic distinction readily collapsing in the face of the history of precious metals, see also Stern and Wennerlind (2014, 8–9).

10 Sutherland (1931). Of crucial importance was the emerging distinction between "reserves" and "resources" according to profitability and certainty of knowledge criteria for the existence and size of resources (see Blondel and Lasky 1956; McKelvey 1972; Pratt and Brobst 1974, 2). Suess made no clear distinction between the two concepts, yet often referred to those "world resources of gold" which would be ultimately accessible to economic extraction ("erreichbare Menge an Gold," Suess 1877, 40; and "Goldvorräthe," 44).

11 Wilhelm Dyes 1916 in: Hessisches Wirtschaftsarchiv HWA, Company Archive "Metallgesellschaft AG," Dept. 119, No. 2113.

12 Suess simplified the picture for the sake of his argument. Not exactly everybody was obsessed with gold. Obviously he himself privileged silver (see pp. 82–83). This was or had been true for several parts of the world, too. In their studies on the early modern global flows of silver, Dennis O. Flynn and Arturo Giraldez (2002, 396–405) argue, for instance, that the over-evaluation of silver compared to gold for monetary reasons in China also implied that silver was a privileged precious metal for nonmonetary uses.

13 The reference is to Ramses II who reigned from 1279 to 1213 BC. In an inscription found in Kuban (and preserved in London), he is said to have considered "the method and way of boring wells on the roads [...] since he had heard that there was much gold existing in the land of Akita, but that the approach to it was accursed on account of the utter want of water" (Brugsch 1877, 436 [Engl. ed. 1879 vol. 2, 81]). See in more detail Suess (1877, 310–312). Suess got his information from Leo Simon Reinisch, professor of Egyptology in Vienna. See Westermann (2014, 25) for the standard establishment of "peak production" by the US Geological Survey's Donnel Foster Hewett in 1929.

14 Conglomerates are coarse-grained clastic sedimentary rock strata composed of a substantial fraction of rounded gravel.

15 Ernst Leuschner, very successful director of the Mansfeld copper mines in Saxony-Anhalt who represented the German state council (*Staats- und Reichsrat*); Wilhelm Hauchecorne, Director of the Prussian Mining Academy on behalf of the Prussian Minister of Commerce and Industry. The delegate for Saxony was Professor Ferdinand Zirkel from Leipzig, and for Wurttemberg, Gustav Klüpfel from Stuttgart.

16 Soetbeer (1878) and Lexis (1879) discuss the typical pitfalls of numerical commensuration and their creative compensation, a thread which I will not further pursue in this chapter: the problem of crafting robust world gold statistics from heterogeneous and unreliable textual sources.

17 Rezension Die Zukunft des Silbers. *Neue Freie Presse*, May 14, 1892, 8–9; almost certainly, Hertzka was the anonymous reviewer.

18 Suess (1893, 56–57); for a similar judgment on Suess's predilection for long-term historical thinking owed to his training as a geologist, see Rezension Die Zukunft des Silbers. *Neue Freie Presse*, May 14, 1892, 8–9.

19 Smith (2015, 45, picture on p. 46). Today, Freiberg's historical silver specimens are highly prized collectibles.

Bibliography

Barnett, Harold, and Chandler Morse. 1963. *Scarcity and Growth. The Economics of Natural Resource Availability.* Baltimore: The Johns Hopkins University Press for Resources of the Future.

Bartels, Christoph. 2013. "The Administration of Mining in Late Medieval and Early Modern Europe (Fourteenth to Eighteenth Centuries)." In *Mining, Monies, and Culture in Early Modern Societies. East Asian and Global Perspectives*, edited by Nanny Kim and Keiko Nagase-Reimer, 115–130. Leiden: Brill.

Blondel, Fernand and Samuel Lasky. 1956. "Mineral Reserves and Mineral Resources." *Economic Geology* 51: 686–697.

Brugsch, Heinrich. 1877. *Geschichte Aegypten's unter den Pharaonen: nach den Denkmälern*. Leipzig: Hinrich.

Bryan, Stephen. 2010. *The Gold Standard at the Turn of the Twentieth Century. Rising Powers, Global Money, and the Age of Empire.* New York: Columbia University Press.

Coen, Deborah R. 2012. "Fault Lines and Borderlands. Earthquake Science in Imperial Austria." In *The Nationalization of Scientific Knowledge in the Habsburg Empire, 1848–1918*, edited by Mitchell G. Ash and Jan Surman, 157–182. Basingstoke: Palgrave Macmillan.

Coen, Deborah R. 2016. "Big is a Thing of the Past: Climate Change and Methodology in the History of Ideas." *Journal of the History of Ideas* 77(2): 305–321.

Conrad, Johannes. 1893. "Gutachten." In *Wissenschaftliche Gutachten über die Währungsfrage*, 30–34. Berlin: Hermann Walther.

de Cecco, Marcello. 1992. "European Monteray and Financial Cooperation before the First World War." *Revista di storia economica* 9(1–2): 55–76.

del Mar, Alexander. 1880. *A History of the Precious Metals.* London: G. Bell and Sons.

Desan, Christine. 2010. "Coin Reconsidered: The Political Alchemy of Commodity Money." *Theoretical Inquiries in Law* 11(1): 361–409.

Desrosières, Alain. 1998. *The Politics of Large Numbers. A History of Statistical Reasoning* Cambridge MA, London: Harvard University Press.

Deutsche Silberkommission. 1894a. *Verhandlungen der deutschen Silberkommission. Stenographischer Bericht der Berathung über den bimetallistischen Hauptantrag, 8.–17. Sitzung*. Vol.1. Berlin: Walther.

Deutsche Silberkommission. 1894b. *Verhandlungen der deutschen Silberkommission. Stenographischer Bericht der Berathung über die Verhältnisse der Gold- und*

Silberproduktion unter Zuziehung von Sachverständigen, 17.-20. Sitzung. Vol. 2. Berlin: Walther.

"Entry: Edelmetalle."1885–1892. *Meyers Konversations-Lexikon*, 307–312. Leipzig, Wien: Bibliographisches Institut.

"Entry: Gold."1885–1892. *Meyers Konversations-Lexikon*, 473–498. Leipzig, Wien: Bibliographisches Institut.

"Entry: Soetbeer, Adolph."1915. In *Palgrave's Dictionary of Political Economy*, edited by Robert Harry Inglis Palgrave, 440–443. London: Macmillan and Co.

Espeland, Wendy N. and Mitchell L. Stevens. 1998. "Commensuration as a Social Process" *Annual Review of Sociology* 24(3): 313–343.

Flandreau, Marc. 2004. *The Glitter of Gold. France, Bimetallism and the Emergence of the International Gold Standard 1848–1873*. Oxford: Oxford University Press.

Flynn, Dennis O., and Arturo Giraldez. 2002. "Cycles of Silver: Global Economic Unity through the Mid-Eighteenth Century." *Journal of World History* 13(2): 391–427.

Frängsmyr, Tore, John L. Heilbron, and Robin E. Rider, eds. 1990. *The Quantifying Spirit in the Eighteenth Century*. Berkeley: California University Press.

Fressoz, Jean-Baptiste. 2016. "L'Anthropocène et l'Esthetique du Sublime." In *Sublime. Les Tremblements du Monde, catalogue d' exposition*, edited by Hélène Guenin, 44–49. Metz: Editions Centre Pompidou Metz.

Grewe, Bernd Stefan. 2013. "The London Gold Market, 1900–1931." In *The Foundations of Worldwide Economic Integration. Power, Institution, and Global Markets, 1850–1930*, edited by Christof Dejung and Niels P. Petersson, 112–132. Cambridge: Cambridge University Press.

Haller, Lea, Sabine Höhler, and Andrea Westermann. 2014. "Rechnen mit der Natur: Ökonomische Kalküle um Ressourcen. Einleitung." *Berichte zur Wissenschaftsgeschichte* 37(1): 8–19.

Hamann, Brigitte 1983. "Eduard Suess als liberaler Politiker." In *Eduard Suess zum Gedenken*, edited by Günther Hamann, 79–100. Wien: Verlag der österr. Akademie der Wissenschaften.

Heise, Ursula. 2008. *Sense of Place and Sense of Planet. The Environmental Imagination of the Global*. Oxford: Oxford University Press.

Helleiner, Eric. 2003. *The Making of National Money. Territorial Currencies in Historical Perspective*. Ithaca and London: Cornell University Press.

Hölscher, Lucian. 1989. *Weltgericht oder Revolution. Protestantische und sozialistische Zukunftsvorstellungen im deutschen Kaiserreich*. Stuttgart: Klett-Cotta.

Hotelling, Harold. 1931. "The Economics of Exhaustible Resources." *Journal of Political Economy* 39(2): 137–175.

Jevons, William Stanley 1865. *The Coal Question: An Inquiry Concerning the Progress of the Nation and the Probable Exhaustion of Our Coal-mines*. London, Cambridge: Macmillan and Co.

Jonsson, Fredrik Albritton. 2011. "Peak Coal and other Bottleneck Panics 1789–1834." Academia.edu. Accessed July 27, 2016. https://www.academia.edu/1064653 Peak_coal_and_other_bottleneck_worries_1789–1834.

Jonsson, Fredrik Albritton. 2014. "The Orgins of Cornucopianism: A Preliminary Genealogy." *Critical Historical Studies* 1(1): 151–168.

Kolbert, Elizabeth. 2015. "The Siege of Miami. As Temperatures Climb, So, Too, Will Sea Levels." *The New Yorker*, December 21.

"La composition de la Circulation Monétaire de la France."1891. *Bulletin de Statistique et de Législative Comparée*: 121–150.

Leith, Charles Kenneth. 1970 (reprint of 1931). *World Minerals and World Politics. A Factual Study of Minerals in Their Political and International Relations.* Port Washington: Kennikat Press.

Lexis, Wilhelm. 1879. "Beiträge zur Statistik der Edelmetalle nebst einigen Bemerkungen über die Werthrelationen." *Jahrbücher für Nationalökonomie und Statistik* 5: 361–417.

Lexis, Wilhelm. 1890. "Review: Zur Geld- und Währungsfrage." *Jahrbücher für Nationalökonomie und Statistik* Neue Folge 21(3): 261–288.

Lindenfeld, David F. 1997. *The Practical Imagination. The German Sciences of State in the 19th Century.* Chicago: The University of Chicago Press.

McKelvey, Vincent E. 1972. "Mineral Resource Estimates and Public Policy." *American Scientist* 60: 32–40.

Meissner, Christpher M. 2002. *A New World Order: Explaining the Emergence of the Classical Gold Standard*, NBER Working Paper No. 9233. Cambridge MA.

Menger, Carl. 1970. *Gesammelte Werke Band IV: Schriften über Geld und Währungspolitik*, edited by F. A. Hayek. Tübingen: Mohr (Siebeck).

Mitchener, Kris James. 2012. "The Classical Gold Standard." In *The Handbook of Major Events in Economic History*, edited by Randall Parker and Robert Whaples, 88–102. London: Routledge.

Muldrew, Craig. 2001. "'Hard Food for Midas': Cash and Its Social Value in Early Modern England." *Past & Present* 170: 78–120.

Nasse, Rudolf. 1893. *Die Kohlenvorräthe der europäischen Staaten, insbesondere Deutschlands, und deren Erschöpfung.* Berlin: Puttkammer und Mühlbrecht.

Northcott, Michael. 2013. *A Political Theology of Climate Change.* Cambridge, UK: Eerdmans.

Officer, Lawrence. 2008. "Gold Standard." EH.Net Encyclopedia, edited by Robert Whaples. Accessed July 27, 2016. http://eh.net/encyclopedia/gold-standard.

Oreskes, Naomi. 2015. "How Earth Science Became Social Science." *Historical Social Research* 40(2): 246–270.

Pelikan, Anton. 1894. "Über die goldführenden Quarzconglomerate von Witwatersrand in Süd-Afrika." *Verhandlungen der kaiserlich-königlichen geologischen Reichsanstalt* 16: 421–425.

Petzholdt, Georg PaulAlexander. 1845. *Geologie.* Leipzig: Carl B. Lorck.

Piatt, Andrew. 1904. "The End of the Mexican Dollar." *The Quarterly Journal of Economics* 18(3): 321–356.

Pratt, Walden P. and Donald A Brobst. 1974. Mineral Resources: Potentials and Problems. *Geological Survey Circular 698.* Washington D.C.: US Government Printing Office.

Reith, Reinhold. 2010. "Ressourcennutzung." In *Enzyklopädie der Neuzeit Bd. 11*, edited by Kulturwissenschaftliches Institut Essen, 122–134. Stuttgart: J. B. Metzler.

Reuss, Christian Friedrich. 1777. "Abhandlung wie die Naturkunde der Grund zu einer wohleingerichteten Oekonomie, und wie groß der Einfluß derselben in diese Wissenschaft ist." *Beschäftigung der Berlinischen Gesellschaft naturforschender Freunde* 3: 3–28.

Rössner, Philipp Robinson. 2012. *Deflation–Devaluation–Rebellion.* Stuttgart: Franz Steiner Verlag.

Rössner, Philipp Robinson. 2015. "Kameralismus, Kapitalismus und die Ursprünge des modernen Wirtschaftswachstums – aus Sicht der Geldtheorie." *Vierteljahrsschrift für Sozial- und Wirtschaftsgeschichte* 102: 437–471.

Sargent, Thomas J., and Francois R. Velde. 2002. *The Big Problem of Small Change.* Princeton: Princeton University Press.

Schabas, Margaret. 2005. *The Natural Origins of Economics.* Chicago: The University of Chicago Press.

Schabas, Margaret, and Carl Wennerlind. 2011. "Retrospectives: Hume on Money, Commerce, and the Science of Economics." *The Journal of Economic Perspectives* 25(3): 217–229.

Schmeisser, Karl. 1894. *Ueber Vorkommen und Gewinnung der nutzbaren Mineralien in der Südafrikanischen Republik (Transvaal), unter besonderer Berücksichtigung des Goldbergbaues. Bericht über eine im Auftrage des Königlichen Preussischen Herrn Ministers für Handel und Gewerbe nach Südafrika unternommene Reise.* Berlin: Reimer.

Smith, Pamela H. 1994. *The Business of Alchemy. Science and Culture in the Holy Roman Empire.* Princeton: Princeton University Press.

Smith, Pamela H. 2015. "The Matter of Ideas in the Working of Metals in Early Modern Europe." In *The Matter of Art*, edited by Christy Anderson, Anne Dunlop and Pamela H. Smith, 42–67. Manchester: Manchester University Press.

Soetbeer, Adolph. 1878. "Zur Kritik der bisherigen Schätzungen der Edelmetallproduktion." *Preußische Jahrbücher* 41: 26–58.

Soetbeer, Adolph. 1892. *Litteraturnachweis über Geld- und Münzwesen.* Berlin: Puttkammer & Mühlbrecht.

Stern, Philip J., and Carl Wennerlind. 2014. "Introduction." In *Mercantilism Reimagined: Political Economy in Early Modern Britain and its Empire*, edited by Philip J. Stern and Carl Wennerlind, 3–22. Oxford: Oxford University Press.

Suess, Eduard. 1877. *Die Zukunft des Goldes.* Wien: Braumüller.

Suess, Eduard. 1892. *Die Zukunft des Silbers.* Wien und Leipzig: Wilhelm Braumüller.

Suess, Eduard. 1893. *The Future of Silver.* Washington: Government Printing Office.

Suess, Eduard. 1902. "Abschieds-Vorlesung des Professor Eduard Suess bei seinem Rücktritte vom Lehramte." *Beiträge zur Paläontologie Österreich-Ungarns* 15: 1–8.

Suess, Eduard. 1904. *The Face of the Earth.* Vol. 1. Oxford.

Sutherland, Alexander C., edit. 1931. *The Gold Resources of the World. An Inquiry Made upon the Initiation of the Organising Committee of the XV. International Geological Congress, South Africa, 1929.* Pretoria: The Bureau of the Congress.

Taussig, Frank William. 1893a. "Review Die Zukunft des Silbers." *Political Science Quarterly* 8(2): 365–366.

Taussig, Frank William. 1893b. "Review Die Zukunft des Silbers." *Science* March 17: 151.

Taussig, Frank William. 1893c. "Why Silver ceases to be money." *Popular Science Monthly* 43(9): 577–585.

The General Secretary of the Congress, ed. 1910. *The Iron Ore Resources of the World. An Inquiry Made upon the Initiative of the Executive Committee of the XI International Geological Congress, Stockholm 1910 with the Assistance of Geological Surveys and Mining Geologists of Different Countries.* Vols. 2. Stockholm: Generalstabens Litografiska Anstalt.

Tresch, John. 2014. "Cosmologies Materialized: History of Science and History of Ideas." In *Rethinking Modern European Intellectual History*, edited by Darrin M. McMahon and Samuel Moyn, 153–172. Oxford: Oxford University Press.

Tschoegl, Adrian E. 2001. "Maria Theresa's Thaler: A Case of International Money." *Eastern Economic Journal* 27(4): 443–462.

Van-Helten, Jean-Jacques. 1982. "Empire and High Finance: South Africa and the International Gold Standard 1890–1914." *The Journal of African History* 23: 529–548.

Wagner, Adolph. 1880 and 1881. "Die Währungsfrage in der neuesten Literatur." *Zeitschrift für die gesammte Staatswissenschaft* 36: 750–776 and 37: 210–233.

Wakefield, Andre. 2014. "Cameralism. A German Alternative to Mercantilism." In *Mercantilism Reimagined. Political Economy in Early Modern Britain and Its Empire*, edited by Philip J. Stern and Carl Wennerlind, 134–150. Oxford: Oxford University Press.

Wennerlind, Carl. 2014. "Money: Hartlibian Political Economy and the New Culture of Credit." In *Mercantilism Reimagined. Political Economy in Early Modern Britain and its Empire* edited by Philip J. Stern and Carl Wennerlind. Oxford: Oxford University Press.

Westermann, Andrea. 2011. "Geologiegeschichte als Verwaltungsgeschichte: Stabilisierungseffekte zwischen Amtshandeln und Forschungshandeln bei Hans Conrad Escher (1767–1823)." *Traverse. Zeitschrift für Geschichte* 18(2): 57–74.

Westermann, Andrea. 2014. "Inventuren der Erde. Vorratsschätzungen für mineralische Rohstoffe und die Etablierung der Ressourcenökonomie." *Berichte zur Wissenschaftsgeschichte* 37(1): 20–40.

Westermann, Andrea. 2015. "Geology and world politics: mineral resource appraisals as tools of geopolitical calculation, 1919–1939." *Historical Social Research* 40(2): 151–173.

4 Gross domestic problem

How the politics of GDP shaped society and the world

Lorenzo Fioramonti

In contemporary governance, policy decisions are generally shaped by considerations of economic growth. In particular, the gross domestic product (GDP) has become an overarching parameter to gauge the acceptability and feasibility not only of policies, but also of development initiatives, social welfare provisions, infrastructure investment, and the like. GDP is also a benchmark via which the global pecking order is defined. Initially designed as a component of a nation's income, this number has become an all-powerful presence in our economic and political debate, as well as in our collective social psyche.

GDP drives macro-economic governmental policies and sets priorities in the social fields. For instance, according to the Stability and Growth Pact of the European Union of 1997 and, more recently, the Fiscal Compact of 2012, member states are constitutionally obliged to respect fixed ratios between GDP and public deficit as well as sovereign debt. In particular, since the outbreak of the European sovereign debt crisis, these rules have tied the hands of democratically elected governments, overriding elections and referenda, and resulting in the enforcement of austerity policies. In the age of economic stagnation, this has meant social tensions throughout Europe, particularly in the Southern member states, from Greece to Portugal.

The efficiency of public revenues strategies and the feasibility of welfare policies have been routinely assessed through the lens of GDP. For instance, the so-called Bush tax cuts in 2001, the largest in the recent history of America, were publicly justified as an efficient strategy to increase GDP growth, while comparable efforts to up the federal living wage have been thwarted by negative forecasts with respect to how a more equitable redistribution of resources would affect the nation's GDP performance (Foertsch 2006).

GDP establishes clear production and consumption boundaries, defining the conceptual (and measured) limits of what activities can be considered of economic value. Because of its methodological approach, it has equated economic growth with the increase in formal market-based transactions, regardless of their social utility. Moreover, it has excluded all economic functions that happen outside the market, including informal exchange at the community level and in households, which often constitute the backbone of economic progress, especially in so-called developing countries. Being a measure of flows, it has ignored the value of stocks, leading to unsustainable consumption of non-renewable resources and incentivizing short-term policy planning.

The close nexus between continuous consumption, policy making and economic development has been triumphant in political discourse since the invention of GDP. In no circumstance was this as explicit as in the "shopping is patriotic" reactions of world leaders to the terrorist attacks of the September 11, 2001. As is well-known, US President George W. Bush's response to a terrified nation was "get on the airlines, get about the business of America," while Tony Blair encouraged his compatriots "to travel and to shop" (Fioramonti 2014a, 17). Similarly, the then Prime Minister of Canada Jean Chrétien argued that sustained consumption was the best way to defeat terrorism: "it is time to go out and get a mortgage, to buy a home, to buy a car. […] The economy of the world needs people to go back to their lives. […] It is the way to fight back" (Fioramonti 2014a, 17).

But how did GDP manage to become so pervasive not only in the economy but also in our political and social life? How did it come into being and acquire its influence? Why have changes to this statistical "gold standard" proved so hard to achieve, despite frequent criticism? This chapter traces the history of GDP and shows how its selective representation of economic growth has served particular interests in society, which in turn contributes to explaining its power and influence in governance. The chapter concludes by charting potential avenues for a post-GDP world.

The dawn of GDP: from the Great Depression to the Second World War

The gross domestic product (GDP), or rather gross national product (GNP, as it was initially known) was invented over eight decades ago (Fioramonti 2013; Coyle 2014; Philipsen 2015). It was indeed in 1934 that an economist by the name of Simon Kuznets, who would later on receive a Nobel Prize for his research on growth and income distribution, presented his first report on the design of national income accounts to the US congress (Kuznets 1934). His work built on the pioneering efforts by economists such as Colin Clark in the UK in the late 1920s and was then followed by Richard Stone and James Meade in the 1940s, when GDP was also introduced in Britain. All these economists had been influenced by John Maynard Keynes' approach to macroeconomic policy, particularly his belief that government had a proactive role to play in managing the business cycle and steering development. The early days of the national income accounts coincided with the hard times of the Great Depression. President Roosevelt's brainchild, the New Deal, rested on the capacity of government to closely monitor the economy's inputs and outputs, so as to align policy stimuli accordingly, and the measurement of national income was essential to its success. Until the mid-1930s, the quantitative analysis based on national income estimates was essentially micro-economic, focusing on retail expenditures for selected agricultural products and predicting demand by key industrial sectors like gasoline, shoe, textile, and the like. By the late 1930s, however, macro-economic considerations began to occupy center stage, in particular to work out what level of economic activity would absorb unemployment and forecast tax revenues.

Since the early stages, Kuznets clarified that his version of national income was an attempt to measure market transactions rather than a comprehensive assessment of the overall production of an economic system. "If market is understood broadly as the meeting place of all buyers and sellers," he wrote in the late 1930s, then gross product "excludes the results of other activities that may supply utilities but are outside the market mechanism" (Kuznets 1937, 3). For instance, his measurement included "payments as wages, salaries, dividends and interest" but did not consider returns to individuals from their activity within the family system "or from other pursuits that are not, strictly speaking, working for the market" (Kuznets 1937, 5). He pointed out clear production and consumption boundaries, excluding "a large volume of services and a substantial volume of commodities produced outside the economic system proper" and neglected "[t]he great contribution to our stock of utilities made within the family system and by numerous activities of mankind engaged in the ordinary processes of life" (Kuznets 1937, 6). Among others, this aspect generated the evident paradox that the same household service would be counted as adding to national income when provided by a waged domestic but not when rendered by a housewife. His market-based approach was, however, not devoid of basic moral requirements. In his first collection of national accounts, Kuznets noted that national income cannot include "activities that have been explicitly recognized by society at large, overtly in the form of legal prohibition, not only as unproductive but also as distinctly harmful" as well as "activities that while legal, represent largely shifts of income among individuals rather than additions to the command over goods" (Kuznets 1937, 5). As a consequence, he excluded profits stemming from crimes such as theft, robbery, prostitution, and drug trafficking. At the same time, Kuznets was aware of the sometimes-arbitrary demarcation between legality and illegality. For instance, the income of official casinos was included in the gross national product, while illegal gambling was taken out. In particular, he was hostile to the idea of including the speculative gains obtained through financial transactions in the computation of national income. After the financial turmoil of the Great Depression, he had come to believe that financial speculation is derived "from the sale of assets that can in no way be interpreted as resulting from skill in the performance of any useful functions that speculative markets may be presumed to render" (Kuznets 1937, 6).

Kuznets's ambition was to find ways to measure the economic welfare of a nation, rather than simply quantifying output. For instance, he argued that "it would be of great value to have national income estimates that would remove from the total the elements which, from the standpoint of a more enlightened social philosophy than that of an acquisitive society present disservice rather than service" (cited in Mitra-Kahn 2011, 239). In particular, he preferred excluding military expenses, something he would later describe as "at best a necessary evil, but still an evil" (Kuznets 1962, 29), as well as all expenditure on advertising, financial, and speculative activities, and "outlays that have been made necessary in order to overcome difficulties that are, properly speaking, costs implicit in our economic civilization" from "subways" to expensive housing, which "do not really represent net services to the individuals comprising the nation but are, from their viewpoint, an evil necessary in order to be able to make a living" (cited in Mitra-Kahn 2011, 239–240).

Needless to say, Kuznets appeared increasingly out of tune with the political needs of a country about to embark on the Second World War. In the early 1940s, the US government began to reveal hostility toward a measurement of national income that would provide a picture of national economic output, but with expenditure on armaments categorized as costs (Coyle 2014). Moreover, other leading economists like Richard Stone disagreed with Kuznets, arguing that "common services such as defence, justice, education and public health" should be included "in the consumption box, being in fact nothing more than agency activities for the body of consumers as a whole" (Stone 1951, 43). A full inclusion of military expenditure in gross national product appeared also in line with Keynes's views as reflected in the essay *How To Pay for the War*, which had explicitly linked national production and economic accounting with a modern approach to military planning (Keynes 1940). Besides scientific pressure, the government also resorted to cooptation. In particular, some of Kuznets's collaborators, namely his best-known students, Robert Nathan and Milton Gilbert, were offered high ranks in the government. Nathan joined the War Production Board, while Gilbert was put in charge of the national income accounts at the Department of Commerce. As noted by Carson (1975, 169),

> The war was the immediate impetus of the rapid development of the product, or expenditure, components. The central question was: given government war expenditures, how much of total product will be left for civilian consumption?

The result was a change in approaches, which led to the publication of the first complete "gross national product" in 1942, fully incorporating "as final product all government output (most conveniently measured by the total of payments to the factors of production)" (Carson 1975, 170). As Gilbert (1948) would later recognize, this was a significant departure from Kuznets's prewar concept of national income.

The availability of regular and detailed statistics on the strengths and weaknesses of the economy helped the American government outpace its enemies in terms of munitions' production, with Roosevelt's Victory Plan closely vetted by Kuznets' former colleagues. More importantly, by using the accounts to closely monitor the economy's productive capacity, the government managed to optimize the conversion of the civilian economy into a war machine without hampering internal consumption, which turned out to be a major advantage in generating revenues for the war and propelling large-scale consumption in the post-war period (Fioramonti 2013; Philipsen 2015). According to the economist John Kenneth Galbraith, the GDP accounts had been the equivalent of "several infantry divisions in their contribution to the American war effort" (Galbraith 1980, 80). For Clifford Cobb, Ted Halstead, and Jonathan Rowe, who led the critique of the national income accounts in the 1980s, the degree to which GDP acquired power "as a war-planning tool is hard to exaggerate" (Cobb et al. 1995, 6).

The evolution of GDP as a global standard

Prior to the war, a few countries had begun to estimate national income using different definitions and methods. But with the Bretton Woods conference of 1944, which redesigned the world system and instituted international financial institutions such as the IMF and the World Bank, the US and the UK took the lead in standardizing the calculations using their pioneering experience. Through aid policies targeted at the reconstruction in Europe and then development funds and technical assistance to the "third world," GDP was exported to the rest of the international community and became the global parameter of good economic policy (Costanza et al. 2014; Fioramonti 2014a). In 1947, the UN issued a technical report outlining the standard parameter for calculations, which was penned by Stone (Coyle 2014). The then Organization for European Economic Cooperation, the forerunner of the OECD, published guidelines in 1951 and 1952, which were used to allocate funds under the auspices of the Marshall Plan. Then in 1953, the first global official System of National Accounts (SNA) was published by the UN.

The influence of GDP on international politics was further reinforced during the Cold War, when the measurement of economic performance turned into a fundamental aspect of the political struggle between the USA and the Soviet Union. Arguably more than the arms race, it was the ambition to ensure economic success that constituted the essence of the capitalism–socialism contest. But assessing prosperity required some commonly agreed measurement. As we have seen, GDP had been invented to gauge the size and scope of market economies and was calculated in terms of market prices. The Soviet Union, by contrast, rejected the market economy and had developed a different metric, the so-called material product, which reflected Marx's focus on industrial labor as the productive core of the economy, considering what we would today call "service industry" ancillary to the production of goods (Marx 1909, III.XIX.39).

Over four decades, each bloc defended the validity of its measurements. Starting in the 1950s, the Central Intelligence Agency (CIA) began to investigate Soviet measures of national income with a view to discrediting them: their objective was to minimize the USSR's alleged economic development and its potential expansion. According to official CIA reports, foreign economic intelligence was essential to estimate the magnitude of present and future military threats, to anticipate the intentions of enemies and undermine their capabilities and, most importantly, to project the relative strength of the West vis-à-vis the East, given that American policy makers were obsessed with the prospect that the USSR would overtake the US in terms of national output (Noren 2003).

By revising Soviet statistics through the GDP lens, the CIA managed to attack the USSR's credibility as an emerging power and its ambition to overtake the US as the largest economy in the world. When party leaders Nikita Khrushchev and then Leonid Brezhnev put forward their economic plans in the 1950s and 1970s respectively, the CIA published GDP estimates to demonstrate how their production goals could not be met (Noren 2003). When in 1958, the Soviet Communist Party declared that the Soviet Union would lead the world in both absolute and per capita output by 1970, the CIA promptly recalculated official statistics and pronounced these plans unfeasible (Noren 2003). In the early 1960s, when the CIA reported that real GDP growth in the Soviet Union had been a fraction of what was officially declared, US President Johnson dispatched a delegation to present the findings in West European capitals and reassure his allies (Noren 2003).

Eventually, the Soviets began to compile SNA-inspired statistics in the late 1980s, partly due to global pressures and partly because of changes in the structures of the economy (Herrera 2011). The stated purpose was to supplement the Marxist-Leninist-based indicators with a new measure that would broaden the analysis of social reproduction, as well as facilitate international comparisons. It may not have been coincidental, however, that the adoption of GDP held the promise of revising economic output upward because of the rapid growth of the services sector (Fioramonti 2013).

In the early 1990s, from "national" the gross product became "domestic." This signalled an important political change in support of economic globalization. Traditional GNP referred to all goods and services produced by the nationals of a given country, regardless of whether the "income" had been generated within or outside its borders. It meant that, for instance, the earnings of a multinational corporation were attributed to the country where the firm was owned and where the profits would eventually return. With the introduction of the gross "domestic" product, this calculation changed. GDP is indeed territorially defined, which means that the income generated by foreign companies is "formally" attributed to the country where it is generated, although the profits may not remain there. This shift in metrics was partly responsible for the economic boom of many developing nations throughout the 1990s. In a sense, one may argue that the very notion of "emerging market" was a by-product of both the shift of production processes away from the more developed countries as well as the introduction of new metrics to capture such transition, rather than a profound change in how wealth was distributed. For some, the statistical reconfiguration produced by GDP simply hides the fact that "the nations of the North are walking off with the South's resources, and calling it a gain for the South" (Cobb et al. 1995, 6).

It was during this period that GDP was "constitutionalized," that is, formally integrated into national and international institutional processes. As mentioned earlier, the European common currency (the Euro) and its economic area (the Eurozone) have been profoundly influenced by fixed parameters between GDP and deficit/debt, a rule introduced in the 1990s allegedly to guarantee stability across the national financial systems of the European Union. As a consequence, countries need a certain GDP "profile" to access the common currency system. As we know, some of them (e.g. Greece) resorted to overstating their economic credentials in order to qualify for membership. Moreover, once countries have been integrated, their macroeconomic management is deeply constrained by GDP trends, which reinforces cyclical downward spirals: a plummeting GDP means more strict conditions and less room to invest and stimulate consumption, which in turn weakens economic recovery even further. Besides Europe, most countries around the world have implicitly accepted the rule of fixed GDP ratios with debt and deficit, a policy long corroborated by the IMF and the World Bank as well as the major credit rating agencies (Chowdhury and Islam, 2012).

The gross domestic "problem"

GDP has dominated public debate and the media in the last century. Countries have been ranked according to GDP, the global definition of "power" has been based on GDP (e.g. superpowers, emerging powers, etc.), access to global governance institutions has been granted on GDP performance (e.g. the G7/8 or G20 members are selected according to their GDP) and development policies have been driven by the GDP formula. Even the traditional distinction between "developed" and "developing" world is dictated by GDP.

The very concept of "growth" is determined by the methodological approach of GDP. For instance, cutting trees and selling them produces output and ultimately growth, but the very natural act of growing trees does not. Cooking and sharing food in the community has no impact on growth, but buying junk food does. It is the measurement itself, with its boundaries in terms of production and assets, which determines what the economy is and, as a consequence, what growth means. Through GDP, our model of growth becomes a sum of market consumption, regardless of whether what is consumed is good for society, for the environment and, as a consequence, for the economy itself.

GDP is not a measure of *all* gains and losses in an economy. It is a "gross" indicator. Not only because it does not include the depreciation of some key assets, but also because it disregards the value of the natural resources consumed in the economic process, as these are obtained free of charge from nature. Moreover, it does not even consider the economic costs of pollution and environmental degradation, which are obvious consequences of industrial development. Finally, whatever good or service is exchanged outside the market (e.g. within households, in the informal economies, through barter, etc.) does not count for GDP.

All these important omissions make this statistic a very inadequate measure of economic performance, let alone social welfare. Household services, for instance, have a fundamental economic impact even though they are not formally priced. If governments or companies had to pay for the innumerable services rendered at the household level (from child and frail care to education), our economies would arguably grind to halt. A study by the Bureau of Economic Analysis estimates that the value of household production in the US accounted for over 30 percent of economic output every year from 1965 to 2010 with a peak of 39 percent in 1965, declining to 25.7 percent in 2010 (Bridgman et al. 2012). In many countries, the "odd jobs" and the goods and services exchanged informally provide the necessary subsistence to millions of people and often constitute the backbone of the real economy, albeit they do not feature in GDP. As reported by the IMF, the informal economy has reached remarkable levels worldwide: in the early 2000s, it accounted for up to 44 percent of economic output in developing nations, 30 percent in transition economies, and 16 percent in the OECD countries (Schneider and Enste 2002).

Similarly, disregarding the input of natural resources just because they are not priced by nature makes us forget that economic growth is only possible because of a continuous provision of "capital" from our ecosystems. When these resources are depleted, however, we risk endangering not only economic progress, but also the very natural equilibrium that makes life possible. Research by Robert Costanza and his team has consistently demonstrated, over several decades, that the economic contribution of natural systems far exceeds that of man-made production and considering the latter of no value to national wealth is disastrous (Costanza et al. 1997; Balmford et al. 2002).

The calculation of GDP is by no means straightforward and uncontroversial. For starters, each national statistical agency uses different formulas and corrective methods to correct for inflation (the so-called GDP deflators). As technological innovation tends to reduce prices (e.g. a laptop today is much cheaper than it was a few years back, even though its performance is much higher), hedonic models have been introduced to account for quality improvements, thus manipulating the pricing principle underpinning the calculation of GDP. The valuation of government expenses is also controversial, as most of these purchases do not happen in the allegedly "open" conditions of the market economy. As discussed, the inclusion of military expenses has long been criticized, but also other sectors have come under scrutiny. In Cuba, for instance, the national statistical office has been correcting the overall contribution of key social services (from education to healthcare) by estimating their impact on social welfare rather than through a calculation of the actual salaries and costs of personnel, as is generally the case (EcuRed 2016). Cubans are indeed concerned that the comparatively low salaries of doctors and teachers, among others, would penalize their GDP and distort the actual impact these services have on economic performance. Indeed, looking simply at the size of expenditures (as conventional GDP methodologies do) rewards countries like the US, which have notoriously expensive yet inefficient healthcare sectors.

Kuznets acknowledged that GDP focuses exclusively on formalized economic transactions, which make it unsuitable to countries largely dependent on informal economic structures (Lundberg 1971). In industrialized countries, by contrast, growth of GDP might be easily over-estimated by counting in goods and services whose sole purpose was to offset the drawbacks of industrialization, such as the increasing cost of traffic, pollution, and security (a phenomenon which economists often refer to as "defensive consumption"). Experts working in developing regions in the early 1950s, after the release of the first SNA guidelines, noted that the "accounting problem is not simply that of the acute scarcity of quantitative data [...] it is also a qualitative problem, which brings into question the fundamental validity for primitive communities of the social accounting concepts themselves" (Deane 1953, 115).

Inconsistencies and different methods across data sources is also a problem. For instance, in 2013, a country like Liberia was Africa's second-poorest, seventh-poorest or 22nd-poorest depending on whether one took the international calculations published by the World Bank (through the World Development Indicators), the Penn World Table or the Maddison Project Database, which combine different data sources to provide aggregate information to most development agencies to design their policies. According to studies of statistical offices' methodologies, "Angola, Central African Republic, Comoros, Congo-Brazzaville, Nigeria and Zambia all make leaps of more than ten places in the rankings from one source to the other," because of different methods and systems of calculation (Jerven 2013, 19).

Even the OECD recognizes that "if ever there was a controversial icon from the statistics world, GDP is it. It measures income, but not equality, it measures growth, but not destruction, and it ignores values like social cohesion and the environment. Yet, governments, businesses and probably most people swear by it" (OECD Observer 2004). The OECD has spearheaded the "beyond GDP" debate since the mid-2000s and has facilitated reforms in member states, while proposing a number of alternative indicators, including the Better Life Index, whose slogan "there is more to life than the cold numbers of GDP" indicates the need to look at a host of wellbeing dimensions to plan economic policies more efficiently. Accounting 101 tells us that profit equals income minus "all" costs. As GDP systematically disregards key sectors in the economy and neglects critical costs, no reasonable businessman would use it to run a company. Yet, it has become the key parameter to run entire societies.

GDP is the "lens" through which policy makers, the media, and often society as a whole see the human economy: what is not counted by GDP becomes valueless to public policies and social debate. No surprise then that the GDP era has been characterized by a relentless privatization of public spaces, commodification of the household (including the ever-decreasing time family members enjoy "together") and destruction of natural beauty.

The struggle to dethrone GDP

Since the early days of the GDP accounts, Kuznets himself had raised doubts about his "invention." For instance, he had warned about the risk of using a "gross" measurement to design policies. He recommended that not only the depreciation of machinery and capital be subtracted from GDP, but also the negative impact on workers' lives. This is what Kuznets called the "reverse side of income," that is, "the intensity and unpleasantness of effort going into the earning of income" (cited in Kaiser 2010). Yet, as GDP focuses only on satisfying consumers' demands for commodities and services, he admitted that "the burden of work and discomfort are ignored" (Kuznets 1946, 127).

Kuznets was also worried about the way in which GDP growth affected the distribution of income. His research showed how rapid growth may be associated with rising inequality, which is partly due to the fact that policies aimed at supporting GDP tend to destroy informal economic structure to replace them with formal (often market-based) systems of production. In the process, many people – especially the most marginalized – lose out. This is something that more recent studies have confirmed, highlighting the widening gap between rich and poor in times of high growth, especially in countries where inequality was not corrected through redistributive policies (OECD 2008 and 2011). Kuznets also raised doubts about the reliability of the accounts, for which data was often missing, and took great pains to single out the disparate sources of error in international comparisons, including the use of prices. Finally, he pleaded with policy makers to always distinguish between the mere "quantity" of economic growth and its actual "quality" in order to clarify what type of growth they want to achieve and "for what" (Kuznets 1962, 29).

Following Kuznets's original focus on a welfare-oriented understanding of growth, over the past decades, progressive economists, ecologically minded think tanks and NGOs have been criticizing GDP with a view to challenging its influence on policy making. A myriad alternative indicators have been produced in an effort to dethrone this "almighty number" and produce more reliable measures of societal wellbeing.

The first attempt at revising GDP was made by Nobel prize–winning economists William Nordhaus and James Tobin in 1971, when they developed an index called Measure of Economic Welfare (MEW). The MEW tried to "correct" GDP by adding the economic contribution of households and excluding "bad" transactions, such as military expenses (Nordhaus and Tobin 1973). The best-known global synthesis of economic, social, and environmental data into a comprehensive measure of economic welfare is the Genuine Progress Indicator (GPI), introduced by Herman Daly and John Cobb (initially with the name of Index of Sustainable Economic Welfare, ISEW) (Daly and Cobb 1994). The GPI sees the current flow of services to humanity from *all* sources as relevant to economic welfare, not just the output of marketable goods and services. For instance, it takes into account positive dimensions such as leisure, public services, unpaid work (housework, parenting, and care giving), the economic impact of negative factors like income inequality, crime, pollution, insecurity (e.g. car accidents, unemployment, and under-employment), family breakdown, and the economic losses associated with resource depletion and long-term environmental damage. The World Bank began to introduce alternative indicators such as the adjusted net savings, which deducts various types of environmental damage from national income while adding gains in education, as far back as the 1990s, highlighting the importance of complementing GDP with the measure of human and natural capital (World Bank 2015). Since 2010, the Bank and various UN agencies have also started to promote data collection processes across the world with a view to integrating the valuation of ecosystem services and natural capital into the mainstream measurements of the economy. Such an approach, although useful for policy decisions, poses a series of conceptual and methodological problems, ranging from the difficulty of establishing monetary values for nature to the always-present risk of commodification (Fioramonti 2014a).

National initiatives have also abounded, following the special commission set up in 2008 by former French President Nicholas Sarkozy and chaired by Nobel laureates Joseph Stiglitz and Amartya Sen and the economist Jean Paul Fitoussi. Besides recommending new indicators, the commission emphasized that "what we measure affects what we do; and if our measurements are flawed, decisions may be distorted" (Stiglitz et al. 2009, 9). In the UK, Canada, the US, and Germany, special task forces were established to reform the national accounts. In 2012, the UN Secretary General Ban Ki-Moon acknowledged that GDP "has long been the yardstick by which economies and politicians have been measured. Yet it fails to take into account the social and environmental costs of so-called progress" and concluded that "We need a new economic paradigm that recognizes the parity between the three pillars of sustainable development. Social, economic and environmental wellbeing are indivisible" (UN News Centre 2012).

Despite all these attempts, GDP is still carrying the day. There seem to be several reasons for this. The first (and, perhaps, most obvious) is that GDP boosted not only the economic relevance, but also the social acceptability of polluting industries and large corporations in general. By disregarding the social and environmental costs of production, it gave society a skewed perception of the contribution made by many industries to the national economy. Against this backdrop, it is not surprising that an early attempt at reforming GDP to account for environmental costs made by the Bureau of Economic Analysis and supported by the Council of Economic Advisers to President Bill Clinton in 1994 was ditched by the coal industry (Bureau of Economic Analysis 1994; Costanza et al. 2014). As warned by a representative of coal-rich states, with GDP accounting for the depletion of coal reserves and the effects of air pollution, "somebody is going to say [...] that the coal industry isn't contributing anything to the country" (Cobb et al. 1995, 6). A global study conducted in 2013 by the agency Trucost in partnership with the UN-sponsored programme on "the economics of ecosystems and biodiversity" challenged the usefulness of GDP showing the massive unaccounted costs generated for society by large businesses, pointing fingers primarily at the extractive industries and commercial farming (Trucost 2013).

A similar statistical revision unfolded in China in the mid-2000s. In response to concerns over pollution and environmental degradation, the Chinese environmental agency piloted a "green GDP" project, which revealed that environmental damage had cost China 8 to 15 percent of its annual economic growth and that the country had lost "almost everything it has gained since the late 1970s due to pollution" (Byrnes 2006). As these results challenged a longstanding practice in the Communist Party to reward officials that had achieved high GDP growth rates in their localities, the political leadership stepped in to halt the project. To assuage the media, the Chinese Academy of Sciences, a government think tank, published a GDP "quality" index to allegedly demonstrate an increase in "true wealth, sustainable development and social harmony" (China Daily 2012). Yet, a few years later, support for a green GDP resurfaced, as the costs of environmental clean-up spiralled out of control, while official GDP growth began to slow down (Lelyveld 2012). Even president Xi Jinping weighed in with a public statement issued in 2013, in which he demanded that GDP no longer be considered a parameter of success for the promotion of public officials in China (Communist Party of China 2013). A year later, over 70 Chinese cities, including Shanghai, announced that GDP would cease to be used as their primary economic policy tool (Wildau 2014).

Ambivalence on the part of policy makers has also played a role in the resilience of GDP to change, especially since the outburst of the global financial crisis. In November 2007, the EU hosted a high-level conference titled "Beyond GDP" and, two years later, the Commission released a communication on "GDP and Beyond: Measuring progress in a changing world," where it argued that GDP has been unduly "regarded as a proxy indicator for overall societal development and progress in general" (European Commission 2009). Yet, when it came to react to the economic instability across the Eurozone, conservative GDP-based policies prevailed, with the Fiscal Compact reinforcing the traditional ratios to debt and deficit for all EU members. Moreover, the European statistical office issued new guidelines for all member states to incorporate estimations of output derived from a series of illicit activities, including prostitution and drugs, into their national income, which was interpreted by some critics as a desperate attempt to "push up" economic figures amid Europe's worst crisis since the end of the Second World War (Alderman 2014).

The power of GDP is also a result of path dependencies, which make statistical reform so hard to achieve and very slow at best. Although the UN Statistics Division has published new guidelines on how to integrate economic and environmental accounting, no clear implementation systems have been put in place. Moreover, countries have been notoriously slow at catching up with global standards, which means that meaningful changes may be decades in waiting unless public pressure is exercised. Even the kingdom of Bhutan, which introduced the concept of gross national happiness back in the 1970s and has been measuring it since 2008, still employs GDP as its main economic indicator to attract foreign direct investment (National Statistics Bureau 2012). Moreover, the existence of a globally accepted parameter of economic success has benefited the discipline of economics as a whole, separating it ever more from the rest of social sciences and contributing to its influence in society (Fioramonti 2013). As remarked by Coyle (2014, 20), "the story of GDP since the 1940s is also the story of macroeconomics. The availability of national accounts statistics made demand management seem not only feasible but also scientific."

As discussed above, GDP has also been instrumental in describing the current model of economic globalization as efficient. Not only has it neglected critical costs, but it has also provided a statistical justification of a system of value chains that is highly problematic. As GDP measures value added in terms of prices, it rewards countries in which the final stages of production occur. While most production in today's world happens in the Far East and in the so-called emerging markets of the Global South, the bulk of market value is added through the cosmetic finishes carried out mostly in the Global North. Most of the GDP is thus "appropriated" in the final stages, purporting an economic performance (and the relative leadership that comes with it) that is largely the result of an accounting trick. Moreover, this method benefits the most "developed" countries also in terms of sustainable development credentials, as demonstrated by recent research published in the Proceedings of the National Academy of Sciences (Wiedmann et al. 2015). Indeed, by retaining the most profitable stages in the value chain, these nations appear very efficient in economic terms, with high volumes of growth apparently generated with little ecological impact.

It must be noted that while a tremendous amount of work has been done by progressive businesses since the Rio +20 summit in June 2012, not all new systems are necessarily indicating a genuine interest in the promotion of social, economic, and environmental wellbeing. In the field of natural capital accounting, for instance, several investment banks and big corporations have been promoting accounting reforms to gauge business performance. On the one hand, this may help a great deal in realizing the environmental costs of our model of growth, thus rewarding companies that put wellbeing at the center of their operations while sanctioning those that do not. At the same time, there is an inherent risk that some corporations (especially those involved in private finance) may interpret this move at measuring the value of nature as putting a "price" on ecosystems and natural assets, thus generating new speculative markets and financial mechanisms to the detriment of the planet (Fioramonti 2014b).

Finally, GDP completely changed the social debate on political accountability and inequality. Being presented as an essential tool for the design of public policies, it contributed to turning the political process into a rather technocratic affair, dominated by central bankers, economic advisors, and business associations. By portraying success in terms of GDP growth, the political economy ceased to be a political struggle over "who gets what" and became a technocratic recipe for the responsible management of the business cycle (Fioramonti 2013). No surprise then that, across the world, governments of different (when not opposing) political traditions adopted similar economic policies, often alienating movements and citizens demanding radical change. Moreover, the growth paradigm based on GDP crowded out important conversations about inequality and redistribution. It presented development as the process of expanding the pool of resources available to the economy (an ever-increasing pie), of which more and more people could get a share without diminishing the relative shares of others. As former governor of the Federal Reserve System Henry Wallich once remarked, "growth is a substitute for equality of income. So long as there is growth there is hope, and that makes large income differentials tolerable" (cited by Street 2014, 70). This is a belief that most politicians, technocrats, and business leaders have traditionally found appealing, in particular as it removes social justice issues from the political debate and supports the dominant distribution of resources while weakening alternative fairness-based approaches.

A post GDP world?

There is no doubt that the invention of GDP has given economics a primary role in society and politics. Conformity among mainstream economists has been pervasive. In 1941, Kuznets admitted that the measurement of national income should not be regarded as a morally neutral process, because it is continuously "affected by implicit or explicit value judgements." Looking at the enthusiasm with which his creation was being welcomed by colleagues, he observed that

> the apparent relative unanimity produced by empirical writings on national income is due largely to the estimators' unconscious acceptance of one social philosophy and their natural reluctance to face such fundamental issues as would reveal that estimates are conditioned by controversial criteria.
>
> (Kuznets 1941, 5)

As Stone put it, national income is not "a primary fact" but "an empirical construct." In order to decide what income is, "it is necessary to set up a theory from which income is derived as a concept by postulation and then associate this concept with a certain set of primary facts" (Stone 1951, 9). The invention of GDP not only marked the era in which economics (and economists) became an all-powerful force in society. It also ushered in a new age of market supremacy. As economic growth became the most important goal of politics, the "producers" of growth felt their reign of uncontested leadership had finally arrived. As GDP masked the negative externalities of industrial production, all industries (especially the heavy polluters) became champions of progress.

GDP growth has not only been criticized by experts, but also by ordinary people. This has been particularly true in industrialized societies, where the GDP creed was first developed before being instituted in the rest of the world. New civil society initiatives and campaigns are being promoted throughout Europe and North America with a view to fighting GDP and radically rethinking our dominant economic model. A variety of community associations, nongovernmental organizations, environmental movements, and other civil society groups have been experimenting with creative models, ranging from alternative currencies to "degrowth" initiatives, in order to promote wellbeing, defend public goods, and preserve our ecosystems. In the Global South, both ecological movements and networks of small businesses and small-scale farmers are demanding radical change. In Africa, too, there is a growing multitude of citizens who are suspicious of the new "Africa rising" discourse and see rising inequality and environmental degradation where the GDP supporters see economic success.

Given that the assessment of a society's economic goals is key to stir its political and social development, Kuznets recommended that each generation should change the way in which progress is measured, "to formulate and reformulate it in response to changing conditions" (Kuznets 1962, 29). The potential impacts of such change are enormous. An institutionalized system of accounting that emphasized the costs associated with highly centralized, polluting, and wasteful production would reveal the way in which many large corporations are taking wealth away from society rather than adding value, thus reducing their acceptability and political influence. Such a system would also highlight the economic contributions and external benefits of forms of production that GDP either downplays or ignores. If the unpaid activity of households and the social benefits to be derived from small businesses were fully accounted for, non-conventional economic actors would gain a much stronger voice in society. Civil society would also benefit: its activities would no longer be perceived as marginal (as implicit in definitions such as "non-profit" and "third sector") but rather as key drivers of wellbeing.

In the same way, looking beyond GDP in economic performance has the capacity to disrupt the balance of opposing forces in a number of key socio-political disputes. Opponents of the fossil fuel industries and others fighting climate change would find their moral and ethical arguments underpinned by solid economic indicators, as would groups mobilized against austerity policies or international trade agreements such as the Transatlantic Trade and Investment Partnership (TTIP) and Trans-Pacific Partnership (TTP). Current arguments for unfettered free trade rest almost entirely on GDP measurements that promote volume over quality in economic activity and do not account for international trade's negative environmental and social externalities, while the austerity policies currently dividing Europe and other regions of the world enforce punitive debt to GDP ratios that prevent social investment.

Whether focusing on genuine progress, wellbeing, and inclusive wealth, all "beyond GDP" indicators highlight the crucial economic contributions made by families, communities, cooperatives, informal and small businesses, organic farmers, fair trade networks, and many similar groups. Even high-tech companies, and especially those providing on-line services, from Google to Facebook, have much to gain from a shift in accounting systems. From a GDP perspective these companies' only value is through selling advertising space, while their overall societal impact in terms of connectivity, social networking, and information sharing has no economic value in GDP terms because it is provided free of charge or at a marginal cost close to zero. This means that the contribution to economic dynamism and wellbeing of information-sharing technologies, some of which provide public goods from free phone calls to global maps to library services, is grossly underestimated by the GDP model.

The "beyond GDP" debate is now high on the agenda. Many international agencies, including the UN, the OECD, the World Bank, and the European Union, are actively engaged, as are a number of national governments. Moreover, the UN 2015 Sustainable Development Goals, although contradictory in their objectives and still including conventional growth in some targets, provide at least an entry point for institutional change at a global level. As more social actors become aware of how a move beyond GDP can assist their causes it is possible that grass-roots social pressure will also grow, connecting bottom-up movements for change with top-down political reform.

Ideally, GDP should be replaced by a "dashboard" of indicators capable of integrating the key dimensions of human and ecological wellbeing. This integration would need to be done carefully, so as to combine both monetary measurements with non-monetary ones. For starters, the economy should be measured in terms of genuine progress, which will require introducing monetary units for dimensions that do not involve formal transactions, such as natural and social capital. This would make both ecosystems and household contributions valuable for economic success. At the same time, the operating boundaries of the economy should be determined by non-monetary measurements of social and environmental wellbeing, indicating the upper and lower limits (that is, the ecological ceiling and the social floor) that cannot be exceeded without endangering wellbeing. This would make sure that sustainability is fully respected in its "strong" version, not allowing econometric calculations to simply offset losses in one field with gains in another (what economists call the "perfect substitutability" of different types of capital). In this proposed system, continuous improvements in wellbeing need not be achieved at the expense of social and ecological conditions.

Ultimately, citizens rather than technocrats should be given the possibility to decide what society's goals are and how to achieve them. The time has come for us to listen to Kuznets and retire GDP. What we need is a growing, popular social movement advocating for a post-GDP world.

References

Alderman, Liz. 2014. "Sizing Up Black Markets and Red-Light Districts for G.D.P." *The New York Times*, July 9. Accessed April 10, 2016. http://www.nytimes.com/2014/07/10/business/international/eu-nations-counting-sex-and-drug-trades-toward-gdp.html?_r=0.

Balmford, Andrew, Bruner, Aaron, Cooper, Philip, Costanza, Robert, Farber, Stephen, Green, Rhys E., Jenkins, Martin, Jefferis, Paul, Jessamy, Valma, Madden, Joah, Munro, Kat, Myers, Norman, Naeem, Shahid, Paavola, Jouni, Rayment, Matthew, Rosendo, Sergio, Roughgarden, Johan, Trumper, Kate, and Turner, R.Kerry. 2002. "Economic Reasons for Conserving Wild Nature." *Science* 297: 950–953.

Bridgman, Benjamin, Dugan, Andrew, Lal, Mickael. Osborne, Matthew, and Villones, Shaunda. 2012. "Accounting for Household Production in the National Accounts, 1965–2010." *Survey of Current Business* 92(5): 23–36.

Bureau of Economic Analysis. 1994. "Integrated Economic and Environmental Satellite Accounts." *Survey of Current Business* 74(4): 33–49.

Byrnes, Sholto. 2006. "The Man Making China Green." *The New Statesman* December 2006–January 2007: 60–61.

Carson, Carol S. 1975. "The History of the United States National Income and Product Accounts: The Development of an Analytical Tool." *Review of Income and Wealth* 21(2): 153–181.

China Daily. 2012. "GDP Growth More Quality Oriented." *China Daily*, July 27, 2012. Accessed April 10, 2016. http://www.chinadaily.com.cn/business/2012-07/27/content_15625077.htm.

Chowdhury, Anis and Islam, Iyanatul. 2012. "Is There an Optimal Debt-To-GDP Ratio?" Vox, Centre for Economic Policy Research. Accessed on April 10, 2016. http://www.voxeu.org/debates/commentaries/there-optimal-debt-gdp-ratio.

Cobb, Clifford, Halstead, Ted, and Rowe, Jonathan. 1995. "If the GDP is Up, Why is America Down?" *Atlantic Monthly* 95/10: 6.

Communist Party of China. 2013. "President Xi Promises to Shake GDP Obsession in Promoting Officials." *News of the Communist Party of China*. Accessed April 10, 2016. http://english.cpc.people.com.cn/206972/206974/8305576.html.

Costanza, Robert, Kubiszewski, Ida, Giovannini, Enrico, Lovins, Hunter, McGlade, Jacqueline, Pickett, Kate E., Ragnarsdottir, Kristin Vala, Roberts, Debra, De Vogli, Roberto, and Wilkinson, Richard. 2014. "Time to Leave GDP Behind." *Nature* 505: 283–285.

Costanza, Robert, D'Arge, Raphael, De Groot, Rudolf, Farber, Stephen, Grasso, Monica, Hannon, Bruce, Limburg, Karin, Naeem, Shahid, O'Neill, Robert, V., Paruelo, Jose, Raskin, Robert G., Sutton, Paul, and Van den Belt, Marjan. 1997. "The Value of the World's Ecosystem Services and Natural Capital." *Nature* 387: 253–270.

Coyle, Diane. 2014. *GDP: A Brief but Affectionate History*. Princeton: Princeton University Press.

Daly, Herman and Cobb, John. 1994. *For the Common Good: Redirecting the Economy Toward Community, the Environment and a Sustainable Future. Second Edition*. Boston: Beacon Press.

Deane, Phyllis. 1953. *Colonial Social Accounting*. Cambridge: Cambridge University Press.

EcuRed. 2016. "Conocimiento con Todos y Para Todos." Accessed April 10, 2016. http://www.ecured.cu/index.php/Producto_Interno_Bruto_en_Cuba.

European Commission. 2009. GDP and Beyond: Measuring Progress in a Changing World, COM/2009/0433 final.

Fioramonti, Lorenzo. 2013. *Gross Domestic Problem: The Politics Behind the World's Most Powerful Number*. London: Zed Books.

Fioramonti, Lorenzo. 2014a. *How Numbers Rule the World: The Use and Abuse of Statistics in Global Politics*. London: Zed Books.

Fioramonti, Lorenzo. 2014b. "The World's Most Powerful Number: An Assessment of 80 Years of GDP Ideology." *Anthropology Today* 30(2): 16–19.

Foertsch, Tracy. 2006. "A Victory for Taxpayers and the Economy." Heritage Foundation, WebMemo#1082. AccessedApril 10, 2016. http://www.heritage.org/research/reports/2006/05/a-victory-for-taxpayers-and-the-economy.

Galbraith, John Kenneth. 1980. "The National Accounts: Arrival and Impact." In *Reflections of America: Commemorating the Statistical Abstract Centennial*, edited by Norman Cousins, 75–80. Washington, DC: US Department of Commerce, Bureau of the Census.

Gilbert, Milton, George Jaszi, Edward F. Denison, Charles F. Schwartz. 1948. "Objective of National Income Measurement: A Reply to Professor Kuznets." *Review of Economics and Statistics* 30(3): 179–195.

Herrera, Yoshiko M. 2011. *Mirrors of the Economy: National Accounts and International Norms in Russia and Beyond*. Ithaca: Cornell University Press.

Jerven, Morten. 2013. *Poor Numbers: How We Are Misled by Africa's Development Statistics and What To Do About It*. Ithaca: Cornell University Press.

Kaiser, Emily. 2010. "Special Report: US Data Dogs on Quest for Sexier Statistics." *Reuters*, July 7, 2010. Accessed April 10, 2016. http://in.reuters.com/article/idINIndia-49928820100706.

Keynes, John M. 1940. *How To Pay for the War: A Radical Plan for the Chancellor of the Exchequer*. London: Macmillan.

Kuznets, Simon. 1934. "National Income, 1929–1932." Report presented to the 73rd US Congress, 2d session, Senate document no. 124. Reprinted as "National Income, 1929–1932." *NBER Bulletin 49*, June 7, 1934.

Kuznets, Simon. 1937. *National Income and Capital Formation (1919–1935)*. New York: National Bureau for Economic Research.

Kuznets, Simon. 1941. *National Income and Its Composition (1919–1938), Volume I*. New York: National Bureau for Economic Research.

Kuznets, Simon. 1946. *National Income – A Summary of Findings*. New York: National Bureau of Economic Research.

Kuznets, Simon. 1962. "How to Judge Quality." *The New Republic*, October 20, 29–31.

Lelyveld, Michael. 2012. "China's Green GDP Resurfaces." *Radio Free Asia*, February 13, 2012. Accessed April 10, 2016. http://www.rfa.org/english/commentaries/energy_watch/greengdp-02132012120520.html.

Lundberg, Erik. 1971. "Simon Kuznets' Contribution to Economics." *Swedish Journal of Economics* 73(4): 444–459.

Marx, Karl. 1909. *Capital: A Critique of Political Economy, Vol. II: The Process of Circulation of Capital*. Chicago: C. H. Kerr & Co.

Mitra-Kahn, Benjamin. 2011. Redefining the Economy. How The 'Economy' Was Invented 1620. Ph.D. thesis, City University of London. Accessed April 10, 2016. http://openaccess.city.ac.uk/1276.

National Statistics Bureau. 2012. "Bhutan at a Glance." October 2012. Accessed July 28, 2016. http://www.nsb.gov.bt/nsbweb/publication/publications.php?id=5.

Nordhaus, William and Tobin, James. 1973. "Is Growth Obsolete?" Reprinted in The Measurement of Economic and Social Performance, special issue of *Studies in Income and Wealth* 38, 1973: 509–532.

Noren, James. 2003. "CIA's Analysis of the Soviet Economy." In *Watching the Bear: Essays on CIA's Analysis of the Soviet Union*, edited by in Gerald K. Haines and Robert E. Leggett. Washington: Central Intelligence Agency.

OECD. 2008. *Growing Unequal? Income Distribution and Poverty in OECD Countries.* Paris: OECD.

OECD. 2011. *Divided We Stand: Why Inequality Keeps Rising*. Paris: OECD.

OECDObserver. 2004. "Is GDP a Satisfactory Measure of Growth?" *OECD Observer* 246–247. Accessed April 10, 2016. http://www.oecdobserver.org/news/archivestory.php/aid/1518/Is_GDP_a_satisfactory_measure_of_growth_.html.

Philipsen, Dirk. 2015. *The Little Big Number: How GDP Came To Rule the World and What To Do About it.* Princeton: Princeton University Press.

Schneider, Friedrich and Enste, Dominik. 2002. "Hiding in the Shadows: the Growth of the Underground Economy." *Economic Issues 30*. Brussels: International Monetary Fund.

Stiglitz, Joseph E., Amartya Sen, and Jean-Paul Fitoussi. 2009. *Report by the Commission on the Measurement of Economic Performance and Progress.* Accessed April 10, 2016. http://www.insee.fr/fr/publications-et-services/dossiers_web/stiglitz/doc-commission/RAPPORT_anglais.pdf.

Stone, Richard. 1951. *The Role of Measurement in Economics.* Cambridge: Cambridge University Press.

Street, Paul. 2014. *They Rule. The 1% Vs. Democracy.* London: Routledge.

Trucost. 2013. *Natural Capital At Risk: The Top 100 Externalities of Business.* London: Trucost.

UN News Centre. 2012. "Ban: New Economic Paradigm Needed, Including Social and Environmental Progress." UN News Centre. Accessed April 10, 2016. http://www.un.org/apps/news/story.asp?NewsID=41685#.VwbzMoU5vP8.

Wiedmann, Thomas O., Schandl, Heinz, Lenzen, Manfred, Moran, Daniel, Suh, Sangwon, West, James and Kanemoto, Keiichiro. 2015. "The Material Footprint of Nations." *Proceedings of the National Academy of Sciences* 112(20): 6271–6276.

Wildau, Gabriel. 2014. "Small Cities Steer Away From GDP as A Measure of Success." *The Financial Times*, August 13, 2014. Accessed April 10, 2016. http://www.ft.com/intl/cms/s/0/a0288bd4-22b0-11e4-8dae-00144feabdc0.html#axzz3FvlTScZh.

World Bank. 2015. *The Little Green Data Book 2015*. Washington, DC: World Bank.

5 Development and economic growth

An intellectual history

Stephen Macekura

In the twenty-first century, people around the world take for granted the concepts of development and economic growth. Leaders and policymakers evoke both concepts when presenting future goals. Experts churn out annual reports of development projects and quarterly reports on growth rates. When citizens assess leaders in power, they often do so by comparing performance to expectation: did the economy grow as hoped and anticipated, or did the country continue to develop? The two concepts have become central to everyday life, and they are two of the most basic terms that many people use to describe change over time. While many may not understand how GDP is calculated nor follow the latest trends in development theories, the notions that countries develop and economies grow are widely held as ironclad truths.

This chapter presents a different approach to studying development and growth. It begins with a historical premise: that the core of both ideas – that nations "develop" through stages or discreet periods of socio-political organization and that something called "the economy" is an object that can be made to grow – are recent products of twentieth-century economic knowledge and political culture. After all, the term "international development" only appeared in widespread use at the turn of the twentieth century and "economic growth" only in the 1940s (Mitchell 2005; Gilman 2003; McVety 2012; Arndt 1978; Collins 2000; Yarrow 2010; Karabell 2014; Fioramonti 2013; Coyle 2014).

This chapter explores how and why the concepts of growth and development emerged and how they evolved in the twentieth-century world. First, I focus on the origins of the development and growth discourse in the United States and Europe. Second, I show how and why intellectuals and policymakers in the United States, Western Europe, and the Soviet Union sought to implement growth and development theories to "modernize" the countries of the Global South. Finally, I highlight some of the criticisms of growth, development, and modernization that have emerged since the 1960s.

In analyzing this history, I make a series of interconnected arguments. First, I argue that both concepts emerged in large part because of the prominence of experts (primarily economists) in twentieth-century political life. The expansion of expert knowledge in governance was particularly important in the 1930s and 1940s because of policymakers' need to explain and shape a transformation taking place: a shift in the United States and Europe toward Keynesian economic policies. Through advances in social scientific theory and economic statistics, experts conceived of theories of socio-cultural and political development and economic growth in order to describe and resolve national problems of economic management that had been laid bare by the Great Depression and the looming international problems that stemmed from the transition of a world ordered by imperial power to one of independent nation-states. In turn, the rise of the economic growth paradigm solidified and strengthened the dominance of economics as a leading social science discipline and a language to describe everyday life (Schmelzer 2016; Speich 2008; Bernstein 2001; Mitchell 2002; Maier 1977).

Second, I demonstrate that the two concepts, economic growth and development, became central to international politics because of decolonization and the early Cold War. From the 1940s through the early 1960s, leaders in the United States, Europe, and Soviet Union drew lessons from their past in the hopes of finding a concrete set of policy prescriptions that could be used to engineer the economic expansion, social transformation, and political allegiance of the "Third World" countries. In the West – especially in the United States – over the 1950s social scientific explorations of "modernization" became popular, drawing elements from research into development and theories of economic growth. Modernization theorists linked socio-cultural and political change with growth-oriented economic theories to provide a framework for analyzing and reproducing in the "underdeveloped" world the same set of processes that they claimed had led to the industrialization and urbanization of much of Western Europe, the United States, and Japan (Chang 2002). Modernization theorists such as Walt Rostow cast their work as an alternative to communism in the global Cold War, a toolkit that post-colonial and other countries in the "Third World" could draw upon as they pursued material wealth and cultural transformation. Thus the discourses of development and growth – often mixed and conflated within the broader umbrella of "modernization" – became inextricably bound with Western attempts to incorporate much of the world into a liberal, capitalist world order (Latham 2000; McVety 2012; Macekura 2015; Cullather 2011; Immerwahr 2015).

Finally, I argue that the development and growth discourses have never been entirely stable nor without challenge. Even during the high tide of modernization theory in the 1950s and 1960s, critics – both from within the social sciences and without – decried the environmental, social, and political consequences of growth-based economics and disputed many of the assumptions that framed development theories. Such criticisms, however, became especially potent in the late 1960s and 1970s as it became clear that various growth models and modernization plans failed to eliminate poverty, unemployment, and led to unexpected social and environmental crises. In many cases, critics of growth, development, and modernization proposed alternative concepts and metrics – sustainability and "green" GDP accounts or "basic human needs" and the human development index – to narrate and assess the process of social change. Yet even as some of these criticisms took hold in many policy circles by the 1990s, they did not replace development and growth thinking. After all, many criticisms of modernization theory, for instance, were still made within the framework of modernization (Gilman 2003, ch. 6). Though the ideas and discourses about development and economic growth had been challenged throughout the late twentieth century, they remain central organizing categories for the twenty-first.

Development and growth: a brief history

Articulating a single definition for "development" is notoriously difficult, because the word has many different meanings that have changed over time. Some scholars have stretched back as far as ancient Greece and Aristotle's thinking about nature, while others have focused on the rise of capitalism in the fifteenth and sixteenth centuries and eighteenth-century attempts by thinkers ranging from Condorcet to Kant to construct an "universal history" that would reveal the ultimate, linear developmental path of humankind (Rist 2008, ch. 1–2; Leys 1996, 4–8). The idea that countries evolve in a linear fashion toward an ideal state of being – the notion of "progress" or "improvement" or "advancement" – found its earliest advocates and most frequent invocations during the Scottish enlightenment of the eighteenth century. Amanda McVety identified David Hume and Adam Smith as two key figures who celebrated Great Britain's peculiar sets of laws and institutions as premier examples worthy of emulation in the non-European world (and especially for much of the world that Great Britain was beginning to colonize). These thinkers believed that individual liberty, trade, protection of property rights, and specialization of labor would generate wealth and help their societies escape a history of deprivation and scarcity (McVety 2012, 5–24).

Notions of economic progress emerged during the long eighteenth century, as well. The phrase economic growth – that the economy was an object that could be made to grow, and that such a process could be managed – only appeared in widespread use in the 1940s, but it had earlier antecedents. Political economists from the eighteenth and nineteenth century envisioned economic activity and material abundance as "progressing" or "increasing" or "improving" through time, often in a linear way similar to how they understood development. This vision of ever-increasing economic activity was not universally accepted, however. Thomas Malthus warned in the late eighteenth and early nineteenth century that population growth would run against material limits to food production, creating not continues improvement but "perpetual oscillation between happiness and misery" (McVety 2012, 24). John Stuart Mill famously contrasted those political economists who envisioned a "progressive state" of ever-increasing economic activity against an ideal "stationary state" where cultural aspirations for economic life moderated considerably (Mill 1926, 746–751). Despite these early warnings about limitless economic expansion, however, over the nineteenth century the industrialization and increasing productivity in Europe and the United States inspired political economists to depict economic activity as progressively moving human society from a condition of scarcity to one of material abundance (McVety 2012, 27).

Over the early nineteenth century, this sense of cultural and institutional superiority of European peoples and the linear course of economic change became matched by a growing faith in managed state power to guide social, political, and economic transformation. The word "development" first came into widespread use in English during the middle part of the nineteenth century to describe how state officials could spur and manage the process of improvement in far-flung parts of the empire. In the 1830s and 1840s, British intellectuals and diplomats rethought their relationship to the settler colonies of Canada and Australia (after the revolutionary break with its settler colony in the United States). In Australia, colonial officials grappled with the vast landscape seemingly bereft of adequate labor needed to use it productively. They worried about the political ramifications of the situation. To maintain allegiance over their burgeoning settler empire, British officials began to speak of accommodating the settler societies by claiming development as a process by which they could make sustained settlement possible through government initiatives to bring people and capital to the distant colony for the purposes of constructing railways, building irrigation canals, and farming the land. Development, in this transitive sense, came to describe a state-guided process of purposeful social, political, and economic change (Hodge 2007, 26–29).

Development discourse further became bound up with the challenges of managing and justifying imperial rule. Over the nineteenth century, many other European thinkers explicitly injected ideas of racial and cultural superiority into their stadial thinking and faith in state power. In particular, the concept of "civilization" came to dominate intellectual discourse. European "civilization," common thinking went, had nurtured the right set of cultural, political, and economic traits while peoples outside Europe had not. For example, French philosopher Henri Saint-Simon and his disciples, most prominently the sociologist Auguste Comte, believed that an elite circle of "trustees" should guide and manage the development of "backward peoples" toward better ends (Ekbladh 2010, 14–16). Scientific racism, notions of white supremacy, and the rising popularity of social Darwinism reinforced the sense that European peoples (and their offshoots in the New World) represented the high-point of human civilization, with all others confined to a lower realm. The notion of a "white man's burden" to "civilize" non-Europeans became popular as colonial rule spread across the world (Ekbladh 2010, 25–29; Rist 2008, 47–58). Though anthropologist Franz Boas and his disciples discredited much of scientific racism in the early twentieth century, the distinction between "primitive" or "backward" societies and "civilized" or "modern" ones persisted. By the early twentieth century, the new anthropological insights argued that civilizational differences were not fixed in time but instead implied that all cultures could fit into the same development path. This thinking, however, further emphasized the importance of European (and American) guidance to ensure the transition from "primitive" to "modern" was a smooth and manageable one (McVety 2012, 36–37).

Amid these intellectual shifts, in practice European countries and the United States began to put forth some protean experiments in promoting this kind of "development." The United States had long experimented with acculturating Native peoples in its territories, but this effort picked up steam in the late nineteenth century. The United States' imperial ventures in the Philippines involved efforts to transform Filipino society through education, agricultural, and land reform, new patterns of dress and social behavior, and new forms of national administration. By the early twentieth century, some European governments also began to experiment with "improvement" schemes in their colonial territories (Westad 2005, ch. 1). Both the French *mission civilisatrice* and the Dutch Ethical Policy, for instance, emphasized hygiene, irrigation schemes, local education, and public works as central to expressing imperial legitimacy (Hodge 2007, 42–43). These schemes, of course, helped European countries grow richer, too. In French colonial policy, for instance, concepts such as *mise en valeur* and "constructive exploitation" linked social improvements in the colonial periphery to increasing wealth in the European core (Rist 2008, 51–55; Conklin 1997).

As European and American colonial ventures focused on development, economic problems at home spawned a revolution in economic statistics and measurement. Efforts to quantify national economic activity reach back centuries, but remained largely inchoate until the late nineteenth century when European countries began to tabulate trade, industry, and agriculture statistics. European countries and the United States kept records of individualistic social statistics, such as crime rates, average caloric intake among workers, and literacy rates, as reformers looked to collect information on poverty and disease amid increasing migration and industrialization (Porter 2001, 17; Bouk 2015). By the 1920s, however, economists in the United States, Great Britain, and a few other wealthy countries moved beyond individualistic indicators to calculate the entirety of national wealth focused largely around the idea of "national income" (Kendrick 1970; Carson 1975; Clavin 2013). In so doing, economists used statistics to represent an object called "the national economy" (Mitchell 2005; Mitchell 2014).

This research became especially important as countries fell into the Great Depression. Experiments in national income accounting by U.S. economist and statistician Simon Kuznets and British economist Colin Clark led to new forms of calculation and ways of describing national economic activity during global crisis. Out of this work came Gross National Product (GNP), which aggregated the total of all products and services produced in a year by citizens of a country. GNP offered policymakers a simple way to see precisely how much the government could spend, and as World War II posed new questions of resource use, how much governments could increase taxes to achieve their military procurement goals. After the War ended, full employment planning depended on GNP metrics and reconstruction efforts in Europe were tied to official GNP estimates for European countries (Speich 2008, 29). Though there was great debate over what GNP should count and how policymakers should use the number, achieving high GNP growth rates quickly became practical policy goals and powerful symbols (Kuznets 1947; Duncan and Shelton 1978). GNP came to stand in for the vitality of the nation, with countries such as Japan, the United States, and postwar Germany holding up rapid GNP increases as markers of national progress (O'Bryan 2009; Yarrow 2010; Schmelzer 2016). Once the UN standardized national accounting in 1953, GNP became central to national policymaking (United Nations 1953).

The widespread use of GNP in this way made possible the concept of economic growth. The idea of material progress and economic expansion became popular during the nineteenth century, but economic growth, premised on a calculable entity called the national economy, only took hold with advancements in quantifying and standardizing GNP as the single best indicator of national economic activity (Schmelzer 2015).[1] Likewise, economists began to take the metric and envisioned ways to make it grow through specific national and international policy interventions. The term "economic growth" appeared in the United States' Full Employment Act of 1946, and it became central to the Truman administration's aspiration for domestic and global security (Collins 2000, 32–39). The growth concept gained cultural power and political significance because it seemed to allow policymakers to redress older distributional conflicts through a superficially neutral language of technocratic consensus. It ensured, in Charles Maier's words, "the primacy of economics over politics, to de-ideologize issues of political economy into questions of output on efficiency" (Maier 1987, 146). Citizens living in the 1940s and 1950s, with vivid memories of the Great Depression and wartime scarcities, embraced growth, too. Agricultural production increased; more consumer goods flooded the markets; unemployment decreased dramatically throughout the United States and Europe. As people came to experience all of these transformations, the idea of a "growing" economy – as the sum of goods produced and purchased and services offered – made perfect sense to those who experienced it and to those who wanted it. By the early 1950s, then, growth defined in terms of GNP increases was a common goal for many governments.

The idea of economic growth was not strictly a Western phenomenon. In the "Second World," economists in the Soviet Union developed a measurement system, the Material Product System, to quantify their country's aggregate production and subsequently crafted theories to grow socialist economies (Spulber 1964; Hatziprokopiou and Valentzas 2002; Barnett 2005; Johnson and Temin 1993). Over the 1920s Soviet economists focused on the principles driving economic expansion and the rates of change in national income, and they linked development with rapid industrialization beginning in the first five-year plan of 1929 (Spulber 1964; Engerman 2010). As the vast agricultural country began to industrialize Soviet leaders trumpeted high growth rates as a symbol of Soviet vitality and by the 1950s Western policymakers began to look at the Soviet economy with trepidation (Engerman 2007).

The development, growth, and modernization of the "Third World"

By the 1940s, thinking about national development and economic growth acquired a powerful strategic purpose for the United States and liberal Western European nations. As the Great Depression swept across the world, liberal capitalism faced two powerful threats, fascism and communism, which offered radically different ways of organizing society. Intellectuals and policymakers began to examine ways in which U.S. and European aid could transform societies around the world to keep their citizens from leaning toward radical alternatives amid the instability of the depression, enlarge the liberal capitalist trading area, and build up allies against fascist and communist expansion. During World War II, colonial improvement schemes picked up in intensity and frequency throughout British territories, and the United States experimented with agricultural, educational, and public health programs in Latin America (Hodge 2007; Rivas 2002). By the war's end, the threat of Nazi Germany and imperial Japan gave way to new concerns in the United States and Western Europe about the Soviet Union. Global decolonization, which loomed in the near future, seemed to pose policymakers with a pressing question: When colonial territories became independent states, which system would they seek to emulate?

In this context, development soon became a widespread term to describe the goals of economic and social policy around the world. U.S. President Harry S. Truman made this commitment explicit in his inaugural address of 1949, where he announced for the first time that the United States would take as a formal objective the economic and social development of what he termed the "underdeveloped" world – the countries of Asia, Africa, and Latin America (Truman 1949). The Point Four program, which emerged from Truman's 1949 inaugural, marked the elevation of development to a primary feature of international politics, placed U.S. aid at the center of international development efforts, and announced the pursuit of development as a goal for nation-states around the world (Macekura 2013).[2] A new array of international institutions supported such development efforts, too, ranging from the Food and Agriculture Organization to several UN commissions which merged in 1965 to form the United Nations Development Programme (Staples 2006).

As development thinking captivated the minds of policymakers from Washington to Geneva, national leaders in the so-called "Third World" countries embraced developmental rhetoric and ideas, too. Nationalist leaders around the globe, such as Tanzania's Julius Nyerere, Ghana's Kwame Nkrumah, India's Jawalrahal Nehru, and Egypt's Gamal Abdel Nasser all spoke of the need for rapid development to overcome the history of colonial exploitation and Western interference and bring their populations out of poverty. Policymakers in Washington and London often looked askance at the strong nationalist claims of these countries, and often considered foreign aid as a way to contain the more revolutionary components of these movements. But in many cases, nationalists translated the ideas and discourse circulating in the international arena to fit their local circumstances. Nationalist leaders often played on post-colonial and emerging Cold War fears to gain either Western or Soviet support for major developmental initiatives, such as Ghana's large dam project on the Volta River (supported heavily by the United States) and Egypt's Aswan Dam (funded by the Soviet Union after Washington and London and the World Bank passed on the project because of its planned high costs) (Latham 2011, ch. 2).

Economists increasingly described this variety of projects in abstract terms to identify how they could contribute to a country's overall economic growth. Over the late 1930s and early 1940s, émigré economist Paul Rosenstein-Rodan began to divide the national economy into discreet sectors and explored how to induce industrialization into largely agricultural societies. In a 1944 article entitled "The International Development of Economically Backward Areas," Rosenstein-Rodan built upon earlier research into industrialization to suggest the need to bring "machinery and capital towards labour" in Asia, Africa, the Caribbean, and Southern and Eastern Europe to spark industrialization to ensure a "stable and prosperous peace" (McVety 2012, 55–56). A few years later, Cambridge economist Roy Harrod and Chicago economist Evsey Domar modified existing Keynesian assumptions by explaining employment as a function of the ratio of national income to overall productive capacity. From this they spoke of an ideal growth rate, determined by the national "propensity to save" and the ratio of capital to output. Like Rosenstein-Rodan, Harrod, and Domar demonstrated that GNP could thus be made to grow at a desired rate. Such thinking became commonplace by the early 1950s (Clark 1961, 15).

Many economists who focused on identifying the factors behind economic growth soon began to seek out the process by which economic growth could "take-off" in the non-Western world. For instance, economists Raúl Prebisch and Hans Singer, working through the United Nations, identified a long-term tendency for the price of agricultural exports to decline relative to manufactured goods. St. Lucian economist W. Arthur Lewis published a widely regarded theory of growth for developing areas that emphasized persistent under-employment in agriculture and argued that rural productivity was low, capital rare, and labor supplies "unlimited" in "underdeveloped areas" – a "dual economy" wracked by a traditional, poverty-stricken agrarian "sector" and a nascent, capitalistic, urbanizing productive one. This dualistic modeling – which divided the economy into sectors by space, time, and/or type – became the foundational assumption behind growth theories that promised to take "backward" or lagging sectors and transform them into production-oriented powerhouses through targeted interventions of external capital, knowledge, and careful planning by technocratic elites. By the start of the 1950s, Singer, Rosenstein-Rodan, and other economists, such as Rangar Nurske, became convinced of the need for a “big push” of large-scale capital investment in the “Third World” to overcome the “gravitational pull of [their] ancient stagnant order” and make them into growing, modern economies (Sackley 2004, 233). These economists became the foundation for what would later be known as “development economics”: a branch of the discipline that focused on explaining and predicting economic change in “developing” countries (Arndt 1978).

In this process, growth thinking went global. In Europe, growth provided the language for escaping from the massive challenges of reconstruction (Milward 2000). In the 1950s, the World Bank focused its lending on large-scale capital projects under the growing belief that “development necessarily occurred through the growth of aggregate indices of the economy” (Alacevich 2009, 145). The pursuit of economic growth defined reconstruction plans and political culture in post-war Japan (O’Bryan 2009). The Organization for European Economic Cooperation (OEEC) used the phrase “economic growth” in the early 1950s, and its successor organization, the Organization for Economic Cooperation and Development (OECD), placed the phrase in its stated aims four years later (Mazower 1998).

Growth talk suffused the rhetoric of post-colonial and nationalist leaders around the Global South as high GNP rates became symbols of developmental success and GNP the “yardstick” by which countries would be judged in the global Cold War (Engerman 2007). Leaders such as Tom Mboye of Kenya, Jawalrahal Nehru of India, or Julius Nyerere of Tanzania looked to GNP increases and rapid economic growth as important dimensions of political independence. Arthur Lewis traveled to Ghana on Kwame Nkrumah’s invitation, and the economist actively planned Ghana’s development model based on prevailing growth theories. Lewis acknowledged the difficulties of doing thorough empirical work under the burden of Nkrumah’s political commitment to achieving growth, but the economist still attempted to organize existing theoretical work to match local conditions (Tignor 2006). Amid global decolonization, economic growth transformed from a statistical construct to a policy goal and political gospel for many leaders worldwide (Speich 2011).

All the while, theorists and advocates for economic growth began to use the concept as a narrative device for describing long-term shifts in economic activity. “As a distinctive epoch in economic organization, modern economic growth, or development,” wrote prominent American economist (and former mentee of Simon Kuznets) Richard Easterlin in the *International Encyclopedia of the Social Sciences* in 1968, “dates from the eighteenth century, when its beginnings in western Europe can first clearly be discerned” (Easterlin 1968). Though the term “economic growth” only dated from the late nineteenth century and the concept as an object of study from the early twentieth century, economists such as Easterlin used the growth concept to characterize the hundreds of years of history as a progressive, linear process of increasing productivity, wealth, and output. The growth story, as Easterlin noted and many more would repeat, had a spatial dimension, as well. It began in

Western Europe, quickly spread to North America, and much as the development discourse had suggested about social and cultural changes, appeared on the verge of "taking off" in the non-Western world after 1945. Easterlin's story simplified the realities of economic, social, and political change that winnowed out distributional conflicts, power relations, and the historical legacies of colonialism. Economic growth was a reductive set of economic theories, a powerful policy goal for the present, an optimistic aspiration for the future, and an alluring explanatory narrative about the past.

In the 1950s and 1960s, intellectuals and policymakers fused econometric theories and quantitative studies of growth with socio-cultural development thinking through the rise of studies in "modernization" in the American and British social sciences. Over the course of the 1950s, development thinkers began to speak about economic growth in the process of modernization. Likewise, economists began to work with other social scientists to identify key aspects of life that might help spark economic growth and the ways in which economic changes might induce broader social change. The main venue for this thinking was the Massachusetts Institute of Technology's (MIT) Center for International Studies (CENIS). At the CENIS, economist Max Millikan and economic historian turned growth theorist Walt Rostow brought together an impressive team of sociologists, including Clifford Geertz, Daniel Lerner, and Lucien Pye, and economists, such as Rosenstein-Rodan, to organize social scientific knowledge on development and growth to help wage the Cold War (Gilman 2003, ch. 5).

In the interdisciplinary setting of MIT, Rostow and many others focused on the relationship between economic growth and the "non-economic" factors behind. As Nils Gilman has shown, in the early 1950s "it became apparent that economic theory and policy could not analyze or induce the changes associated with industrialization" (Gilman 2003, 82). Development economics thus became intertwined with a growing literature on the sociology and psychology of development. In a few years, "modernization" became the catchall term to describe such synthetic analyses that linked social and cultural traits with economic growth to help steer countries and societies on a path from "traditional" society to the "modern" world. The most influential study came from Walt Rostow in his 1960 book *The Stages of Economic Growth: A Non-Communist Manifesto*. Fusing economics with history, anthropology, sociology, and psychology, Rostow linked social and cultural changes with economic theory to produce a blueprint for how outsiders (namely, the United States) could engineer the process of modernization in developing countries. Relying on "big Push" thinking, Rostow advocated for large-scale projects – dams, factories, railroads, schools – that simultaneously served as expressions of the external capital necessary to spark the industrial growth process and cultural showpieces that would transform the psychology of the seemingly tradition-bound peasantry by inducing them into the wonders of industrial, urban life (Rostow 1960; Cullather 2011, 151). Rostow linked scholarship on socio-cultural development with the abstract, statistics-driven theories of economic growth and presented them as a ready-made toolkit for policymakers to remake the "Third World."

After all, Rostow and many other modernization theorists worried that the United States – and the West in general – was losing the battle for hearts and minds. Following Nikita Khrushchev's rise to power, the Soviet Union began aiding strategically important countries such as India, Egypt, and Indonesia in their quest for development and touting the Soviet Union as a model for rapid economic growth and transformative development (Latham 2011, 42). By 1958, Soviet policymakers defined a clear plan for "socialist development" of "Third World" countries. The model was based on the Soviet experience of attempting to "develop" the Soviet Central Asian and Caucasian Republics over previous decades through mechanized agriculture premised on collective and state farms, investments in large-scale infrastructure and industrial plants, and limiting foreign capital and nationalizing existing private enterprises. In the late 1950s the Soviet Union sought to replicate this model in Ghana and Guinea, for instance, though these efforts ultimately unraveled by the mid-1960s (Iandolo 2012). In many cases, both Soviet and Western experts operated in the same country. In India during the 1960s, Indian planners welcomed waves of official Soviet delegations, Second World economists such as Oskar Lange, and First World economists such as Jan Tinbergen and Simon Kuznets (Engerman 2013). China likewise began to court developing countries by claiming solidarity with similarly rural countries and offering billions of dollars in aid, particularly to post-colonial African countries (Weinstein and Henriksen 1980).

As this geopolitical competition over development expertise intensified in the late 1950s, modernization theories found a receptive home in the foreign policy apparatus of the John F. Kennedy administration. Kennedy wholeheartedly embraced the modernization paradigm and Walt Rostow, who had previously served as a consultant and speechwriter to President Eisenhower, became the State Department's head of policy planning. With Rostow as a close advisor, Kennedy created the Agency for International Development (AID), the Alliance for Progress, and the Peace Corps – new government programs that promoted long-term growth planning (AID, Alliance for Progress) as well as programs designed to change the habits and attitudes of people living in the "Third World" (Peace Corps). By the mid-1960s, when experts in the United States and Europe spoke of development they often implied a process of modernization premised on sparking economic growth. The two terms were often conflated in official discourse, blurring earlier distinctions and linking the notion of international development to the idea of endless economic growth. As many scholars have demonstrated, U.S. officials sought to modernize many "Third World" countries with elaborate aid programs designed to spark economic growth and guide the development of whole societies along the path from "traditional" to "modern." Modernization was a critical part of international politics during the 1960s (Latham 2011).

Development and growth: the reckoning

For all their popularity in the 1960s, modernization, growth, and development did have detractors too. By the late 1960s, many observers were beginning to suggest that the focus on development and growth had created unintended and deleterious consequences for countries and the world. Critics assailed growth and development in a variety of ways. Popular intellectuals and writers such as John Kenneth Galbraith, David Reisman, Ezra Mishan, and Vance Packard identified many of the social downsides of pursuing growth such as rampant consumerism, increasing waste, and social alienation (Galbraith 1958; Riesman 1964; Mishan 1967; Packard 1960). Another group of critics focused on the ecological consequences of pursuing growth and development through industrialization, urbanization, and mechanization, highlighting how the pursuit of growth defined in terms of GNP increases led to pollution and resource exhaustion (Macekura 2015, ch. 3). Others took an even more critical stance, questioning whether growth should remain a central goal at all for the wealthy countries or for the globe as a whole because of ecological "limits to growth" on "spaceship earth" (Meadows et al. 1972; Boulding 1966; Daly 1971; Georgescu-Roegen 1971; Woodhouse 2010). Even some economists, including Simon Kuznets and development theorists such as Dudley Seers and Hans Singer, began to question the suitability of relying on aggregate statistics in policymaking and the pursuit of growth worldwide (Speich 2011; Morgenstern 1963; Seers 1972). Criticizing GNP became mainstream fodder when Robert F. Kennedy, President Kennedy's brother and popular candidate for the 1968 Democratic Party presidential nomination, gave a speech bemoaning GNP for "measuring everything [...] except that which makes life worthwhile" (Kennedy 1968). Though still supporting economic growth as the end goal, many economists tried to correct GNP's identified flaws to include environmental degradation, welfare, and indicators of social life in national accounts (Nordhaus and Tobin 1972; Stanton 2007; Mayumi 2001).

Within the field of international development, critics argued over whether growth and development could be reformed or whether they should be abandoned. Some reformers, such as Mahbub ul Haq and Paul Streeten argued that development and growth remained important goals, but believed the means to achieve them need to shift to focus on the "basic human needs" of the poor, to pursue "redistribution with growth," or promote more participatory planning in development. These reformers succeeded in reshaping development policies of key institutions, such as the World Bank during Robert McNamara's leadership in the early 1970s (Streeten 1981; Chenery et al. 1974; Sachs 1978; Rahnema 2010). Such criticisms varied over the extent to which overall national economic growth should remain a dominant goal, or whether interventions should instead focus on individuals or communities. Other thinkers, many of whom followed Western counter-culture figures such as E.F. Schumacher, more pointedly criticized growth and dominant approaches to development, envisioning alternative ways of living premised on "smallness," the use of contextually "appropriate" technologies and decentralized decision-making removed from national objectives (Schumacher 1989; Macekura 2015, ch. 4). Such aspirations, however, relied on romantic notions that conflicted with leaders from the Global South who argued that the problems with growth and development stemmed from the Global North's historical exploitation of the South, the unequal structure of the global economy, and the unwillingness of wealthy countries to give sufficient aid untethered from Western political or military objectives. In the early 1970s, as many Western intellectuals debated limits to growth and reforming international development policies, Global South countries banded together to demand a New International Economic Order that demanded the right of the Global South to develop and grow as it saw fit and demanded aid without political or military strings attached (Gilman 2015).

Modernization theory, too, fell out of favor: from scholars who criticized its reductive simplifications, from those who saw the United States' disastrous war in Vietnam as evidence for the failure of the West to transform other societies in their images, and from more conservative intellectuals who questioned the power of the technocratic state to pursue any kind of top-down social engineering (Gilman 2003, ch. 6). In some cases, criticisms of growth, development, and modernization theory cross-fertilized; the economist Dudley Seers, for instance, questioned the pursuit of growth in the wealthy countries and Global South, the reliance of technocratic thinking and statistical reasoning, and the virtues of large-scale modernization schemes in the Global South (Seers 1972). But in many cases, reformers focused on various elements of economic growth models or development and modernization plans, with many seeking to reform growth and development by making the pursuit of both more equal, just, and ecologically sustainable. In all these ways, support for unheeded development and growth frayed over the late 1960s and early 1970s.

Amid these widespread criticisms of development and growth, however, in the 1980s and 1990s a new "antistatist growthmanship" revived the discourses of growth and development with a new focus on the free market (Collins 2000, ch. 6). Over the 1970s many factors contributed to a collapsing faith in the state-based growth paradigm. Western countries faced high unemployment and inflation; the collapse of the Bretton Woods system diminished state controls over capital flows; and many development economists lamented that state intervention to drive economic growth had not eliminated poverty (Latham 2011, ch. 6; Mazower 2012, ch. 12; Lal 1983). Politicians such as Margaret Thatcher and Ronald Reagan denigrated big governments and economists from Milton Friedman to Deepak Lal decried state planning and government intervention in markets. Economic growth in the 1950s and 1960s relied on national governments to boost growth through targeted policy interventions in multiple sectors and provide a complex social safety net to ensure the welfare of the citizens. The neoliberalism of the 1980s and beyond sought "non-inflationary" growth based on free trade, liberalization of capital controls, privatization of state goods, and redirecting state fiscal policy from providing social security toward structuring increased market activity. Neoliberal growth justified higher unemployment, declining wages, and welfare cuts in order to promote more rapid short-term economic growth that would "trickle-down" in the long run by creating more jobs and higher wages for workers. Growth remained the goal, although in this era policymakers and economists often valorized market forces and criticized Keynesian interventions (Schmelzer 2015, 267). State-led development, premised on large top-down technological projects, persisted, too, in the development thinking of elites and planners in countries such as China (Prashad 2012, ch. 3).

That is not to suggest that criticisms of growth, development, or modernization went away. Environmental critiques of growth underwrote growing interest in global climate change, the most powerful symbol that industrialization and faith in ever-expanding productive capacity have wrought many unintended consequences and imperiled the material basis on which development and growth depend. Efforts to remake GNP (and its successor, Gross Domestic Product, or GDP) continue to this day (Stiglitz et al. 2010). The Basic Human Needs movement gave birth to a renewed focus on poverty eradication in the development community and helped create alternative metrics such as the Human Development Index (HDI) (Stanton 2007). Alternative concepts emerged, too, such as "sustainable development" or "human development," or "inclusive growth" or "green growth." But many critics have been quick to point out that much of these ideas have superficially incorporated earlier criticism of growth and have become so broad or generalized as to limit their challenge to existing paradigms (Macekura 2015; Schmelzer 2015). Post-development scholars have increasingly highlighted such trends and the persistent flaws of growth and development, and more recently, advocates of "degrowth" or "post-growth" have challenged the basic tenets of the growth paradigm (Demaria et al. 2013). Many historians have now critiqued modernization theory, with a number of historians criticizing both the theory's assumptions and how it was applied during the Cold War world (Gilman 2003; Latham 2011). Yet for all these efforts, development and growth have remained powerful ideas, dominant discourses, and policy objectives.

A century of development and growth

How should we assess the concepts of development and growth and their place in twentieth-century life? That question has become all the more pressing in recent years as awareness of global climate change has increased. With the aid of historical perspective, scholars have begun to show that many common but flawed assumptions lurked beneath the two discourses that have reshaped the entire planet. One set of assumptions related to energy and the environment. Economic growth depended on unprecedented access to cheap fossil fuels. World energy use in 1900 amounted to 800 million metric tons of oil equivalent; in 2000, that number had soared to 10,000 (in 1800 the number was 250 million metric tons, by comparison) (McNeill 2000, 15). Pursuing growth and development required mobilizing vast stores of energy for human use, and the consequences of doing so have largely driven global climate change.

Moreover, while both development and growth discourse presented visions of a long-term future, in practice short-term returns dominated expectations and inhibited a broader understanding of large-scale changes over time. Project cycles are short; so too are most leaders' time in office. The politics of development and growth demanded short-term results, and thus there was only dim understanding of the cumulative effects of long-term trends. Global climate change, by contrast, demanded understanding of a longer time scale. Scientists have begun to understand a set of profound ecological changes born from the industrial revolution that have only accelerated dramatically since 1945. Long-term climate change, only dimly understood for much of the twentieth century, has proven difficult for countries to manage and may be the ultimate long-term consequence of the widespread pursuit of development and economic growth defined in terms of GNP. Contending with climate change requires policies based on historical responsibilities for carbon emissions, current inequalities between countries, and long-term empathy for the future of the planet and those who live on it – a wide variety of temporal scales far beyond the kind of short-term thinking that too often framed development and growth plans (Macekura 2015)

Today, anxieties abound over whether development and growth will continue. Those concerns are not likely to ebb anytime soon. Development and growth were two of the most powerful categories of twentieth-century international history, and the pursuit of both has reshaped the world in countless ways. These categories shaped the parameters of political debate and policy choice for much of the twentieth century, and they held because they suited the political circumstances and economic context of the times. But now new categories will be needed to contend with the world that the push for development and growth has created.

Notes

1 One of the earliest uses of the phrase "economic growth" appeared in an 1875 article in the *Times* about the state of the United Kingdom's fiscal difficulties. "The Revenue," *Times*, December 29, 1875, 3. "Economic growth" does not appear in the title of an English-language book until 1940, when economist historian Fred Shannon revised the title of his 1933 book, *Economic History of the People of the United States*, to *America's Economic Growth* (Shannon 1940).

2 On the rise of international development discourse within international institutions during the 1940s, see Helleiner (2009).

Bibliography

Alacevich, Michele. 2009. *The Political Economy of the World Bank: The Early Years*. Stanford: Stanford University Press.

Arndt, Heinz W. 1978. *The Rise and Fall of Economic Growth: A Study in Contemporary Thought*. Melbourne: Longman Cheshire Pty Limited.

Barnett, Vincent. 2005. *The History of Russian Economic Thought*. London and New York: Routledge.

Bernstein, Michael A. 2001. *A Perilous Progress: Economists and Public Purpose in Twentieth-Century America*. Princeton: Princeton University Press.

Bouk, Dan. 2015. *How Our Days Became Numbered: Risk and the Rise of the Statistical Individual*. Chicago: Chicago University Press.

Boulding, Kenneth E. 1966. "The Economics of the Coming Spaceship Earth." In *Environmental Quality in a Growing Economy*, edited by Henry Jarrett, 3–14. Baltimore: John Hopkins University Press.

Carson, C.S. 1975. "The History of the United States National Income and Product Accounts: the Development of an Analytical Tool." *The Review of Income and Wealth* 21(2): 153–181.

Chang, Ha-Joon. 2002. *Kicking Away the Ladder: Development Strategy in Historical Perspective: Policies and Institutions for Economic Development in Historical Perspective*. London: Anthem Press.

Chenery, Hollis B., Montek S. Ahluwalia, C.L.G. Bell, Jack H. Duloy, and Richard Jolly, eds. 1974. *Redistribution with Growth*. Oxford: Oxford University Press.

Clark, Colin. 1961. *Growthmanship: A Study in the Mythology of Investment*. London: Institute of Economic Affairs.

Clavin, Patricia. 2013. *Securing the World Economy: The Reinvention of the League of Nations, 1920–1946*. Oxford: Oxford University Press.

Collins, Robert. 2000. *More: The Politics of Economic Growth in Postwar America*. Oxford: Oxford University Press.

Conklin, Alice L. 1997. *A Mission to Civilize: The Republican Idea of Empire in France and West Africa, 1895–1930*. Stanford: Stanford University Press.

Coyle, Diane. 2014. *GDP: A Brief But Affectionate History*. Princeton: Princeton University Press.

Cullather, Nick. 2011. *The Hungry World: America's Cold War Battle Against Poverty in Asia*. Cambridge: Harvard University Press.

Daly, Herman E. ed. 1971. *Essays Toward a Steady-State Economy*. Cuernavaca, Mexico: CIDOC.

Demaria, Frederico, Francois Schneider, Filka Sekulova, and Joan Martinez-Alier. 2013. "What is Degrowth? From an Activist Slogan to Social Movement." *Environmental Values* 22: 191–215.

Duncan, Joseph W. and William C. Shelton. 1978. *Revolution in United States Government Statistics, 1926–1976*. Washington, DC: GPO.

Easterlin, Richard. 1968. "Economic Growth: Overview," in *International Encyclopedia of the Social Sciences*. Accessed September 12, 2015. http://www.encyclopedia.com/topic/Economic_growth.aspx#1.

Ekbladh, David. 2010. *The Great American Mission: Modernization and the Construction of an American World Order*. Princeton: Princeton University Press.

Engerman, David C. 2007. "Bernath Lecture: American Knowledge and Global Power." *Diplomatic History* 31(4): 620–621.

Engerman, David C. 2010. "The Price of Success: Economic Sovietology, Development, and the Costs of Interdisciplinary." *History of Political Economy* 42 (suppl.): 234–260.

Engerman, David C. 2013. “Learning from the East: Soviet Experts and India in the Era of Competitive Coexistence.” *Comparative Studies of South Asia, Africa and the Middle East* 33(2): 227–238.

Fioramonti, Lorenzo. 2013. *Gross Domestic Problem: The Politics Behind The World's Most Powerful Number*. London: Zed Books.

Galbraith, John Kenneth. 1958. *The Affluent Society*. Boston: Houghton Mifflin.

Georgescu-Roegen, Nicholas. 1971. *The Entropy Law and the Economic Process*. Cambridge: Harvard University Press.

Gilman, Nils. 2003. *Mandarins of the Future: Modernization Theory in Cold War America*. Baltimore: Johns Hopkins University Press.

Gilman, Nils 2015. “The New International Economic Order: A Reintroduction.” *Humanity* 6(1): 1–16.

Hatziprokopiou, Michalis and Kostas Valentzas. 2002. “Preobrazhensky and the Theory of Economic Development.” In *The Canon in the History of Economics: Critical Essays*, edited by Michalis Psalidopoulos, 180–195. London and New York: Routledge.

Helleiner, Eric. 2009. “The Development Mandate of International Institutions: Where Did it Come From?” *Studies in Comparative International Development* 44(3): 189–211.

Hodge, Joseph Morgan. 2007. *Triumph of the Expert: Agrarian Doctrines of Development and the Legacies of British Colonialism*. Athens: Ohio University Press.

Iandolo, Alessandro. 2012. “The Rise and Fall of the ‘Soviet Model of Development’ in West Africa, 1957–1964.” *Cold War History* 12(4): 683–704.

Immerwahr, Daniel. 2015. *Thinking Small: The United States and the Lure of Community Development*. Cambridge: Harvard University Press.

Johnson, Simon and Peter Temin. 1993. “The Macroeconomics of NEP.” *The Economic History Review* 46(4): 750–767.

Karabell, Zachary. 2014. *The Leading Indicators: A Short History of the Numbers That Rule Our World*. New York: Simon and Schuster.

Kendrick, J.W. 1970. “The Historical Development of National-Income Accounts.” *History of Political Economy* 2(2): 284–315.

Kennedy, Robert F. 1968. “Remarks at the University of Kansas.” Accessed August 19, 2015. http://www.jfklibrary.org/Research/Research-Aids/Ready-Reference/RFK-Speeches/Remarks-of-Robert-F-Kennedy-at-the-University-of-Kansas-March-18-1968.aspx.

Kuznets, Simon. 1947. “Measurement: Measurement of Economic Growth.” *The Journal of Economic History* 7 (suppl.): 10–34.

Lal, Deepak. 1983. *The Poverty of ‘Development Economics’*. London: The Institute for Economic Affairs.

Latham, Michael. 2000. *Modernization as Ideology: American Social Science and “Nation Building” in the Kennedy Era*. Chapel Hill: University of North Carolina Press.

Latham, Michael 2011. *The Right Kind of Revolution: Modernization, Development, and U.S. Foreign Policy from the Cold War to the Present*. Ithaca: Cornell University Press.

Leys, Colin. 1996. *The Rise and Fall of Development Theory*. Nairobi: East African Educational Publishers.

Macekura, Stephen. 2013. “The Point Four Program and International Development Policy.” *Political Science Quarterly* 128(1): 127–160.

Macekura, Stephen. 2015. *Of Limits and Growth: The Rise of Global Sustainable Development in the Twentieth Century*. New York: Cambridge University Press.

Maier, Charles S. 1977. "The Politics of Productivity: Foundations of American International Economic Policy after World War II." *International Organization* 31(4): 607–633.

Maier, Charles S. 1987. *In Search of Stability: Explorations of Historical Political Economy.* Cambridge: Cambridge University Press.

Mayumi, Kozo. 2001. *The Origins of Ecological Economics: The Bioeconomics of Georgescu-Roegen.* London: Routledge.

Mazower, Mark. 1998. *Dark Continent: Europe's Twentieth Century.* London: Penguin Press.

Mazower, Mark. 2012. *Governing the World: The History of an Idea.* New York: The Penguin Press.

McNeill, John R. 2000. *Something New Under the Sun: An Environmental History of the Twentieth Century World.* New York: W.W. Norton.

McVety, Amanda Kay. 2012. *Enlightened Aid: U.S. Development as Foreign Policy in Ethiopia.* New York: Oxford University Press.

Meadows, Donella, H., *et al.* 1972. *The Limits to Growth: A Report for the Club of Rome's Project on the Predicament of Mankind.* Washington: Potomac Associates.

Mill, John Stuart. 1926. *Principles of Political Economy with Some of their Applications to Social Philosophy.* London: Longmans, Green and Co.

Milward, Alan S. 2000. *The European Rescue of the Nation-State.* London: Routledge.

Mishan, Ezra J. 1967. *The Costs of Economic Growth.* New York: Staples Press.

Mitchell, Timothy. 2002. *Rule of Experts: Egypt, Techno-Politics, Modernity.* Berkeley: University of California Press.

Mitchell, Timothy. 2005. "Economists and the Economy in the Twentieth Century." In *The Politics of Method in the Human Sciences: Positivism and Its Epistemological Others,* edited by George Steinmetz, 126–141. Durham: Duke University Press.

Mitchell, Timothy. 2014. "Economentality: How the Future Entered Government." *Critical Inquiry* 40: 479–507.

Morgenstern, Oskar. 1963. *On the Accuracy of Economic Observations.* Princeton: Princeton University Press.

Nordhaus, William D. and James Tobin. 1972. "Is Growth Obsolete?" in *Economic Research: Retrospect and Prospect Vol 5: Economic Growth.* New York: National Bureau of Economic Research.

O'Bryan, Scott. 2009. *The Growth Idea: Purpose and Prosperity in Postwar Japan.* Honolulu: University of Hawaii Press.

Packard, Vance O. 1960. *The Waste Makers.* London: Longmans.

Porter, Theodore M. 2001. "Economics and the History of Measurement," *History of Political Economy* 33 (suppl.): 4–22

Prashad, Vijay. 2012. *The Poorer Nations: A Possible History of the Global South.* London: Verso.

Rahnema, Majid. 2010. "Participation." In *The Development Dictionary: A Guide to Knowledge As Power,* edited by Wolfgang Sachs, 127–144. London: Zed Books.

Riesman, David. 1964. *Abundance for What and Other Essays.* London: Chatto.

Rist, Gilbert. 2008. *The History of Development: From Western Origins to Global Faith.* London: Zed Books.

Rivas, Darlene. 2002. *Missionary Capitalist: Nelson Rockefeller in Venezuela.* Chapel Hill: The University of North Carolina Press.

Rostow, W.W. 1960. *The Stages of Economic Growth: A Non-Communist Manifesto.* Cambridge: Cambridge University Press.

Sachs, Igancy. 1978. "Crises of Maldevelopment in the North: A Way Out." *IFDA Dossier no. 2*.

Sackley, Nicole. 2004. "Passage to Modernity: American Social Scientists, India, and the Pursuit of Development, 1945–1961." Ph.D. Dissertation, Princeton University.

Schmelzer, Matthias. 2015. "The growth paradigm: History, hegemony, and the contested making of economic growthmanship." *Ecological Economics* 118: 262–271.

Schmelzer, Matthias. 2016. *The Hegemony of Growth. The OECD and the Making of the Economic Growth Paradigm*. Cambridge: Cambridge University Press.

Schumacher, E. F. 1989. *Small is Beautiful: Economics as if People Mattered*. New York: Harper & Row Publishers.

Seers, Dudley. 1972. "What Are We Trying to Measure?" In *Measuring Development: The Role and Adequacy of Development Indicators*, edited by Nancy Baster, 21–36. London: Frank Cass and Co.

Shannon, Fred Albert. 1940. *America's Economic Growth*. New York: Macmillan Co.

Speich, Daniel. 2008. "Travelling with the GDP through Early Development Economics' History." *Working Papers on The Nature of Evidence: How Well Do Facts Travel?* No 33/2008. London School of Economics, Department of Economic History.

Speich, Daniel. 2011. "The Use of Global Abstractions: National Income Accounting in the Period of Imperial Decline." *Journal of Global History* 6(1): 7–28.

Spulber, Nicolas. 1964. *Foundations of Soviet Strategy for Economic Growth: Selected Soviet Essays, 1924–1930*. Bloomington: Indiana University Press.

Stanton, Elizabeth A. 2007. "Human Development Index: A History." *Working Paper Number 127*, Political Economy Research Institute, University of Massachusetts Amherst.

Staples, Amy L. S. 2006. *The Birth of Development: How the World Bank, Food and Agriculture Organization, and the World Health Organization Changed the World, 1945-1965*. Kent: The Kent State University Press.

Stiglitz, Joseph E., Amartya Sen, and Jean Paul Fitoussi. 2010. *Mismeasuring our Lives: Why GDP Doesn't Add Up*. New York: The New Press.

Streeten, Paul. 1981. *First Things First: Meeting Basic Human Needs in the Developing Countries*. New York: Oxford University Press.

Tignor, Robert L. 2006. *W. Arthur Lewis and the Birth of Development Economics*. Princeton: Princeton University Press.

Truman, Harry S. 1949. "Truman Inaugural Address, January 20, 1949." Accessed September 21, 2015. http://www.trumanlibrary.org/whistlestop/50yr_archive/inagural20jan1949.htm.

United Nations. 1953. *A System of National Accounts and Supporting Tables*. Studies in Methods, No. 2. New York: United Nations Department of Economic Affairs.

Weinstein, Warren and Thomas H. Henriksen. 1980. *Soviet and Chinese Aid to African Nations*. New York: Praeger Publishing.

Westad, Odd Arne. 2005. *The Global Cold War*. Cambridge: Cambridge University Press.

Woodhouse, Keith. 2010. A Subversive Nature: Radical Environmentalism in the Late-Twentieth-Century United States. *Ph.D. Dissertation*, University of Wisconsin-Madison.

Yarrow, Andrew L. 2010. *Measuring America: How Economic Growth Came to Define American Greatness in the Late Twentieth Century*. Amherst: University of Massachusetts Press.

6 Economic growth and health

Evidence, uncertainties, and connections over time and place

Iris Borowy

The question whether economic growth is good for human health is not one for the academic ivory tower. It has tangible policy repercussions.[1] People universally value their health highly. If evidence for this statement is necessary at all, it was provided by a global survey conducted before the UN Millennium Summit in 2000, which found that good health was the first desire of people around the world (Commission on Macroeconomics and Health 2001, 21). It is not surprising, therefore, that references to health act as powerful arguments in political debates, particularly with regard to decisions on broad policy directions. A recent case in point was the Brexit campaign in the United Kingdom in the spring of 2016: the Brexit supporters argued that leaving the EU would benefit the health of Britons since the funds, otherwise transferred to the European Union, would go to the National Health Service instead (an argument which evaporated into thin air almost instantly after the vote had been taken), while opponents warned of health risks of the Brexit because of fewer research funds and less rigorous environmental policies (Thompson and Hunt 2016; Birt 2016; Saksena 2016). Other examples directly tied health to decisions affecting economic policies and fostering economic growth. In his inaugural address in January 1949, a speech which is widely credited as forming the basis for international efforts of development aid, President Truman cited disease among people in low-income countries as a primary reason that industrial countries had a moral duty to share technological knowledge and "foster capital investment in areas needing development" (Truman 1949). Half a century later, Thomas Gale Moore (2000, 40) of the Hoover Institution insisted that "most diseases are related more to income than to climate" in order to argue against the Kyoto Protocol and against policies designed to mitigate climate change:

> All steps that lower economic growth or reduce incomes make people more vulnerable to the inevitable natural disasters that routinely strike parts of the globe. The Kyoto Protocol would lower incomes and reduce growth for every country attempting to meet its goals. [...] Thus the entire globe would be made poorer and more vulnerable to diseases, earthquakes,

> storms, and floods. We must continually remind ourselves that richer is safer, richer is healthier, and richer is cleaner.
>
> (Moore undated)

Similarly, a paper written in preparation of the 1993 World Bank Development Report dedicated to health insisted on the need for growth-oriented policies arguing that "in 1990 alone, more than half a million child deaths in the developing world could be attributed to poor economic performance in the 1980s. Wealthier nations are healthier nations" (Pritchett and Summers 1993). In 2009, a publication of a World Bank commission, dedicated to the connection between economic growth and health summed up its interpretation data of past years as follows: "We can say with confidence that economic growth improves health. It increases the availability of food, makes health spending affordable, and raises the demand for good health" (Spence 2009, xii). By contrast, scholars affiliated with the degrowth movement have sought to disprove a positive correlation between economic growth and health by drawing on the apparent connection between falling growth rates during economic crises and declining mortality rates (De Vogli and Owusu 2014), or by pointing out that the "[v]olume and increase of spending in the health sector contribute to economic growth, but do not consistently relate with better health" (Missoni 2015). Others have analyzed past experiences with economic crises and their effects on health for possible lessons for the future (Borowy 2011; 2013). In the process, the perceived relation between health and economic growth has become part of the debate about the perceived value of economic growth and, implicitly or explicitly, all sides make a historical argument, evoking past data.

At first sight, the relation between economic growth and health seems simple enough. Graphs pairing per capita GDP and life expectancy for the countries of the world show a clear positive correlation, with people in high-income countries enjoying longer lives. The connection appears particularly strong at the low-income end of the curve, where small differences in income translate into large differences in life expectancy, and weakens at the higher end, where higher incomes appear to show little or no relation to higher life expectancy. This correlation has been shown repeatedly for different times of the twentieth century, and it can freely be reproduced by any interested reader on www.gapminder.org, an organization dedicated to informing the public about the basic facts of global development based on reliable international statistics.

The connection is intuitively plausible. In rich countries, people tend to have access to better quality health care, better housing, better food, generally better living conditions and a better public infrastructure. However, interpreting the graph as evidence that economic growth improves population health entails a series of crucial assumptions: that correlation equals causation, that causation flows from high incomes to better health rather than vice versa, that other factors affecting health (not shown in the graph) are of secondary importance, that per capita GDP is an accurate expression of economic performance, that life expectancy is an accurate expression of health, that the effect of income on health shows in their simultaneous status and that the economic status of a country, rather than regional constellations or economic relations between different countries, is the suitable framework for the question.

None of these assumptions rests on solid ground. Correlation clearly does not establish causation. Without further information it is impossible to decide whether one factor is influenced by the other or whether both are subject to the impact of one or more further factors not included in the picture. In this particular case, the assumption of causation is weakened by the fact that pairing per capita GDP and life expectancy of individual countries over time, instead of across countries at the same time, produces markedly different results: In many countries, positive correlations only began after 1950 or later and earlier periods were characterized by phases of economic growth without improvements in population health or, conversely, of health improvements without simultaneous economic growth. This can also be tried out on the gapminder website, and the results are corroborated by historical studies, discussed below. The fact that healthy people can work better and more than people suffering disabilities or diseases is plausible and has been long recognized. Using the clear connection between working capacity and health status as grounds for passionate calls for more efforts to improve health worldwide, the Commission on Macroeconomics and Health, in 2001, called health "one of the cornerstones of human capital" (Commission on Macroeconomics and Health 2001, 21). Any discussion which treats the relation between economic growth and health as uni-directional, is therefore simplistic at best. Nevertheless, the positive correlation between higher income and longer life expectancy is too strong and consistent to be discarded as a mere statistical artifact.

The questionable and, in many ways, arbitrary or even absurd nature of GDP as a measurement of economic performance has repeatedly been pointed out. As the chapter by Lorenzo Fioramonti in this volume makes clear, GNP/GDP is anything but a representation of some objective reality. Rather, it is a construct which entails political and often interest-driven decisions about which factors are included and which are not and about how they are priced (see also Coyle 2014). This is true for all countries, but particularly so for countries in Africa, whose bureaucracies face a series of additional problems of value assessment, which stand in the way of reliable economic data (Jerven 2013).

However, even if GDP as a measurement of economic growth can easily be discredited, this does not mean that something like an "economy" does not exist, consisting of the sum of interacting economic activities, however they may be defined. If such economic activities exist, their increase can be conceptualized as economic growth and, presumably, it has some bearing on health. For the most part, available data refer to a conventional understanding of economic growth as increases in GDP, and this chapter will use them as far as it seems helpful. But it assumes that even beyond the vagaries of GDP there is a phenomenon which involves increasing income, material wealth, and financial means and which affects health, even though a reliable quantification is beyond the scope of this chapter and may not be possible at all.

Health is even more difficult to define and to quantify. Several proxy numbers are in use, all of which come with their own strengths and weaknesses. A frequent choice is mortality rate or, conversely, life expectancy. Their advantage is that births and deaths have been the relatively most widely and most reliably registered life events, data have been collected for relatively the longest time, and at a basic level they do seem to express health. After all, ill health, in its extreme form, results in death. However, this is precisely also its disadvantage, since many forms of ill health are not extreme and often death is not very informative about the health status people had during their lives. Mortality says little about chronic malnutrition, non-lethal infectious or chronic diseases, mental illness, disabilities, or other forms of compromised health, thus leaving a distorted perspective. This weakness shows in the way mortality and morbidity data have been shown to diverge, indicating that declining death rates and higher life expectancy can result in higher rates of reported illness, partly because declining mortality rates lead to aging societies (Riley 1990; Riley 1997; Gorsky and Harris 2005). A variation focuses on child or infant mortality rates. Implicitly, this choice reflects the intuitive moral value judgment that, though all people must die at some point, ideally after long and fulfilled lives, the death of children is wrong. Though historically, high infant mortality rates have been the norm rather than the exception, in the twentieth century they have increasingly come to be considered an indication of societal or political failures. Besides, small children are particularly vulnerable to social factors that endanger health, ranging from unhygienic living conditions to malfunctioning health care systems. On the other hand, children are little affected by some factors that are important for the health of adults and of society at large such as cardio-vascular diseases, occupational hazards, or abuse of alcohol or other drugs. Thus, infant and child mortality rates fail to reflect large parts of societal health.

Arguably, a better measurement is provided by anthropometric data, using people's height as an expression of health. To some, albeit unclear, degree, physical height is apparently influenced by genetic predispositions. Beyond that, it reflects the accumulated nutritional and health experience during the years of growing up: good food and healthy living conditions increase height, while hunger, malnutrition, and a high disease burden impede physical growth. Height, therefore, reflects the health status a given cohort experienced during childhood and adolescence, though it cannot directly express the health conditions of these people as adults. However, it can reflect the long-term effects of early life deprivation. Thus, height has been found to be related to mortality in Norwegian men and to chronic health conditions of men examined for the US Union Army (Fogel 2012, 73). Data on physical height are not as widely available as those on births and deaths but are still frequent, often found in documents on army conscription, but also from other public services such as schools or from skeletal remains. Meanwhile, more recent numbers such as the Disability or Quality Adjusted Life Years (DALYs/QALYs) have been in use since the 1990s but are unavailable for historical periods (and also come with their own sets of complications). This chapter will use mortality rates and heights as they are available, keeping in mind that neither is a perfect description of "health."

Furthermore, an accepted definition of economic growth and health is merely the beginning of an analysis about how the two are connected. Given the complex nature of health, where one determinant can be related to several health effects and one health outcome can be influenced by several determinants, simple answers are bound to be incomplete, misleading, or just plain wrong. The current state of research indicates that health depends on numerous factors with varying connections to economic performance. Some, like genetic disposition, are independent of economic status; some, like social support systems, social equality, or healthy workplaces, don't necessarily have to but can be and frequently are affected by economic development, and many determinants are influenced by economic development in that they involve private or public money: the quantity and quality of available food, education, living conditions (notably the quality of air and water and protection against climatic and social dangers), road safety, and effective administrative, social, and health services (WHO 2008). But effects are rarely in simple and clear-cut ways. In every case, how more funds play out depends on how they are used and how they interact with other, potentially contradictory effects of increased income. Determining which factors become active in which instance, at what time and under which circumstances and what role has been played by economic growth is difficult and usually involves an element of informed guesswork. At the end of the day, there is a lot we simply do not know about the determinants of health, their interactions, and the impact of economic growth. However, having said that, there is a lot we do know, and this chapter attempts to take stock of some of the existing knowledge and debates and to link them to a broader consideration of long-term connections in history.

The historical record of economic growth and health: the bare numbers

Economic growth was virtually non-existent for long parts of human history. Measured as retroactively calculated per capita GDP, annual growth rates in Western Europe changed little between 1000 and 1820, showing a mere increase from 0.13 to 0.15 percent over several centuries. However, in the period from 1820 to 1998, average annual growth rates increased 10-fold to a spectacular 1.51 percent. The highest rates occurred during the "golden age" of economic growth between 1950 and 1973, with average global per capita growth rates of almost 3 percent per year (Maddison 2006, 48, 71). Measured in terms of mortality, health developments were similar but not identical. Though the record differs for different industrializing countries, in broad strokes, Western Europe began seeing a slow and irregular decline of mortality around 1750, which accelerated in the nineteenth century. On average, life expectancy at birth jumped from 36 years (1820) to 46 (1900), 67 (1950), and 78 years (1999) (Maddison 2006, 31–32).

There are two aspects to keep in mind when beginning the analysis: Historically, wealth did not always coincide with better health, or at least with longer lives. In the sixteenth and seventeenth century, English noblemen experienced similar or lower life expectancy than their subjects, for reasons that are not well understood. If wealth alone guaranteed good health, these noblemen should have outlived the people they ruled. However, from the eighteenth century onwards, the situation changed and noblemen did begin to live significantly and increasingly longer than their subjects (Harris 2004, 389). If wealth played no role, privilege should not have made a mortality difference after 1750. Apparently, higher status and income has had some effect which, however, could only begin to play out under conditions from the mid-eighteenth century onwards. Second, one should not underestimate the low level of health considered normal until relatively recently and, consequently, the extent of health improvement which humanity has experienced since. There is evidence that, prior to the twentieth century, the majority of people lived in chronic malnutrition, which showed in stunted growth, low weight, impaired immune systems, and high risk of chronic disabilities and premature death. Over the past 300 years, people in today's OECD countries have increased their average body weight by more than half and have more than doubled their life expectancy. These improvements have been accompanied by substantial gains in their physical robustness and their economic productivity (Fogel 2012, 91–95). In what Roderick Fogel and Dora Costa have termed the "techno-physio evolution, based mainly on improved food production and distribution and improved means of reducing the disease burden, people in all high-income countries in the global North and almost all countries in the global South have "become much taller and heavier and now experience lives which are much healthier, as well as longer, than ever before in human history" (Floud et al. 2011, 1, cf. 5)

Statistically, there is broad consensus that increases in life expectancy in today's industrialized countries resulted from two distinct immediate causes: a spectacular reduction in infant mortality from between 150 and 200 per 1,000 population in 1830 to about seven in the 1990s. This cause dominated increases in life expectancy until approximately 1950. Subsequently, with infant mortality already reasonably low, Europeans gained years by addressing chronic diseases mainly in old age, involving high and rising health expenditures (Maddison 2006, 36). However, this simple periodization obscures highly complex stories of different causes of death falling at different times and places and for different reasons. Questions remain about what caused those changes in mortality and stature and how they have been related to economic growth. These questions have been the object of protracted debate among historians of health, and the course of this debate has provided the frame for current approaches to this issue.

How did economic growth affect population health (in the short run)? The historical debate

Historians began discussing the question in the 1970s in reaction to a few pivotal publications.

In 1975, sociologist Samuel Preston paired life expectancy and national per capita income for numerous countries for the years 1900, 1930, and 1960. He found three parallel curves, each of which showed a positive correlation between per capita GDP and life expectancy with a strong effect of increased income at its low end and a weaker effect towards the high end. The different positions of the curves along the y-axis showed that the same income correlated with longer life expectancy in 1960 than in 1930, when it was higher than in 1900. He concluded that 1) the shape of the curves demonstrated that rising incomes improved population health, with declining marginal effects, and 2) the positions of the different curves demonstrated that there were other relevant factors such as improvements in medical technology or in health care infrastructure. Preston speculated that increases in income per se accounted for only 10 to 25 percent of the mortality decline (Preston 1975). But inadvertently, he had established a convention of a visualization which survives until gapminder today, and his curve took on a life of its own. The Preston Curve became widely endorsed and cited, not in its original form, whose several lines indicated that economic growth constituted one factor among others, but as a single curve, suggesting a simple causal relation. In the process, it changed from a demonstration of the multifactorial nature of health to a powerful argument in favor of economic growth as the central motor for health improvements.

Almost simultaneously, medical historian Thomas McKeown published an article, followed by a book (McKeown 1975, 1976), arguing that the population increase in nineteenth century Britain had resulted from declining mortality which, in turn, was primarily due to improved nutrition, made possible because industrialization had increased private and national incomes, i.e. economic growth. These publications unleashed a protracted debate among historians of health and demography. The discussion focused specifically on whether public health intervention, mainly sanitation, or increased income, mainly improved nutrition, had been the main causes of falling mortality rates. The McKeown theory, in particular, sparked vivid discussions since, ironically, it resonated both with scathing criticism, which writers of the political left were directing against organized medicine at that time, including such radical critics of growth-centered orthodoxy as Ivan Illich, and with the emerging neo-liberal agenda of the 1980s. Indeed, it could be – and was – used as an argument to reject targeted state intervention and, instead, to rely on invisible economic forces to improve population health. This reading was a simplification of what McKeown had written, but the seeming sub-text of strengthening free market forces at the expense of public services added vehemence to the debate. Subsequent research discredited much of the original McKeown thesis: early population growth in Britain turned out to have been driven mainly by increasing fertility, the record regarding increased food supplies and improved nutritional status was murky, several forms of health intervention, notably sanitation, could be shown to have had a bearing on health, and declines in mortality, which began in a modest way in the eighteenth century, stalled between approximately 1820 and 1870, a period of strong economic growth and rising wages. Instead of reducing mortality, the rapid economic growth of industrialization, on the contrary, brought substantial stress and new health burdens to vulnerable urban groups, harming population health at large (Szreter 2004; Szreter 2002; Colgrove 2002). Simon Szreter, probably the most passionate opponent of McKeown's theory, pointed to "disruption, deprivation, disease and death" brought by early industrialization and argued that "economic growth should be understood as setting in train a socially and politically dangerous, destabilizing, and health-threatening set of forces" (Szreter 2005, 204).

Indeed, more detailed research on periods of economic expansion and contraction strongly contradicted a simple positive effect of economic growth on health. The take-off points of economic growth and of mortality declines did not coincide in six European countries studied and the conditions of economic growth, urbanization, and crowded living conditions without simultaneous sanitation efforts burdened rather than improved health. Richard Easterlin (1999) concluded that it was not improved living conditions brought about by economic growth, which acted as primary cause of decreasing mortality, but "new techniques of disease control based on new knowledge of disease," for whose funding no economic growth was necessary. One discovery that baffled scholars in this context was the "early-industrial-growth-puzzle": the finding that rapid economic expansion in Sweden, in the Habsburg Empire, Bavaria, the UK, and the US coincided with stunted growth, particularly among the lower classes of the population. Explanations drew on a combination of points: rising prices, which forced people to turn to cheaper, less nutritious food, but also (in the US) the effects of national and international migration, which coincided with economic growth and broadened the disease spectrum (Komlos 1997; Haines 2003). This connection seems to hold true for more recent times as well. Decreases in unemployment during economic expansion were linked to increases in mortality in the United States during the 1980s and 1990s (Ruhm 2007) as well as in 23 OECD countries over the 1960–1997 period (Gertham and Ruhm 2002).

Conversely, health, measured in mortality rates, repeatedly improved during periods of economic crisis. With the notable exceptions of deaths from suicide and traffic accidents, gains in life expectancy or reduction in age-specific mortality rates were consistently negatively correlated with GDP growth and positively correlated with increases in the unemployment rate (Tapia Granados 2004; Tapia Granados and Diez Roux 2009). Even the most recent crisis of 2008–2012 resulted in mortality declines in the countries in Southern Europe that were hardest hit (Tapia Granados 2014).[2] These findings have led to the "counterintuitive hypothesis that [...] population health tends to evolve better during recessions than in expansions" (Tapia Granados and Diez Roux 2009).

A number of reasons have been put forward for an apparent negative impact of economic expansion on health in addition to price rises and migration, mentioned above, including social disruptions leading to stress, increased air pollution, smoking and alcohol consumption, sleep reductions, increases in work stress related to overtime and faster and more strenuous labor, more traffic and industrial injuries, declines in home care and generally in social support as a result of greater employment, and work-related migration. Collectively, these effects appear to be stronger than the undoubted negative health effects of unemployment (Ruhm 2007; Tapia Granados and Diez Roux 2009). However, in a frank admission rarely found in a scholar who has spent many years studying a topic, José Tapia Granados recently admitted that, in the end, this phenomenon was still not well understood (Tapia Granados 2014).

Nevertheless, though there seems to be a pattern of mortality evolving parallel to economic performance, it is not an iron-clad rule. Historically, experiences both with economic expansion and with crisis have been diverse. Increasing income has been shown to have had a directly positive impact on health when it translated into tangible beneficial expenditures. Thus, stunting in nineteenth-century France decreased with rising industrial wages, with increased expenditures per child for primary education and, to a lesser extent, with increases in private land ownership and with a growing number of health workers (Postel-Vinay and Sahn, 2010). Meanwhile, crises could tangibly damage health. In Yugoslavia, the economic decline after the late 1970s saw an increase in all-cause and in cardiovascular disease mortality rates, especially among the elderly and in all-cause mortality among infants and children. Kunitz (2004) attributes these developments to increasing "erosion of real incomes, to the increased cost of imported pharmaceuticals and medical technologies, and to the withdrawal of government support from the health and social services sector" forced both by financial constraints and IMF demands. Economic crises during the 1990s have led to a devastating mortality crisis among men in Russia, but have had no discernible health effects in Cuba (Borowy, 2011). Crises have tangibly increased mortality rates in Mexico among children and the elderly and have increased low-weight births and infectious diseases among children in Thailand (Cutler, 2002). Finally, a juxtaposition of the accumulated economic growth rates of numerous countries between 1950 and 2005 with infant mortality rates showed no apparent correlation, either positive or negative (Deaton 2013, 117–120). Apparently, the question of whether economic crises benefit or harm health depends on how they affect important determinants of health such as nutrition, social services, and access to medical care.

Even this interpretation hardly does justice to the diversity of factors now known to play a role in health. In a meticulous meta-analysis, Bernard Harris (2004) reviewed the discussion on mortality declines and revealed a confusingly multifaceted picture, in which wage rises, the nutritional status (a function of the quantity and quality of food, physical activities, and infectious diseases), changing pathogen virulence, urbanization, housing, social disruption, expenditure patterns, and sanitation, all played some roles. His paper seemed to prove Szreter's earlier conclusion that the assessment of numerous determinants of health, which often interact in complicated and poorly understood ways, result in a complex relationship between public health, social and economic change, creating a "devilishly complicated story" (Szreter 2002, 724).

And still, it is only part of the story, since it only looks at those effects of economic growth which show in the population health almost immediately. A predominantly negative or even indifferent effect of economic growth on health would be difficult to reconcile with the dramatic health improvements, which have taken place worldwide over the decades and centuries. Though improvements have been uneven and have repeatedly included setbacks, life expectancy and health status are manifestly better everywhere than 200 years ago, including in the poorest countries (Deaton 2013, 56). Given that unprecedented economic growth rates were one of the most distinctive features of global history during the same period, there must have been something in the overall effects of this economic development which, at the very least, did not prevent these health improvements and, more probably, provided some help. Apparently, changing the time frame of the analysis changes both findings and related questions.

How did economic growth affect population health (in the long run)?

Strangely enough, to date scholars have not debated the long-term effects of economic growth on health with anything approaching the passion of the McKeown debate. This does not mean that there is a broad consensus. Twenty years ago, Easterlin (1996) denied any discernible effects. He argued that, in a long-term perspective, the health difference was determined by increasing knowledge and health technology, whose "pattern of diffusion" was "similar to but largely independent from the spread of" economic growth. Similarly, in his analysis of 12 low-income countries with high life expectancies, Riley (2008) argues that each country had chosen its own trajectory, with public participation as the most widespread common denominator and apparently a general prerequisite. Otherwise, methods included vaccination programs, anti-malaria campaigns or, in one case a successful campaign by the Rockefeller Foundation to encourage people to build their own latrines near their home. However, even knowledge and health technology require money, and various interventions are cheap only after years of research and/or implementation elsewhere have made them cheap. (In the case of latrine building, it involved an actor whose existence goes back to lucrative engagement in the oil industry decades earlier.) Finances clearly play a tangible albeit indirect role.

As already mentioned, most if not all factors which allow long and healthy lives, have to do with private and national income: food security improved with rising private incomes, increasing agricultural productivity through mechanization, and a better transportation infrastructure. Housing and clothing (including shoes all year, traditionally a luxury item for children of poor farmers) likewise improved with increasing incomes, providing better protection against the cold, rain, and parasites; widespread education only became possible when keeping children from manual labor was affordable; public health infrastructure was costly, notably the provision with piped drinking water, the removal of solid and liquid waste, the control of food, water, and occupation standards and also the administration of preventive medical services such as vaccinations or prophylactic examinations and scientific research, which form the basis for preventive or therapeutic practices. And, as many people know who wear glasses or use a wheelchair, even genetic dispositions will affect health differently depending on whether compensatory aid is affordable and available.

Since economic growth increases available finances, and increased financial means widen options for successful health policies, economic growth can be good for health. However, the outcome is not automatic. If rising incomes are funneled into extraordinary privileges of the few instead of health infrastructures for the many, if the medical sector is characterized by absenteeism of medical staff or by an emphasis on unneeded prestige objects or equipment (Deaton 2013, 122–123), simply more money will not help. As Szreter insisted, the "potential capacity of post-industrial economic growth to provide the material basis for generally enhanced population health is not intrinsic to the process of industrialization or of economic growth in itself" (Szreter 2004, 82). Rather, in the past, he maintained that a positive effect of economic growth on health had required policy decisions, brought about only after election reforms had expanded the vote to larger societal groups and often against the opposition or inertia of the privileged classes. But he also acknowledged that, irrespective of the disruptions and death immediately caused by economic growth, in the long run increasing financial means could and usually did benefit population health (Szreter 2005). Thus, even if short- and long-term changes in behavior and circumstances are taken into account, which affect health negatively, the historical record suggests that in the long run the outcome is positive (Stuckler, 2009). Thus, Floud et al. comment that, regardless of uncertainties about the short- and medium-term health effects of industrialization, it "nevertheless laid the foundations for the long-term improvement in both health and living standards of the population since the end of the eighteenth century" (Floud et al. 2011, 296)

In short, while there is no guarantee that economic growth will improve population health, generally it has done so in the past. Populations in industrialized countries have benefitted from economic growth in recent decades and centuries because it has improved their living conditions and it has allowed administrations to pursue policies which have improved health either directly (such as sanitation, public health services, the education of medical doctors and medical research) or indirectly (through education, especially of women, and through increasing wages). In practice, this means that the determinants of people's health do not begin from scratch every time a child is born. Rather, every generation builds on the material and immaterial health resources it inherits from the people who lived before them. In this sense, the people who lived through periods of rapid economic growth amassed resources, which mainly benefitted their descendants, while suffering increased health burdens themselves. Floud, Fogel, Harris, and Hung explain this intergenerational connection during European industrialization as a process of successive layers of health-resources building on one another:

> the health and nutrition of one generation contributes, through mothers and through infant and childhood experience, to the strength, health, and longevity of the next generation; at the same time, increased health and longevity enable the members of that next generation to work harder and longer and to create the resources which can then, in their turn, be used to assist the next, and succeeding, generations to prosper.
>
> (Floud et al. 2011, 1–2)

However, this finding must be viewed in context. It refers mostly to Europeans and US Americans roughly between 1700 and today. During most of that period, people were far poorer, shorter and short-lived than their descendants today, similar to people living in low-income countries today who "have been starved and deprived of care and have therefore, despite their best efforts, been unable to achieve their full potential, either physical or cognitive," a fate they frequently share with their mothers and grandmothers, placing them at a disadvantage even before birth (Floud et al. 2011, 365). So, while there is ample room for this pattern in low-income countries in the future, it is questionable to what extent it is useful in countries where people have already come close to reaching their health potential. Though it seems that even in affluent countries today, further economic growth increases life expectancy, per capita GDP has to increase ever more in order to further extend the lives of already long-living populations (Deaton 2013, 20–21). Since life cannot be prolonged indefinitely, this process will at some point come to an end, though when exactly this will be is, at present, impossible to tell. Besides, even historically, this perspective may benefit from some complementary qualifications.

While the long-term benefits of economic growth for health have been real, they have also been uneven. As mentioned, part of the health outcome of economic growth depends on where policy makers and private citizens choose to invest the funds gained through increasing incomes. Another part depends on who gets to have the necessary funds and knowledge first. As Deaton emphasizes, all improvements initially benefit only a minority of people, usually the wealthiest and the most educated (Deaton 2013, passim). This can be seen as a relatively benign part of health inequalities resulting from economic growth, since the improvements among the wealthy pave the way for those of the less privileged. However, there is a less friendly side to this. Creating wealth not only involved people in the place whose per capita income would eventually grow, so that the benefits gained at the price of health burdens of those living through rapid economic growth would accrue to their children and grandchildren, a connection many people might happily accept even if they were given the choice. But sometimes, the long-term health-wealth connection spreads further across time and space, forming part of a global web of health connections. Clearly, more devastating repercussions of economic growth were felt not by contemporary workers in England, the cradle of industrialization, or continental Europe, but elsewhere.

How did economic growth affect population health (across time and space)?

A. Early industrialization

Global economic growth began with industrialization, and industrialization began in Britain. Therefore, the following discussion will focus on Britain with a tacit understanding that the significance of these developments subsequently went far beyond the economic development of the British Isles.

Britain's economic development in the nineteenth century was tied to its ability to make use of an unprecedented amount of resources, both on its own soil and beyond. This would not have been possible to the same extent if land, labor, and other resources from other continents had not become available in the Americas, Africa, and Asia. The appropriation of non-European resources for the benefit of European wealth was no British invention. It began well before the eighteenth century and involved, among other aspects, South American gold and silver going into Portugal and Spain, and Asian spices going into the Netherlands, Portugal, and France. These transfers represented a massive shift of wealth from the Americas and India to Europe, but during several centuries they were unrelated to a sustained development of industrialization and systemic economic growth. Global exchanges gained a new function when the British economy tied foreign resources to its domestic economic development, which, eventually, shifted the world from a biological to a fossil fuel energy regime. This development benefitted from the established and new regimes of resource transfers, both of which depended on prior massive depopulation of the New World.

In the Americas, large stretches of land could be incorporated into a European production system because of the virtual collapse of the native population following the arrival of Europeans. Though precise figures are contested, the general picture indicates that the native population of North America began a massive population decline due to the introduction of infectious diseases, especially smallpox, in the sixteenth century. This was not the result of a master plan.[3] Rather, the introduction of contagious Eurasian diseases into immunologically naïve populations could not but wreak havoc among the native inhabitants of the Americas, whose slow original migration into the American continent thousands of years earlier and scarcity of domesticated animals had shielded them from all but a few infectious diseases (probably only tuberculosis and syphilis). Forced labor, warfare, and the destruction of livelihoods by Europeans added to the demographic catastrophe. Effects differed, ranging from complete eradication of the native population in the case of the Caribbean Taino to far more benign developments elsewhere. Overall, the Amerindian population dwindled to anywhere between 50 and 5 percent of its original size between 1492 and 1650. In North America, the decline continued throughout the nineteenth century, as the remaining native population suffered large-scale forced removals from their areas of settlement in the eastern states to remote and infertile reservations in the west (Webb 2015; Thornton 2000; McNeill and McNeill 2003; Livi Bacci 2008). It was certainly an example of health deterioration for the population of numerous Indian societies on a gigantic scale.

This depopulation of North America provided several important preconditions for industrialization in Britain: it offered land for a plantation economy for the production of sugar and cotton, important contributions to British food and industrialization; and it offered land for British settlers, facilitating the large-scale emigration of British subjects.

Emigration had a strong influence on development in the United Kingdom. Approximately 572,000 people left the United Kingdom between 1700 and 1820, a number that increased substantially during the following decades, reaching over 5.5 million people between 1820 and 1869 and 6.4 million between 1870 and 1913 (Maddison 2006, 37). These numbers represented substantial relief for the British population, which began an explosive growth in the early nineteenth century from 12.5 million in 1811 to just under 30 million in 1861 (ChartsBin 2009). Emigration of this scale was only possible because depopulated North America offered a continent available for settlement. It had immediate effects on British health in that it mitigated the negative health effects of urbanization and industrialization by providing some demographic relief, making British cities a little less overcrowded and less of epidemic hotspots than they undoubtedly were (see e.g. Hardy 1993). It also spurred the economic development in Britain. By reducing the potential labor force, emigration affected wage levels, though the degree is difficult to quantify. British wages relative to capital were in line with those in France and Austria until the early eighteenth century but began a substantial increase then until wages relative to capital were 60 percent more expensive in Britain than on the continent. (Allen 2011, 31). These high wages were crucial for investments into the mechanization of production processes, an essential precondition for a dramatic increase of labor productivity and economic growth based on industrialization.

In addition, the decimation of population in North and Central America provided land for incorporation into the British economy. Kenneth Pomeranz famously conceptualized transcontinental production as "ghost acres." According to his calculation, the cotton, sugar, and timber which Britain received from the New World, added somewhere between 25 and 30 million "ghost acres" to the country, land which, though it did not physically belong to

Britain, contributed its production to the British economy. Given that Britain only had approximately 17 million acres of arable land at the time, these "ghost acres" represented a massive contribution to British wealth. They provided valuable calories to population nutrition, helped keep British bodies warm through affordable clothes and, by providing goods whose production would otherwise have required work outside, they advanced work indoors, further reducing population calorie requirements. Undoubtedly, these "ghost acres" strengthened population health in Britain at the time, both directly, by providing food and clothing, and indirectly, by providing material for the budding British industry (Pomeranz 2000, 274–276, 126). Sugar and cotton, in particular, stand out in this regard.

Both were products produced on plantations making use of slave labor, so that Pomeranz's concept ties into an older approach to a similar idea of transatlantic production acting as an important or even essential input into British – and, in a larger sense, European – industrialization and economic growth. Slaves had long formed a fact of life in many parts of the world but the emerging industrialization increased their numbers (McNeill & McNeill 2003, 252) and changed their function within an overriding economic system.

The pioneering work, which introduced slavery into the history of industrialization, was Eric Williams's 1944 study on *Capitalism and Slavery*. As one of several theses,[4] with which he broke with the conventional historiography of slavery, he argued that Caribbean sugar plantations provided much of the capital used for investments in the emerging industries in Britain, so that slave labor in the Caribbean either caused or contributed substantially to British industrialization (Williams 1944). These theses were discussed for decades, including in two volumes reassessing its ideas in light of subsequent research after, respectively, 40 and 50 years (Solow and Engerman 1987; Cateau and Carrington 2000). After more than half a century of further research in that field, there is broad consensus that slavery contributed to industrialization in Britain, but disagreements remain on the degree of its importance.

Opponents of the Williams theory argue that the profits and additional market opportunities generated through slave trade and the Caribbean sugar production in the late seventeenth and eighteenth century formed too small a percentage of total economic income in Britain at the time to have a substantial effect on the British economic development (Anstey 1975). For instance, Eltis and Engerman (2000, 132–133) calculate that by 1805, the output of Caribbean plantations accounted for no more than 2.5 percent of national income, which was more than the coal industry but only about a third of the iron industry. Even including British refining enterprises, they conclude that "sugar production was no more important than were several other industries."

By contrast, the supporters of the thesis of slave labor as a significant, possibly essential, element of British industrialization disagree not only on the numbers, but also argue that the importance went beyond mere monetary data. Thus, Blackburn (1997) calculates that, counted comprehensively, the profits related to plantation slavery in 1770 accounted for between 21 and 55 percent of gross capital formation in Britain. Besides, slave-produced sugar supplied essential calories for the growing English population during crucial decades before larger quantities of grain could be produced with chemical fertilizers or imported from North America. In the course of the nineteenth century, sugar may have accounted for anything between 4 and 22 percent of daily intake of calories (Pomeranz 2000, 274–276, 126). Indeed, Eltis and Engerman (2000, 132) agree that during that period "the British consumed more sugar than any other people in the world," but do not try to assess its effect on nutritional status or working productivity. However, the real significance may not have been financial or nutritional, but structural. Blackburn goes to great lengths to explain how British sugar production in Barbados and Jamaica contributed significantly to establishing a capitalist approach to agricultural investment with slaves as central production factors. This new organization of production, trade, and consumption was at the heart of the shift of the British economy from an agrarian to an industrial regime. Similarly, Joseph Inikori (2002) argues that the Caribbean plantation economy formed an essential component of a specifically British Atlantic trade system, which connected Britain, West Africa, the Caribbean, and the North American settlements into a new economic network. Given the high transportation costs and high land–labor ratio, low-cost slave labor was the only way to establish this Caribbean leg of that system. Regardless of whether the slave-sugar economy caused or merely contributed to industrialization and economic growth in seventeenth-century Britain, slavery played some role, and plausibly this role was significant (see e.g. Morgan 2000).

In the nineteenth century, the central connection between slavery and industrialization shifted to cotton. Cotton supplied the raw material for the textile industry, a key building block of the emerging industrialization. By 1830, cotton was the largest British industry, accounting for 8 percent of British GDP and 16 percent of manufacturing jobs. It was the first industry transformed by factory production (Allen 2011, 32). Mysteriously, a country in Europe, one of the few places where cotton had been virtually unknown, used the material as its "launching pad for the broader Industrial Revolution." Cotton, Beckert (2014, xiv) argues, led to "the origins of the modern world, industrialization, rapid and continuous economic growth, enormous productivity increase and staggering social inequality." To move from relative unimportance to central status between the end of the seventeenth century and the mid-nineteenth century required technical innovations such as the cotton gin, the spinning jenny, the flying shuttle and, eventually, the steam-powered power loom. Collectively, these innovations vastly increased the speed of transforming cotton fibers into cloth, and, thereby, increased the demand for cotton. In this context, slave plantations in the Southern states of the USA gained importance. Merely 1.5 million pounds of cotton were produced in the US in 1790. By 1830, it was 331 million pounds and by 1860 the number had risen to 2,275 million pounds. During the same period, the number of slaves in the US South increased from under 700,000 in 1790 to just over two million in 1830 and almost four million in 1860. In the process, North American cotton replaced cotton imports from India and Egypt, which had originally been used in the British textile industry. While US cotton represented a minuscule 0.04 percent of British cotton imports in 1790, the proportion virtually exploded to 17 percent in 1800, 52.6 percent in 1820, 76.5 percent in 1830 and 88.5 percent in 1860. Though some of this cotton was produced by white farmers, the vast majority involved slave labor (Bailey 1994, 35–38). In the second part of the nineteenth century, slave-produced cotton also began feeding an emerging textile industry in the northeastern states of the USA, especially Massachusetts and Rhode Island (Bailey 1994, 45). Generally speaking, by the nineteenth century at the latest, slavery had become a central part of a large trans-Atlantic production system (Zeuske 2012, 104–106). It was easily combined with the evolving modern machinery, turning slavery into part of the cutting edge of economic modernization (Kaye 2009). In the process, it fed into the largest development of economic growth in human history. It is tempting to follow Beckert in seeing slavery at the core of the development of global capitalism (Beckert 2014, xv).

While economically productive, slavery was not healthy for slaves. Frequently, it was lethal. About a third of captured slaves died in Africa before even setting foot on a ship. An estimated 5 to 25 percent of the 10 to 11 million slaves transported from Africa into the New World over the course of several centuries died during the crossing. Between 10 and 30 percent died within their first three years in the Americas. Thus, less than half of the people originally enslaved in Africa survived long enough to become adapted to plantation life. Even then, mortality remained high (Johnson 1999, 4). Sugar plantations both in Louisiana and the Caribbean stand out as consistently requiring additional slaves, pointing to the deadly nature of the work (Kaye 2009, 637). Otherwise, the slave population in the Americas generally increased, due to higher fertility than mortality (how much of this development was the result of routine rape is difficult to assess).

The health record for slaves working on plantations in antebellum United States varied. Working adult slaves apparently received adequate food and care, so that they were as tall as or even taller than whites in different regions in Europe and North America. However, they represented only the survivors of dismal health prospects early in life. Roughly half of all slave pregnancies seem to have ended in stillbirths or infant and early childhood deaths, largely reflecting the harsh living conditions of slave women. Slave children were severely stunted, representing virtually the slowest growing population ever studied. Apparently, slave owners invested food in working slaves, so that adolescent slaves apparently caught up with growth when they began physical labor. However, modern research suggests that they may not have been able to compensate for the cognitive and mental deficiencies suffered from severe malnutrition during childhood (Steckel 1986a, 1986b).

Just like the health benefits people enjoy as a result of economic growth and more funds available for public and private health expenditures today cannot be separated from the health burdens experienced by people working during periods of rapid economic expansion, they cannot be separated from the health burdens suffered by Amerindians and African slaves of former centuries. This is not to say that anyone enjoying the health advantages of good food, good housing, and good education today is responsible for the large-scale death of the native population in the Americas or for slavery and its brutality. Nor does this chapter argue that the availability of American land or slavery were the only or even sufficient reasons for industrialization and resulting high economic growth. But this chapter does argue that "ghost acres" and slave labor have been integral components of industrialization, first in Britain and then in Europe and beyond. Thereby, the premature deaths, and high disease burden borne by workers in early and disruptive periods of industrialization, of Amerindians and of African slaves form part of the collective health effects of economic growth. Therefore, they must be added to a comprehensive assessment of the health effects of economic growth as much as the undoubted and valuable health effects of improvements in income and living standards on secular improvements in life expectancy, nutrition, and overall health status.

By the same token, a comprehensive assessment of the effect of economic growth on health must acknowledge that health effects of fossil fuels, reaching both into the past and the future. Between the nineteenth and the twentieth century, i.e. between early and later phases of industrialization, hard manual labor, especially forced labor, was increasingly replaced by fossil fuels. The connection between fossil fuels and industrialization is so close as to be almost synonymous. Without coal, no steam engine would have driven steam-powered looms, trains or ships, essential elements of increasing production, trade, and income. The use of coal and later oil provided the energy for production and services on a totally unprecedented level. It provided the basis for unprecedented economic growth. In historical terms, this shift represented a massive transformation both in the economic and the social sphere (McNeill and McNeill 2003, 258). But it also created a connection between economic growth and new health burdens.

How did economic growth affect population health (across time and space)?

B. Advanced industrialization

Similar to the other preconditions for economic growth discussed above, the use of fossil fuels placed a heavy health burden on those involved in its making. Obtaining coal has required extracting it from the ground through mining, making use of the manpower of miners (men, women, and children), who engaged in work entailing a list of series health risks. In a depressingly monotonous repetition of events miners have borne the burden of working overly long hours in dusty, moist, dark, and dangerous environments, suffering from silicosis, other respiratory diseases, hookworm disease, and disablement and premature death through accidents (Rainhorn 2014). Contrary to expectations, modernization and the growing use of machinery did not necessarily improve health conditions. In fact, it could increase the health burden, for instance when the growing use of heavy machinery and of explosives in Scottish mines during the 1930s increased the amount of dust miners breathed, thus amplifying the risk of lung damage (McIvor 2014, 289).

Coal has retained an important role in global industrialization to this day, with China, whose explosive economic growth rates in the last 30 years are legendary, becoming the world's largest importer (Cao et al. 2015). But after 1950, it has been complemented and in many ways overtaken by oil as the prime energy basis for economic growth. Collectively, fossil fuels form the backbone of the global economy as we know it today, and while the developments of the eighteenth and nineteenth century formed an essential precondition for the unprecedented growth of the global economy in recent decades, in its dramatic form it only took off after 1950. During this "Great Acceleration" or "1950s Syndrome" more people became affluent during a single generation than ever before in human history. Largely based on abundant energy through cheap oil, this period saw the emergence of mass consumption on a hitherto unimaginable scale, an explosive growth of a broad range of products and services, and a restructuring of physical and social lives that took the easy availability of transportation for granted and turned aspiration to travel and to enjoy leisure time into perceived entitlements. (Pfister 2010).

Burning fossil fuels substantially contributed to ambient air pollution, which, according to World Health Organization (WHO 2014) estimates, caused 3.7 million premature deaths worldwide in 2012 alone, mainly due to ischaemic heart disease and strokes and, to a lesser extent, to respiratory diseases and lung cancer. Eighty-eight percent of these deaths occurred in low- and middle-income countries. However, the most important emerging risk is climate change with a potential to affect human health furthest into the future. The projections about possible health effects of future climate change are, indeed, alarming. Several studies predict serious health risks for hundreds of millions of people (McMichael 2013; Bauchner 2014, Myers and Bernstein 2011). Expected health threats include increasing malnutrition, resulting from decreases in food production, drowning in more frequent instances of flooding, and an increase in various diseases ranging from health-related heart diseases, vector-borne diseases (notably malaria), stress-related mental illness to injuries received in rising violence as conflicts about scarce resources increase. These effects will disproportionately affect people in vulnerable groups in low-income tropical countries, further exacerbating existing socio-economic inequalities (WHO and WMO 2012; Smith et al. 2014). A recent WHO fact sheet estimated that between 2030 and 2050 climate change might cause approximately 250,000 additional deaths per year resulting from malnutrition, malaria, diarrhea, and heat stress (WHO 2016). Outcomes beyond that date will obviously depend vitally on the climate-related policies taken during the following years. Thus, nobody knows how exactly a changing climate will affect the health of people in the future. But it is certain that it will have a profound effect and that this effect will be connected to the way people have made their incomes grow and their economies increase in the past and our present. In 2009, the UCL-Lancet Commission on Climate Change simply called climate change "the biggest global health threat of the 21st century" (Costello et al. 2009).

Tentative conclusions

Global economic growth has not ended, nor have the health effects, and our understanding of how one has affected – and continues to affect – the other is far from complete. Besides, even with a better understanding it is doubtful that this relation would ever lend itself to an easy tally of the positive and negative effects. Conclusions, therefore, can only be tentative.

What seems safe to say is that economic growth has affected health in more far-reaching and complex ways than is often acknowledged. The economic growth gained through industrialization has brought important health gains to millions of people, who have been able to enjoy the benefits of sanitation, high living standards, as well as of vaccinations and drugs borne from medical research. Maybe a similar scale of economic growth would have been possible without large-scale industrialization or without industrialization taking a form that depended heavily on fossil fuels. This chapter does not argue that this has been the only possible form of economic growth or that no other form may be possible in the future. But it does argue that in its actual historic form it has taken a substantial toll on many people's health, ranging from Amerindians to slaves and from miners to unnamed people living and working at times of rapid economic expansion and living through the effects of climate change in the future. Thus, to sum up, economic growth has enabled many people to live longer and healthier lives, relatively less burdened by death, incapacitation, and disease than that of others. These improvements have often come about a long time after the beginnings were laid, and they have affected people in many parts of the world, including those that had not themselves undergone substantial economic growth.

But these benefits have always been bought at the price that the lives of other people, living at other times and places, have been cut short or burdened with contingent disability and disease. In historical perspective, therefore, exploring positive and negative effects is manageable only in a very limited framework or focused on an isolated group of people. But people rarely live isolated from the rest of the world. Their activities have an impact on the lives of others, living on other continents and living in the future, just as their lives have been affected by activities of others in foreign lands and in the past. Amerindians and slaves do not usually appear in Preston curves or in discussions on the effects of economic growth on population health in North America, let alone in Britain and Europe at large, either because their deaths occurred long before the onset of industrialization or because they were not counted as part of the population. Including their numbers would substantially change the picture of the relation between economic growth and health. A more suitable approach may be to consider trade-offs between the helpful and the burdensome. Justifying policies designed to foster economic growth on the grounds that this will improve some people's health without considering how it may harm other people's health is certainly simplistic. Considerations of future health policies should focus on the profound challenge of how to spread or even maintain the health benefits brought by economic growth while avoiding its health costs.

Notes

1 I would like to thank Martin Gorsky for his extremely helpful comments on an earlier version of this chapter.
2 This is not to say that the crisis and subsequent austerity measures did not have negative health effects. But the 2014 debate in the Lancet about the extent to which changes in stillbirths, suicides, HIV, and infant mortality rates result from austerity or are part of other longer-term developments (Kentikelenis et al. 2014 and follow-up printed correspondence) demonstrates the difficulty of measuring the effects of economic contraction.
3 The narrative that the epidemics were generally caused by blankets contaminated with smallpox pathogens, which whites gave to Amerindians in a deliberate effort to spread the disease, has been one of the most powerful legends of the European takeover of the North American continent since its beginnings. Indeed, at least one case of such a deliberate infection has been documented, but the historical record hardly backs up the argument that this was a general strategy nor that such measures would have been necessary to cause large-scale epidemics (Mayer 1995).
4 The others focuses on the relations between slavery, on the one hand, and racism, economics, and abolitionism, on the other.

Bibliography

Allen, Robert. 2011. *Global economic history*. Oxford: Oxford University Press.

Anstey, Roger. 1975. *The Atlantic Slave Trade and British Abolition*. London: Macmillan.

Bailey, Ronald. 1994. "The Other Side of Slavery: Black Labor, Cotton, and Textile Industrialization in Great Britain and the United States." *Agricultural History* 68(2): 35–50.

Bauchner, Howard. 2014. "Climate Change. A Continuing Threat to the Health of the World's Population." *JAMA*. 312(15): 1519.

Beckert, Sven. 2014. *Empire of Cotton*, New York: Alfred A. Knopf.

Birt, Christopher. 2016. "How Brexit Could Damage Our Health." *The Guardian*. June 21. Accessed July 22, 2016. https://www.theguardian.com/commentisfree/2016/jun/21/brexit-damage-health-drug-research-funding-free-treatment-europe.

Blackburn, Robin. 1997. *The Making of New World Slavery: From the Baroque to the Modern, 1492–1800*. London: Verso.

Borowy, Iris. 2011. "Similar but Different: Health and Economic Crisis in 1990s Cuba and Russia." *Social Science and Medicine* 72(9): 1489–1498.

Borowy, Iris. 2013. “Degrowth and Public Health in Cuba: Lessons from the Past?” *Journal of Cleaner Production* 38: 17–26.

Cao, Shixiong, Yuan Ly, Heran Zheng and Xin Wang. 2015. “Research of the Risk Factors of China’s Unsustainable Socioeconomic Development: Lessons for Other Nations.” *Social Indicators Research* 123: 337–347.

Cateau, Heather and Selwyn Carrington, eds. 2000. *Capitalism and Slavery Fifty Years Later: Eric Eustace Williams. A Reassessment of the Man and His Work*. New York: Peter Lang Publishing.

ChartsBin. 2009. Historical Population of United Kingdom, 43 AD to Present. *ChartsBin.com*. Accessed February 3, 2016. http://chartsbin.com/view/28k

Colgrove, James. 2002. “The McKeown Thesis: A Historical Controversy and Its Enduring Influence.” *American Journal of Public Health*, 92(5): 725–729.

Commission on Macroeconomics and Health. 2001. *Macroeconomics and Health: Investing in Health for Economic Development*. Geneva: WHO.

Costello, Anthony *et al.* 2009. “Managing the Health Effects of Climate Change.” *The Lancet* 373(9676): 1693–1733.

Coyle, Diane. 2014. *A Brief but Affectionate History of GDP*. Princeton: Princeton University Press.

Cutler, David, Felicia Knaul, Rafael Lozano and Beatriz Zurita Garza. 2002. “Financial crisis, health outcomes and ageing: Mexico in the 1980s and 1990s.” *Journal of Public Economics* 83: 279–303.

Deaton, Angus. 2013. *The Great Escape. Health, wealth, and the origins of inequality*. Princeton: Princeton University Press.

Easterlin, Richard. 1996. “Is Economic Growth the Engine Driving Improved Life Expectancy?” ASSA: Cliometric Society Sessions. Accessed July 20, 2016. http://cliometrics.org/conferences/ASSA/Jan_96/easterlin.shtml.

Easterlin, Richard. 1999. “How Beneficent is the Market? A Look at the Modern History of Mortality.” *European Review of Economic History* 3(3): 257–294.

Eltis, David. 2000. *The Rise of African Slavery in the Americas*. Cambridge: Cambridge University Press.

Eltis, David, and Stanley Engerman. 2000. “The Importance of Slavery and the Slave Trade to Industrializing Britain.” *Journal of Economic History*, 60(1): 123–144.

Floud, Roderick, Robert Fogel, Bernard Harris and Sok Chul Hong. 2011. *The Changing Body. Health, Nutrition, and Human Development in the Western World since 1700*. Cambridge: Cambridge University Press.

Fogel, Robert. 2012. *Explaining Long-term Trends in Health and Longevity*. Cambridge: Cambridge University Press.

Gapminder, created by Hans Rosling. https://www.gapminder.org. Accessed July 20, 2016.

Gertham, Ulf-G. and Christopher Ruhm. 2002. “Deaths Rise in Good Economic Times: Evidence from the OECD.” NBER Working Paper Series 9357. Accessed July 20, 2016. http://www.nber.org/papers/w9357.

Gorsky, Martin and Bernard Harris. 2005. “The Measurement of Morbidity in Interwar Britain: Evidence from the Hampshire Friendly Society.” In *Facing Illness in Troubled Times*, edited by Iris Borowy and Wolf Gruner, pp. 129–163. Berlin: Peter Lang.

Griffin, Emma. 2013. *Liberty’s Dawn. A People’s History of the Industrial Revolution*. New Haven and London: Yale University Press.

Haines, Michael, Lee Craig and Thomas Weiss. 2003. “The Short and the Dead: Nutrition, Mortality, and the ‘Antebellum Puzzle’ in the United States.” *The Journal of Economic History* 63: 382–413.

Hardy, Anne. 1993. *The Epidemic Streets.* Oxford: Oxford University Press.

Harris, Bernard. 2004. "Public Health, Nutrition, and the Decline of Mortality: The McKeown Thesis Revisited." *Social History of Medicine* 17(3): 379–407.

Inikori, Joseph. 2002. *Africans and the Industrial Revolution in England: A Study in International Trade and Economic Development.* New York: Cambridge University Press.

Jerven, Morten. 2013. *Poor Numbers: How We are Misled by African Development Statistics and What to Do About it.* Ithaka: Cornell University Press.

Johnson, Walter. 1999. *Soul by Soul.* Cambridge Mass.: Harvard University Press.

Kaye, Anthony. 2009. "A Second Slavery: Modernity in the Nineteenth-Century South and the Atlantic World." *The Journal of Southern History* 75(3): 627–650.

Kentikelenis, Alexander *et al.* 2014. "Greece's Health Crisis: From Austerity to Denialism." *Lancet* 383(9918): 748–753.

Komlos, Jürgen. 1997. "Warum wurden die Leute kleiner in einer wachsenden Volkswirtschaft?" *Historical Social Research* 22: 150–162.

Kunitz, Stephen. 2004. "The Making and Breaking of Yugoslavia and its Impact on Health." *American Journal of Public Health* 94(11): 1894–1904.

Livi Bacci, Massimo. 2008. *Conquest: The Destruction of the American Indios.* Cambridge: Policy Press.

Maddison, Angus. 2006. *The World Economy.* Paris: OECD.

Marks, Robert. 2006. *Die Ursprünge der modernen Welt.* Darmstadt: Wissenschaftliche Buchgesellschaft. (*The Origins of the Modern World.* Lanham MD: Rowman & Littlefield Publishers. 2002.)

Mayer, Adrienne. 1995. "The Nessus Shirt in the New World: Smallpox Blankets in History and Legend." *The Journal of American Folklore* 108(427): 54–77.

McIvor, Arthur. 2014. "Quand les corps parlent: faire de l'histoire orale pour étudier la santé et l'invalidité au travail dans les houillères britanniques au vingtième siècle." In *Santé et travail à la mine XIXe-XXIe siècle*, edited by Judith Rainhorn, 281–301. Villeneuve d'Asq: Presses Universitaires du Septentrion.

McKeown, Thomas. 1975. "An Interpretation of the Decline of Mortality in England and Wales during the Twentieth Century." *Population Studies* 29: 391–422.

McKeown, Thomas. 1976. *The Modern Rise of Population.* London/New York: Academic Press.

McMichael, Anthony. 2013. "Globalization, Climate Change, and Human Health." *NEJM* 368: 1335–1343.

McNeill, John, and William McNeill. 2003. *The Human Web. A Bird's-Eye View of World History.* New York/London: W.W. Norton.

Missoni, Eduardo. 2015. Degrowth and Health: Local Action Should be Linked to Global Policies and Governance for Health. *Sustainability Science* 10(3): 439–450.

Moore, Thomas Gale. Undated. "The Red Cross Morphs into Chicken Little.". Accessed July 20, 2016. http://www.stanford.edu/~moore/RedCross.html.

Moore, Thomas Gale. 2000. "In Sickness and in Health: The Kyoto Protocol versus Global Warming." Hoover Press: EPP 104. Accessed July 20, 2016. http://www.hoover.org/sites/default/files/uploads/documents/epp_104.pdf.

Morgan, Kenneth. 2000. *Slavery, Atlantic Trade and the British Economy, 1660–1800.* Cambridge: Cambridge University Press.

Myers, Samuel, and Aaron Bernstein. 2011. "The Coming Health Crisis: Indirect Effects of Global Climate Change." *F1000 Biology Reports*, 3(3).

Pfister, Christian. 2010. "The '1950s Syndrome' and the Transition from a Slow-Going to a Rapid Loss of Global Sustainability." In: *The Turning Points of Environmental History*, edited by Frank Uekoetter, 90–118. Pittsburgh: University of Pittsburgh Press.

Pomeranz, Kenneth. 2000. *The Great Divergence*. Princeton: Princeton University Press.

Postel-Vinay, Gilles and David E. Sahn. 2010. "Explaining Stunting in Nineteenth Century France." *Economic History Review* 63(2): 315–334.

Preston, Samuel. 1975. "The Changing Relation between Mortality and Level of Economic Development." *Population Studies* 29(2): 231–248, reprinted in *International Journal of Epidemiology* 36, 2007: 484–490.

Pritchett, Lant and Lawrence H. Summers 1993. "Wealthier is Healthier." *Policy Research Working Paper Series*, no. 1150. Accessed June 20, 2015. http://www-wds.worldbank.org/servlet/WDSContentServer/WDSP/IB/1993/06/01/000009265_3961004215604/Rendered/PDF/multi0page.pdf.

Rainhorn, Judith, ed. 2014. *Santé et travail à la mine XIXe-XXIe siècle*. Villeneuve d'Asq: Presses Universitaires du Septentrion.

Riley, James. 1990. "The Risk of Being Sick: Morbidity Trends in Found Countries." *Population and Development Review* 16(3): 403–432.

Riley, James. 1997. *Sick, Not Dead: The Health of British Workingmen during the Mortality Decline*. Baltimore: Johns Hopkins University Press.

Riley, James. 2008. *Low Income, Social Growth, and Good Health: A History of Twelve Countries*. Berkeley: University of California Press.

Ruhm, Christopher. 2007. "A Healthy Economy can Break your Heart." *Demography* 44(4): 829–848.

Saksena, Rhea. 2016. "Brexit – What Might it Mean for Global Health?" Medical Press. June 26. Accessed July 22, 2016. http://medicalxpress.com/news/2016-06-brexitwhat-global-health.html.

Smith, Kirk *et al.* 2014. "Human Health: Impacts, Adaptation, and Co-benefits." In Chris Field *et al.* eds., *Climate Change 2014: Impacts, Adaptation, and Vulnerability*. Part A: Global and Sectoral Aspects. Contribution of Working Group II to the Fifth Assessment Report of the Intergovernmental Panel on Climate Change, Cambridge: Cambridge University Press, 709–754.

Solow, Barbara and Stanley Engerman, eds. 1987. *British Capitalism and Caribbean Slavery: The Legacy of Eric Williams*. Cambridge: Cambridge University Press.

Spence, A.Michael. 2009. "Introduction." In *Health and Growth* edited by Michael Spence and Maureen Lewis. Washington: World Bank.

Steckel, Richard. 1986a. "A Peculiar Population: The Nutrition, Health, and Mortality of American Slaves from Childhood to Maturity." *The Journal of Economic History* 46(3): 721–741.

Steckel, Richard. 1986b. "A Dreadful Childhood: The Excess Mortality of American Slaves." *Social Science History* 10(4): 427–465.

Stuckler, David *et al.* 2009. "The Health Implications of Financial Crisis: A Review of the Evidence." *The Ulster Medical Journal* 87(3): 142–145.

Szreter, Simon. 2002. "Rethinking McKeown: The Relationship between Public Health and Social Change." *American Journal of Public Health* 92(5): 722–725.

Szreter, Simon. 2004. "Industrialization and Health." *British Medical Bulletin* 69: 75–86.

Szreter, Simon. 2005. *Health and Wealth*. Rochester: Rochester University Press.

Tapia Granados, José. 2004. "Increasing Mortality during the Expansions of the US Economy, 1900–1996." *International journal of Epidemiology* 34(6): 1194–1202.

Tapia Granados, José. 2014. "La crisis y la salud en España y en Europa: ¿Está aumentando la mortalidad?" *Salud colectiva* 10(1): 81–91. On-line version ISSN 1851–8265.

Tapia Granados, José and Ana V. Diez Roux. 2009. "Life and Death during the Great Depression." *Proceedings of the National Academy of Sciences of the USA* 106(41): 17290–17295.

Thompson, Mark and Katie Hunt. 2016. "Brexit's Broken Promises: Health Care, Immigration and the Economy." CNNMoney (London) First published June 27, 2016: 7:03 AM ET. Accessed July 22, 2016. http://money.cnn.com/2016/06/27/news/economy/brexit-broken-promises/index.html.

Thornton, Richard. 2000. "Population History of Native North Americans," in *A Population History of North America* edited by Michael Haines and Richard Steckel, 9–50. Cambridge: Cambridge University Press.

Truman, Harry. 1949. Inaugural Address, January 20, 1949. Accessed July 15, 2016. https://www.trumanlibrary.org/whistlestop/50yr_archive/inagural20jan1949.htm.

De Vogli, Roberto, and Jocelynn Owusu. 2014. "The Causes and Health Effects of the Great Recession: From Neoliberalism to 'Healthy De-growth'." *Critical Public Health*. Pre-published online January 2015;25(1) 15–31.

Webb, James. 2015. "Globalization of Disease, 1300 to 1900." In *The Cambridge World History Volume 6: The Construction of a Global World, 1400–1800 CE, Part 1: Foundations, edited by*Jerry H. Bentley, Sanjay Subrahmanyam, and Merry E. Wiesner-Hanks, 54–75. Cambridge: Cambridge University Press.

WHO. 2014. "Ambient (Outdoor) Air Quality and Health." Fact sheet No.313. Accessed July 25, 2016. http://www.who.int/mediacentre/factsheets/fs313/en.

WHO. 2016. "Climate Change and Health." Fact sheet. Accessed July 25, 2016. http://www.who.int/mediacentre/factsheets/fs266/en.

WHO, Commission on Social Determinants of Health. 2008. *Closing the Gap in a Generation. Health Equity through Action on the Social Determinants of Health*. Geneva: WHO.

WHO and WMO. 2012. *Atlas of Health and Climate*. Geneva: WHO.

Williams, Eric. 1944. *Capitalism and Slavery*. Chapel Hill: University of North Carolina Press.

Zeuske, Michael. 2012. *Die Geschichte der Amistad*. Stuttgart: Reclam Verlag.

Zhang, Junfeng *et al.* 2010. "Environmental Health in China: Challenges to Achieving Clean Air and Safe Water." *Lancet* 275(9720): 1110–1119.

7 An incompatible couple

A critical history of economic growth and sustainable development

Jeremy L. Caradonna

There is a growing sense amongst both historians and sustainability advocates that the ambivalence toward economic growth that characterized the early formation of sustainable development (circa 1980 to 1992) ended up benefitting the status quo and essentially failed to change the course of unsustainable global development.[1] This murky attitude toward growth can be glimpsed in the many reports, meetings, declarations, and conferences – some of which are discussed below – that gave sustainable development its first and most lasting identity. Although sustainable development appeared, in the context of the 1980s, to be a radical departure from the status quo of industrial growth, in hindsight it often seems like little more than an ecologically sensitive form of neoclassical economics and old-style Westernized development, with deep roots in Gross Domestic Product (GDP) expansion, increased material consumption, and the monetization and internationalization of low-impact, localized economies. As one group of degrowth economists has argued recently, "in the context of increased global environmental problems, the 'sustainable development' discourse [...] has been unable to produce the overarching policies and radical change of behavior needed at individual and collective scales" (Martinez-Alier et. al. 2014, 78). These economists go on to assert that "economic growth, even if disguised as sustainable development, will lead to social and ecological collapse" (ibid., 87).

This chapter is an attempt to historicize and contextualize the complex debates over growth and to understand how its perceived role within sustainable development has changed over time. How did economic growth go from being largely acceptable, albeit controversial, in the milieu of 1980s-era sustainable development, to being largely unacceptable and even an object of scorn by the 2010s? Although there were many people involved in sustainable development who criticized growth for depleting resources, generating pollution and destructive technologies, facilitating urbanization, unraveling traditional societies, and creating the conditions for unsustainable population growth, their voices were largely drowned out in the 1980s, for reasons discussed below. What emerged was a "muddled middle," in which the potent attacks on endless economic expansion from the 1960s and 1970s were largely set aside in favor of a rather tepid compromise position that was tacitly (or even openly) supportive of the neoclassical economic assumption that a bigger economy is necessarily a better one.[2] For instance, the dominant belief within the World Commission on Environment and Development (WCED), which produced the groundbreaking *Our Common Future* (the Brundtland report) in 1987, was that there was a fundamental "compatibility of economic growth with environmental protection" (Borowy 2014, 84).

But by the twenty-first century, those involved in the economics of sustainability had begun to see sustainable development as a failed attempt to address the problem of economic growth. Scholars such as Giorgos Kallis, François Schneider, Christian Kerschner, Joan Martinez-Alier, and Richard Heinberg have argued in recent years that growth and environmental protection, pace the Brundtland report, are *not* compatible, and that unchecked economic expansion is a root cause of the world's complex ecological crises (Schneider et. al. 2010; Kallis et. al. 2012; D'Alisa et. al. 2014; Heinberg 2010). Although the broader discourse on sustainability is alive and well, as demonstrated by its growing acceptance in universities, governments, NGOs, and corporations, the concept of *sustainable development* is increasingly burdened by its troublesome links to the growth paradigm (Caradonna 2014, ch. 5). The world economy in the 2010s is the biggest that it has ever been in world history, topping 70 trillion per annum (IMF 2012; UNPop 2010), and yet the biggering of the Gross World Product has failed to prevent financial disasters (The Great Recession 2007–2009), the transgression of key planetary boundaries (cited below), staggering increases in population, or rising levels of global inequality. The goal of the WCED was to "achieve sustainable development by the year 2000," a goal that was clearly not reached (WCED 1987, "Chairman's Foreword").[3] Did sustainable development fail to meet its lofty objectives because it was too wedded to the business-as-usual growth model that exacerbated the rate of environmental decline?[4]

Historiography of the growth question within sustainable development

Scholars have recognized since at least the early 1990s that sustainable development has suffered a Janus-faced identity problem in which economic growth plays both protagonist and antagonist in the story of development. Donald Worster (1993) first took aim at this inconsistency in an essay called "The Shaky Ground of Sustainable Development," in which he argued that growth is an "economic concept on which economists are clear and ecologists are muddled" (Worster 1993, 153). He expressed his concern that the sustainable development relies on overly "utilitarian, economic, and anthropocentric definitions," and that, unless defined differently, economists would naturally assume that a sustainable society equates to a continuously growing *economy* (ibid., 153 and 147). Carl Mitcham argued shortly thereafter (1995) that sustainable development, as a philosophy and an agenda for the international community, was a constructive response to the challenges posed by the Club of Rome's paradigm-challenging *Limits to Growth* (1972; updates in 1992 and

2004). This MIT-based team of systems theorists famously demonstrated through complex computer modeling that exponential growth could not continue forever (Meadows et. al. 1972). For international committees, such as the WCED, sustainable development was supposed to bridge the gap between the position of the "no-more-growth" environmentalists, who had imbibed the lessons of the Club of Rome and ecological economics, and the predominantly Third World economists, who sought to level the global playing field via development-as-growth. Thus in the milieu of sustainable development in the 1980s, growth was viewed simultaneously and contradictorily as the *cause* of and *solution to* the interlocking social, environmental, and economic problems of the twentieth century. The upshot, though, is that the WCED and other organizations ended up in a state of "ambivalence" that was anything but hostile toward growth (Mitcham 1995, 317). The *Limits to Growth* (the book and the data) was a problem that had to be addressed and dealt with rather than a scientific truth to be accepted and put to good use. In the following year, 1996, the respected environmentalist Bill McKibben derided sustainability (a term sometimes used synonymously with sustainable development), calling it a "buzzless buzzword" that was "born partly in an effort to obfuscate" and which would never catch on in mainstream society (McKibben 1996).

By the end of the millennium, Desta Mebratu (1998) could reasonably suggest that the ambiguity of sustainable development had generated widespread "disenchantment" within the international community. She showed that the idea of "sustainable growth" played an important role in the reports, mission statements, and conferences that gave sustainable development its basic character, including the International Union for Conservation of Nature's hugely important *World Conservation Strategy* (1980), the WCED's *Our Common Future* (1987), the various documents that emerged from the Rio Earth Summit (1992), the International Institute of Environment and Development (IIED), the World Bank's report *Sustainable Development Concepts* (1992), and the World Business Council for Sustainable Development (WBCSD), the latter of which summed up the mainstream view in the following terms: "Economic growth in all parts of the world is essential for improving the livelihood of the poor, for sustaining growing populations, and eventually for stabilizing population" (Mebratu 1998, 505). It is important to keep in mind that the adjective "sustainable" became well-known in English via a dictionary of economics (1965) that popularized the phrase "sustainable growth," so the ongoing coupling of these terms is perhaps not surprising (Caradonna 2014, 7).[5]

In 1998, the physicist Albert A. Bartlett suggested that "sustainable growth" was misleading and oxymoronic, since if something is being "sustained," it cannot simultaneously be growing (Bartlett 1997–1998). In fact, the critique that sustainable development conflates "development" and "growth" goes back at least as far as 1991, when Robert Goodland, Herman E. Daly, and other economists published *Ecologically Sustainable Development: Building on Brundtland*, a book that argues for the need to distinguish between the chrematistic economic growth of the industrialized North, which was mostly superfluous economic biggering, and the sustainable development of poorer countries, which would require both qualitative improvements in living standards, in addition to some measure of economic expansion. Yet these economists did not want sustainable development to become merely another moneymaking scheme used by the North to profit from social and environmental exploitation in the South (Goodland et. al. 1991).

By the twenty-first century, the concept of sustainable development had been around long enough to divide into different micro-stages. Anne Dale (2012) has split sustainable development into first-generational (1987–1995), second-generational (1995–2005), and third-generational (2005–present) phases or "responses," each of which, according to her, had its own character, goals, and preoccupations (Dale 2012, 3–5). Dale contends that first-generational sustainable development set the stage for the next 20 years or more of development policy by advocating for a revival of economic growth, rather than confronting its contradictions and corollaries, even if the "quality of [that] growth" was expected to change from high-impact, high-emissions, material throughput, to a low-impact, low-emission, and largely dematerialized economy.[6] Dale has also argued quite cogently that sustainable development has done nothing to slow the spread of free trade agreements and neoliberal organizations that depend upon growth and exploitation of the global South, a list that would include NAFTA, GATT, the IMF, the World Bank, and the Trans-Pacific Partnership (Dale 2001, 82).

Jacobus A. Du Pisani, in an insightful essay (2006) on the "historical roots" of sustainable development, reviewed the mounting conflicts in the twentieth century between the critics and advocates of growth, showing that the very idea of modern "progress" hung in the balance. According to Du Pisani, sustainable development was supposed to be a *via media*, a "compromise between growth and conservation. It was not ideologically neutral, because it was intended as an alternative for the zero-growth option and was therefore positively inclined towards the growth and modernization viewpoints." Du Pisani goes on to argue that "sustainable development was not fully embraced by either side in the debate about growth and conservation," and that, from the outset it was "open to criticism from both the left and the right" (Du Pisani 2006, 94).

John A. Robinson's oft-cited article, "Squaring the Circle? Some Thoughts on the Idea of Sustainable Development" (2004), puts forth the contention that the compromise over growth accounts for the relative inability of sustainable development organizations and policies to create real change at the international level. The problem for Robinson is that "development," in this discourse, often seems like little more than a euphemistic synonym for industrialization and "growth," and if that is the case, then "sustainable development" is not a concept that favors a steady-state economy, as ecological economists and critics of growth had proposed in the late 1960s and 1970s, but rather a greenwashed vehicle for business-as-usual growth policy. In his words, "development is seen as synonymous with growth, and therefore [...] sustainable development means ameliorating, but not challenging, continued economic growth." Further, he adds, it is "vague, attracts hypocrites, and fosters delusions" (Robinson 2004, 370). In this way, Robinson echoes earlier critiques of sustainable development from Albert Bartlett, Herman Daly, Robert Goodland, and others; more recently (2010) Gilbert Rist has made similar points about the pitfalls of coupling "sustainable" with "development" (Rist 2010).

But where Robinson's article was truly unique was in untangling the strand of environmental thought that created the intellectual conditions for sustainable development. His contention is that "sustainability" and "sustainable development," although often conflated in the 1980s and 1990s, represent two different environmental discourses in the Western world. For Robinson, sustainability ultimately derives from John Muir's notion of "preservationism," whereas sustainable development traces its lineage back to Gifford Pinchot's pro-business and pro-resource-development conception of "conservationism" (Robinson 2004, 369–371). (The idea of "conservation" has changed considerably since the early decades of the twentieth century.) What's striking about Robinson's historical interpretation is that he suggests that sustainable development was not so much a compromise between growth-skeptics and growth-maniacs as it was a subtle departure from an intellectual and economic tradition that runs from John Stuart Mill in the 1840s to John Muir in the 1890s to Herman Daly in the 1970s, in which ecological reality was seen as the basis of the human economy (especially for Daly), and the ultimate purpose of an economy was to create stability, foster life satisfaction, and use resources sustainably (Mill 1848; Muir 1901; Daly 1973; Daly 1977; Dryzek 2005). That is, one could view the concept of sustainable development as a co-optation by neoclassical economists (or those favorable to this brand of capitalism) of an older and quite different sustainability discourse. As I have argued elsewhere, "there were some important differences between the concepts of sustainability and sustainable development. The systems theorists and ecological economists of the 1970s [...] had not focused very much on 'development,' concentrating instead on rethinking growth-based economics and establishing a society that lived within ecological limits" (Caradonna 2014, 151).

The final books to cite are Stephen Macekura's *Of Limits and Growth: The Rise of Global Sustainable Development in the Twentieth* Century (2015) and Iris Borowy's recent *Defining Sustainable Development for Our Common Future: A History of the World Commission on Environment and Development (Brundtland Report)* (2014), both of which have made crucial contributions to the historiography. Macekura's work focuses on the role played by NGOs since WWII in creating an international movement for sustainable development. He has excellent chapters on the Stockholm Conference, the *World Conservation Strategy*, and the Rio Earth Summit, and shows the extent to which debates about the character of sustainable development hinged on the sticky issues of ecological limits and economic growth (Macekura 2015, chs. 3, 6, 7). Borowy situates the work of the WCED (1983–1987) within a dense cluster of contexts, including the insular world of United Nations meetings and diplomacy, the reality of environmental disasters (Bhopal, Chernobyl), and the economic coups and political upheavals of the 1980s.

Through interviews and careful textual analysis, Borowy uncovers the disagreements that the WCED suffered on numerous issues, ranging from nuclear power to the idea of ecological limits. But no disagreement was more important than that of economic growth, which took center stage in the context of debates between delegates from the North and South over the character of "development" and whether the South had a kind of "right" to grow its way out of poverty and get in on the higher levels of consumption enjoyed in the North (Borowy 2014, 5 and 127). Although some of the 22 members of the WCED had read and appreciated the *Limits to Growth*, such as Jim MacNeill, a Canadian and a veteran of the Organization for Economic Cooperation and Development (OECD) Environmental Directorate, the majority of committee members, including the outspoken Slovenian economist Janez Stanovnik, believed not only that economic growth and environmental conservation were "compatible," but that the world would have to grow its way out of the current environmental crisis (ibid., 86, 97–98, 113). The ideology of growth ultimately benefitted from the WCED's ambiguous position. The final draft of the WCED's *Our Common Future* "implied that economic growth, when it was not misdirected, was helpful and, indeed, necessary," and the committee steered clear of "the vocabulary of the limits-to-growth approach" (ibid., 111 and 127). Borowy elaborates here on the WCED's contradictory attitude toward growth:

> The text acknowledged that the idea of continued economic growth evoked concerns about an increased environmental burden, so that the result might merely replace the degradation of poverty with the degradation of affluence without being any more sustainable. But it brushed aside these fears with references to promising trends in a tangible "dematerialization" of Northern economies and to apparent "moves to other, newer kinds of growth, involving higher levels of personal development, physically, intellectually and spiritually." Unlike growth in a traditional sense, this new kind of growth would know no limits.
>
> (ibid., 135–136)

In other words, *Our Common Future* wanted to have its cake and eat it, too: It wanted to shed the negative aspects of growth while creating the conditions for endless economic expansion (Caradonna 2014, ch. 4; Du Pisani 2006, 87–88). Although it is not, properly speaking, a work of neoclassical economics, it did share with mainstream economic thought the assumption that growth is not *inherently* a problem and that, given the right circumstances, it could continue indefinitely.

Key texts

Ambiguity about economic growth appears in numerous documents, committee proceedings, and conferences from the 1980s and 1990s, all of which helped give sustainable development its original, core identity. What follows is an analysis of three key texts that played a central role in forging the character of sustainable development.

One can locate ambiguous views toward growth and economic policy in what is perhaps the first document to offer a concrete definition of sustainable development: The *World Conservation Strategy: Living Resource Conservation for Sustainable Development* (1980), written by the International Union for the Conservation of Nature (IUCN). The United Nations Environment Programme (UNEP) had commissioned this scientific body, an organization made up of some 700 scientists from over 100 countries, to produce a report that would "help advance the achievement of sustainable development through the conservation of living resources" (IUCN 1980, iv). The report defined development as "the modification of the biosphere and the application of the human, financial, living and non-living resources to satisfy human needs and improve the quality of human life. For development to be sustainable," the report continues, "it must take account of social and ecological factors, as well as economic ones" (ibid., Introduction, n.p.). This definition, and this project, is important because it reflects a shift in environmental consciousness from strict conservationism to a more integrative philosophy of social transformation that recognized the dynamic interplay between environmental, economic, and social factors. The IUCN played no small part in helping to establish sustainable development as an identifiable discourse and a lens through which to view the world's complex problems.

But the *World Conservation Strategy* offers conflicting ideas on the role of economics in changing the course of global development. It presses for a "new international economic order," making allusion to the UN's 1974 Declaration on the Establishment of a New International Economic Order, and advocates for the need to "regulate international trade" to ensure that resources in developing countries are not exploited. But then, a few pages later, the report lauds growth policies and suggests that "trade be liberalized, including the removal of all trade barriers to goods from developing countries," echoing the logic of free-trade agreements, such as GATT, which existed until it was supplanted by the World Trade Organization in 1995 (ibid., 32–33; Dale 2001, 82). This inconsistency reflects the fact that the *World Conservation Strategy*, as with many of these UN-backed documents, was written by numerous individuals, often with incommensurable points of view. But the key point here is that the IUCN did *not* narrow in on economic growth, or free trade, as a root cause of the decline in "living resources" that it chronicled. What stands out the most in this report is often what is left out.

Our Common Future, which was produced by the WCED (1983–1987), itself backed (albeit lukewarmly) by UNEP and many national governments, is even more contradictory on matters of economic strategy, in part reflecting the different views of its 22 constituent members, 12 of whom came from the South, seven from the West, and three from the East. The report, at times, defends the notion of ecological limits and denounces growth for producing environmental degradation, industrial pollution, and resource overconsumption in the developed world. But it often vacillates back toward a mainstream economic position and even calls for a "new era of economic growth" (WCED 1987, 12). At one point, the report uses the dreaded term "sustainable economic growth" that came to symbolize sustainable development's image in the 1990s as a troubling and oxymoronic form of groupthink (ibid., ch. 4). In fact, *Our Common Future* mentions "economic growth" on at least 42 occasions, and mostly in favorable terms. It even defends growth in the sentence following its famous definition of sustainable development: "Sustainable development seeks to meet the needs and aspirations of the present without compromising the ability to meet those of the future. Far from requiring the cessation of economic growth, it recognizes that the problem of poverty and under-development cannot be solved unless we have a new era of growth in which developing countries play a large role and reap large benefits" (ibid., ch. 1).[7] Thus the idea is that the impoverished Southern countries are meant to grow their way out of poverty, but the report never really squares the circle between this apparent imperative and the broadly defined "costs" of growth. Nor does it seriously address the need for the global North to consume less.

In certain places, the report is more sobering about the externalized costs of growth, noting the human economy's "profound impacts upon the biosphere [...]. Much of the economic growth pulls raw materials from forests, soils, seas, and waterways"[8] (ibid., 4). But the prevailing, if altogether muddled, message of the report is that growth and conservation are compatible and that growth is "absolutely essential to relieve the great poverty that is deepening in much of the developing world" (ibid., 1). Elsewhere: "We have in the past been concerned about the impacts of economic growth upon the environment. We are now forced to concern ourselves with the impacts of ecological stress – degradation of soils, water regimes, atmosphere, and forests upon our economic prospects" (ibid., 5). Why are concerns about growth relegated to "the past"? This passage makes it clear that the WCED, parting ways with the Club of Rome and the ecological economics of the 1970s, ultimately did not view growth as a necessary cause of "ecological stress," but rather a matter largely separate from it, given the Commission's faith in future dematerialization and economic decoupling. The report does not do enough to explain how growth is supposed to continue without access to cheap and abundant fossil fuels or without deepening the ecological crises that began with the Industrial Revolution and only magnified in the great age of post-War growth. It also does not explain how the developing world is supposed to reap the benefits of growth without taking the same destructive path as the global North, much of whose growth was based upon cheap labor and resources extracted from the global South. The Commission found it very difficult, indeed, to reconcile poverty reduction imperatives, the desire to empower the South, and the reality of global environmental limits.

The third and final example to cite is the UN Rio Earth Summit of 1992, along with *Agenda 21*, the non-binding, voluntary action plan for sustainable development that emerged out of the conference. This much-publicized gathering included representatives from 172 countries, along with thousands of NGOs, and reproduced, on a larger scale, many of the same divisions that plagued the WCED, the most important of which was the divide between the global North and South (Borowy 2014, 188).[9] Yet the enduring message at Rio was that "it would be possible to have economic growth, eliminate poverty and safeguard the environment all at the same time, a position," according to Borowy, "which even some participants were skeptical about" (Borowy 2014, 91). The Rio summit often addressed the corollaries of industrialism and economic growth, such as the troubling concentration of greenhouse gases in the atmosphere – the summit gave birth to the Framework Convention on Climate Change (UN 1992c) – but it stopped short of criticizing economic growth itself. It also produced the Convention on Biological Diversity (UN 1992b) but avoided, in this document, economic growth altogether, and did not suggest that the biggering of the human economy had played a major role in reducing diversity or contributing to mass species extinction. In fact, if the documents that the summit generated are any testament, then the Rio gathering was often less critical of growth than the IUCN or the WCED, despite the fact that by 1992 the base of research that demonstrated links between industrial growth and environmental degradation had only grown.[10]

Agenda 21 uses the term "economic growth" on at least 21 occasions, and employs "sustainable economic growth" intermittently throughout. The multiple authors of this 700-page document subscribed, for the most part, to the same compatibility thesis associated with the WCED. That is, this UN-backed plan wanted policies that "make economic growth and environmental protection mutually supportive" (UN 1992a, §2.9, 136). But whereas the WCED, and the IUCN before it, had acknowledged, at the very least, that economic growth could produce negative consequences to human societies and the natural world, *Agenda 21* largely avoided this pesky reality. The best it could muster was a brief allusion to the fact that dissenting voices existed within the world of economics and development theory. "Some economists are questioning traditional concepts of economic growth and underlining the importance of pursuing economic objectives that take account of the full value of natural resource capital," the plan states (ibid., §4.6). However, the subject is quickly changed and the document returns to more saccharine statements about the possibility and utility of growth. "Investment is critical to the ability of developing countries to achieve needed economic growth to improve welfare of their populations and to meet their basic needs in a sustainable manner, all without deteriorating or depleting the resource base that underpins development" (ibid., §2.23). As was the case with *Our Common Future*, the plan says little about how one is supposed to achieve the twin goals of growth and environmental integrity, when the history of human development suggests that bigger economies necessarily use more energy and resources.[11] The only solution that the agenda could conjure was less "wasteful" and "material-intensive economic growth," repeating the WCED's fantastical notion of a dematerialized economic future.

Contexts

The context of 1980s geopolitics is crucial to understanding how it came to be that a "limits to growth" perspective was so politically unfeasible in the early formation of sustainable development, and conversely, why a favorable attitude toward growth was so normal and predictable. In this short chapter it would be impossible to describe exhaustively the dynamics at play that contributed to a normalization of pro-growth attitudes, but one can at least sketch out the most important contextual factors. It is also important to remember that attitudes toward growth in such organizations as UNEP, the WCED, and the OECD were ambiguously pro-growth, meaning that there was not a consensus, but rather a divided community, peppered with a vocal minority of individuals who questioned the logic, feasibility, and costs of growth, in broadly social, financial, and ecological terms. Borowy's book, for instance, is excellent at showing the dissenting voices on the question of growth that existed within the WCED, revealing just how impossible it was in this period to truly challenge the status quo (Borowy 2014, part 2).

The first contextual factor was the ongoing legacy of 1970s-era stagflation, when low growth rates and high inflation combined to create high unemployment rates and widespread disillusionment. Exacerbated by the first (1973) and second (1979) oil shocks, the economic difficulties of the 1970s exposed problems in Keynesian economics and ultimately led to the rise of Milton Friedman and his monetarist school of thought, in which governments tightly controlled the money supply and sought new ways to weaken financial regulation and spur growth (Victor 2008, 12; Borowy 2014, 46; Mirowski and Plehwe 2009). In the early 1980s, relatively few people were excited by a future without economic growth, given the difficulties of the preceding decade. It was less acceptable in the capitalist West to criticize growth in 1980 than it had been in, say, 1968, when Robert F. Kennedy, shortly before his assassination, roundly attacked the social utility of the Gross National Product (Kennedy 1968).[12] Even though first-wave ecological economists had used stagflation to discuss the inherent problems of a growth-obsessed economy, the lack of viable alternatives led to a redoubling of efforts among national governments to revive growth (Daly 1977; Schumacher 1973; Stivers 1976). Moreover, the idea of economic growth had become so normal within mainstream economic theory, and especially in the wake of Bretton Woods, that it was naturally a challenge to dispute mainstream beliefs about the need for a busier economy.

Second, the political winds had shifted in the 1980s, blowing in a strongly rightward direction. Ronald Reagan and Margaret Thatcher embodied this shift to political conservatism, monetarism, and privatization, and both leaders created regimes that excelled at "reducing taxes and welfare spending, curbing the influence of unions, privatizing state enterprises, minimizing subsidies and price controls and deregulating central economic sectors" (Borowy 2014, 44). The idea of limits fell by the wayside and fossil fuels were embraced like never before (Caradonna 2014, ch. 5).[13] Wall Street and the world of corporate finance found enthusiastic political backing, and a revival of commercialism, materialism, and corporate values defined the decade (Scheer 2010). Moreover, the Latin American debt crisis and the Volcker Shock, in which the US Federal Reserve suddenly and dramatically increased interest rates, sent much of the developing world into a paralyzing debt spiral that meant impossibly onerous debt payments and the need for yet more loans (Klein 2007, 199; Dienst 2011; Mason 2010; Ocampo 2014). Naomi Klein calls this economic maneuvering "disaster capitalism," and argues that disasters (both environmental and man-made) have been used since at least the 1980s to undermine global stability and produce economic growth through the manipulation of difficult circumstances. Further, much of this "economic shock therapy" has occurred with the help of powerful multinational corporations, relatively few of which cared much about sustainable development in the first place, and would have cared even less if the concept had not implied obvious financial benefits for private investors. Thus the defenders of sustainable development, and especially those in the "limits to growth" camp, had to cope not only with an emergent Washington Consensus, in which pro-growth policies, "deregulation and privatization came to be seen as the only reasonable economic policy option," but they also had to take into account the entrenched interests of corporations involved in international development, especially in the domains of manufacturing and resource extraction (Borowy 2014, 46; Hawken 1993).

A third, related factor is the decline of Communism and sudden growth of neoliberalism, itself spurred on by Reagan and Thatcher. The teetering and collapse of the Soviet Bloc created an unparalleled public relations victory for capitalism, which in any case was in the process of radical transformation in the late 1980s and early 1990s.[14] As Klein argues, "as long as Communism was a threat, the gentleman's agreement that was Keynesianism would live on; once the system lost ground, all traces of compromise could finally be eradicated, thereby fulfilling the purist goal [Milton] Friedman had set out for his movement [Chicago School of economics] a half century earlier." Thus for her, "neoliberalism" was "not some new invention but capitalism stripped of its Keynesian appendages, capitalism in its monopoly phase, a system that has let itself go – that no longer has to work to keep us as customers, that can be as antisocial, antidemocratic and boorish as it wants" (Klein 2007, 319). David Harvey has showed the degree to which neoliberalism became a force to reckon with by the 1980s. Those in the milieu of sustainable development had to deal with the apparent reality that the "fundamental mission" of development in this period was "to create a 'good business climate' and therefore to optimize conditions for capital accumulation no matter what the consequences for employment or social well-being," or, one might add, for the natural environment (Harvey 2006, 24). In many ways, the 1980s was the worst possible decade to seek significant changes to traditional forms of development.

A fourth and final contextual factor to mention is the simmering hostility between the industrialized North and the poorer countries of the global South. Tensions between North and South cropped up in the proceedings of the WCED and especially at the Rio Earth Summit. The debt crisis had increased the social and economic gulf separating richer and poorer countries, and many in the global South wanted either a shift in economic growth from North to South, and/or increased aid from the North, as a means of balancing out the benefits the North derived from labor and resources in the South.[15] (Macekura 2015, ch. 7). The WCED briefly weighed the possibility of suggesting reparation payments from North to South, but dropped this proposal when it proved too divisive (Borowy 2014, 60). Du Pisani has argued, "less-developed countries," especially at Rio, "were suspicious that sustainable development might be an ideology imposed by the wealthy industrialized countries to enforce stricter conditions and rules on aid to developing countries. There were fears that sustainable development would simply be employed to sustain the gap between developed and underdeveloped countries" (Du Pisani 2006, 93). Jim MacNeill wrote recently that Southern representatives to the WCED and other international organizations largely saw growth as something that the South had missed out on, and sought sustainable development as a means to rectify this apparent injustice (Borowy 2014, ix). Borowy sums it up nicely: "For countries [in the South] whose foremost goal was rapid development based on industrialization and substantial economic growth, the prospect of a shift to a non-growing economic system appeared like a sudden and unfair change of rules to their disadvantage" (ibid., 31; also Rice 2009).

Thus the early framers of sustainable development (1980–1992) had to contend with strong pressures on all sides to include favorable positions on growth in these various declarations and action plans. This pressure took multiple forms, ranging from the demands of neoliberal institutions to conservative political regimes to Chicago School ideologues to Third World governments and economists, the latter of whom wanted less growth up North and more down South. But all of the contextual factors described in this section made it so that growth became a central value and permanent feature within the agenda of sustainable development, where it has remained since the 1990s.[16] The purpose of this chapter is not to suggest that things could have been different, but rather to understand why and how growth came to play such a prominent role in ideas about sustainable development.

The fact that sustainable development was not particularly radical on the question of growth is confirmed by *Our Common Future*'s largely favorable reception amongst the cronies of Reagan and Thatcher. Although then-US Secretary of the Treasury James Baker disapproved of the traces of "'Limits to Growth' philosophy" in the document, many in the conservative establishment endorsed its message, and loved that it called for an annual economic growth rate of 3 percent – a rate that was not radically different from the 4–5 percent targeted by many neoclassical economists of the twentieth century (Borowy 2014, 172, 181; Schumacher 1973, 46). Sir Crispin Tickell, who represented the Thatcher government in a meeting with the WCED, lauded the Brundtland report for supporting "long-term economic growth," and Reagan's people found it similarly amenable to a neoliberal worldview (Borowy 2014, 160). Conservatives often cherrypicked passages from *Our Common Future* and *Agenda 21*, but ultimately realized that what became the Ur-texts of sustainable development presented, at worst, an alternative approach to endless economic biggering, which now had to take stock of environmental worries, but did not consider growth a problem in and of itself.

Conclusion: the thing about growth

The thing about growth is that it has many forms and multiple effects. According to the environmental historian J. R. McNeill, growth had many faces in the twentieth century and affected virtually every meaningful, measurable indicator. The world economy grew by factor-14 and industrial output by factor-40; world population (factor-4), urban population (factor-13), coal production (factor-7), water consumption (factor-9), air pollution (factor-5), carbon dioxide emissions (factor-17), all grew precipitously; forested land decreased by 20 percent and the blue whale population, hunted to near extinction for its oil, declined by 99.75 percent (McNeill 2000, 360–361). Anthropogenic climate change, which is already wreaking havoc on ecosystems, and which has been studied intensively since the 1980s, is a direct consequence of the industrial growth that the world has produced since the dawn of the Industrial Revolution. Per the US Environmental Protection Agency, "increases in concentrations of [greenhouse] gases since 1750 are due to human activities in the industrial era" (US EPA 2013). According to the 2005 Millennium Ecosystem Assessment, 15 of 24 crucial ecosystem services are severely damaged, mostly because of human behavior (MEA 2005). More recently, a team of eminent scientists has collaborated to measure and assess the Earth's "planetary boundaries." They contend the Earth has at least nine such boundaries – climate change, biodiversity loss, nitrogen cycles, freshwater use, phosphorous cycles, land change rates, ocean acidification, chemical pollution, and atmospheric aerosol loading – with the first three boundaries already dangerously surpassed as of 2009 (Rockström et. al. 2014, 51–52). The team concludes that "the exponential growth of human activities is raising concern that further pressure on the Earth System could destabilize critical biophysical systems and trigger abrupt or irreversible environmental changes that would be deleterious or even catastrophic for human well-being" (ibid., 52). Clearly, growth is a complex problem and one that has direct consequences for the natural world and the human *oikonomia* that relies upon it. That is, growth magnifies pressures on biophysical systems and vitiates efforts to establish an egalitarian and stable global society. In short, sustainable development has not proven to be very compatible with aggregate economic growth.

Further, we now have new evidence that neither relative nor absolute decoupling (of economic growth from energy use, emissions, and resource consumption) has occurred if one sets aside national accounting methods for a more global perspective that internalizes the import sector; nor has the world experienced the long-hoped-for shift to a dematerialized economy.[17] The ecological economist Peter A. Victor has shown through modeling the Canadian economy that economic growth makes the job of fighting climate change all the more difficult. "For example, if an economy grows at 3% per year for 40 years, an average annual reduction in GHG intensity of 7.23% is required if GHG emissions are to be reduced by 80%. This compares with an average annual reduction in GHG intensity of 4.11% if there is no economic growth during that period" (Victor 2012, 207). To date, there has been no known society that has simultaneously expanded economic activity and reduced absolute energy consumption, and the only known periods in which global or regional emissions of carbon dioxide have declined were during instances of economic recession or disruptions to normal economic activity (Heinberg 2011; Schneider et al. 2010; Broder 2009).

The problem with the "compatibility thesis" endorsed by many actors within sustainable development is that it either ignores or misunderstands the multifaceted consequences of growth. There has been no shortage of data since the 1960s to show that economic growth brings with it a whole range of environmental and social costs that are poorly captured by conventional economic metrics, and that growth can be "uneconomic," in the sense that it brings short-term gains at the expense of long-term socio-economic stability. Far from being separate issues, economic growth and "ecological stress" are closely related, and scholars have known as much for nearly 50 years. Growth depletes resources and vitiates ecosystem functionality, both of which are necessary for the existence of a healthy economy, as the Canadian maritime provinces discovered after the collapse of the Atlantic northwest cod fishery in 1992 (Kurlansky 2010). Indeed, a steady stream of works has exposed the endemic problems of a growth-oriented economy, and the list of scholars and organizations that have addressed this issue is a long one.[18]

First-wave diplomats, commissioners, and policymakers of sustainable development had access to much of this scholarship – that is, to serious works by ecologists, ecological economists, and systems theorists who cast doubt on the role played by growth (especially in terms of material throughput and consumption) in the establishment of a sustainable society. But for a range of contextual reasons elicited above, the framers of sustainable development "chose" growth, and in doing so created a core identity for this philosophy that lacked the ability to truly redress conventional forms of development. The key documents associated with sustainable development largely avoided direct criticism of growth, choosing not to see economic expansion as an inherent problem, but only its *attendant corollaries*, which were (mostly) viewed as incidental to economic activity. Growth was so integral to the identity of industrialized society that to criticize it was as close to heresy as one could come in a secularized world. Moreover, the advocates for the global South often assumed that sustainable development meant reproducing (in fast forward) the development path taken by the global North, as though the pyrrhic victory of conventional industrialization was the only measuring stick of human advancement. In any case, the "limits to growth" camp clearly lost the debate, even if this defeat was not immediately apparent, and even though the idea of growth limits remains enduringly important (Turner 2012; Turner 2008; Bardi 2011).

A lot was at stake in this debate, and one consequence was that sustainable development ultimately (and often despite itself) remained within the broader ideological universe of mainstream economics. Sustainable development simply was not radical enough to challenge the status quo of industrial growth. Indeed, if we cite the UN's 2015 Sustainable Development Goals as evidence, then it is clear that a fundamentally favorable attitude toward growth still characterizes this approach to development. As we saw in this chapter via discussions of historiography, textual assessment, and contextual analysis, those behind sustainable development have not done enough to put growth *itself* under the spotlight.[19] It is, of course, impossible to say how things might have been different, but in choosing growth, the framers of sustainable development set back efforts to remake growth-oriented economics by at least a few decades. In general, sustainability economists of the present day do not believe that the vision of sustainable development provides workable solutions to our interlocking social, environmental, and economic problems (Martinez-Alier et. al. 2014; Borowy 2014, 10–11). And sustainable development will likely remain ineffective and unable to uproot the ultimate causes of environmental decline as long as it avoids the inherent problems of our sprawling industrial economy.

Notes

1 This claim is made by numerous historians, all of whom are cited in the section on historiography.
2 To be clear, the obsession with growth was not limited to neoclassical economic theory in the late twentieth century, and even the Soviet bloc countries sought economic expansion. However, given that neoclassical economic theory dominated conventional capitalist thought, I will use the term in this chapter as a kind of shorthand for mainstream economic theory. But growth played a prominent role in Keynesianism, neoliberalism, Soviet bloc Communism, and so on.
3 This was, in fact, one of the agenda items proposed to the WCED by the General Assembly of the UN.
4 Harding (2006, 232) shows that even the UN was calling sustainable development a failure by the early 2000s. The stalemates in international development policy at Johannesburg (2002), Copenhagen (2009), and Rio de Janeiro (2012) have only added to this sentiment. It is too soon to know whether the agreement at Paris (2015) will change this view.

5 However, the term "sustainable growth" goes back at least to 1960, and probably existed before that.
6 Dale (2012, 3–5); Dale (2001, 5). Note that the periodization that I use for the history of sustainable development differs from the one employed by Dale. I date the early formation of the concept between 1980 and 1992, not 1987 and 1995.
7 Note that the WCED offers variants of this definition of sustainable development a couple of times in the report. The definition gives priority to the needs of the poor and stresses the "limits" of the environment, hampered by the state of technology and social organization. See, e.g., beginning of ch. 2, 43.
8 The report has a section called "Industrial growth and its impact," but focuses mostly on the benefits of expanded industrial output in the twentieth century.
9 Note that it was at the Rio Earth Summit that the UN created the Sustainable Development Commission.
10 Between 1987 and 1992, the journal *Ecological Economics* came about and William E. Rees and Mathis Wackernagel began publishing on ecological footprint analysis, to give only two examples.
11 See discussion of this subject in the Conclusion of this chapter.
12 As far as I know, Kennedy was the last mainstream American political figure to openly criticize the value of economic growth, although Jimmy Carter might have come close at times.
13 In a highly symbolic move, newly elected president Ronald Reagan removed the solar panels from the roof of the White House that former President Jimmy Carter had installed.
14 The irony is that the Communist countries were also ardent disciplines of growth, albeit from a somewhat different point of view. They invested heavily in industry to drive up growth without regard for the environment.
15 See Macekura (2015, ch. 7). It is one of the central arguments of Macekura's book that environmentalists in the global North accepted and accommodated, mostly for political reasons, the aspirations for economic growth in the global South.
16 UN Sustainable Development Goals 2015. Goal number 8 cites "sustainable economic growth" as an objective.
17 Victor (2008); Jackson (2009); Monbiot (2015). One of the sources cited by Monbiot "reveals that while the UK's carbon dioxide emissions officially fell by 194 million tonnes between 1990 and 2012, this apparent reduction is more than cancelled out by the CO_2 we commission through buying stuff from abroad. This rose by 280m tonnes in the same period." Elsewhere: "A recent paper in the journal *Resources* found that the global consumption of materials has risen by 94% over 30 years, and has accelerated since 2000. 'For the past ten years, not even a relative decoupling was achieved on the global level.'" However, the report does reveal that there is a huge range of "domestic material consumption" between countries that rank high on the Human Development Index. The bottom line is that decoupling is a difficult thing to achieve and an even trickier thing to measure.
18 There are too many sources to mention in the text, since this literature is vast. Certainly the list of key texts would have to include the following: Boulding (1966); Mishan (1967); Mishan (1977); Georgescu-Roegen (1971); the Club of Rome 1972, 1992, 2004; Schumacher (1973); Daly (1973); Daly (1977); Odum and Odum (1976); Lovins (1977); Brown (1981); Rees and Wackernagel (1992); Heinberg (2003); Heinberg (2011); Victor (2008); Jackson (2009); Monbiot (2009); O'Neil (2012); Skidelsky and Skidelsky (2012); also, the many works by degrowth scholars from 2010 to 2015, including works by G. Kallis, F. Schneider, J. Martinez-Alier, C. Kerschner, and S. Latouche, some of which are cited in the bibliography.
19 It is important to keep in mind that even the economists most critical of growth, from Herman Daly (1977) to Daniel O'Neil (2012), acknowledge that some parts of the world, including Sub-Saharan Africa, could benefit from busier economies.

But they approach the issue from the point of view of ecological reality and also with the assumption that growth requires complex qualitative assessments. It is not a question of being absolutely pro or con but rather having a critical understanding of when growth is necessary, when it is not, when uneconomic growth is occurring, what the complex effects of growth are on society and the environment, and a clearer understanding of what it is that actually grows in a growing economy.

Bibliography

Bardi, U. 2011. *The Limits to Growth Revisited.* New York: Springer.

Bartlett, A. A. 1997–1998. "Reflections on Sustainability, Population, Growth, and the Environment – Revisited." *Renewable Resources Journal* 15(4): 6–23.

Borowy, Iris. 2014. *Defining Sustainable Development for Our Common Future: A history of the World Commission on Environment and Development (Brundtland Report).* New York: Earthscan.

Boulding, Kenneth E. 1966. "The Economics of the Coming Spaceship Earth." In *Environmental Quality in a Growing Economy*, edited by H. Jarret, 3–14. Baltimore: Resources for the Future/JHU.

Broder, J. M. 2009. "Emissions Fell in 2009, Showing Impact of Recession." *New York Times*, February 16.

Brown, Lester R. 1981. *Building a Sustainable Society.* New York: Norton.

Caradonna, Jeremy. 2014. *Sustainability: A History.* Oxford: Oxford University Press.

Dale, Ann. 2001. *At The Edge: Sustainable Development in the 21st Century.* Vancouver: UBC Press.

Dale, Ann. 2012. "Introduction." In *Urban Sustainability: Reconnecting Space and Place*, edited by A. Dale, W. T. Dushenko, P. Robinson. Toronto: Univ. of Toronto Press.

D'Alisa, Giacomo, Frederico Demaria and Giorgos Kallis, eds. 2014. *Degrowth: A Vocabulary For a New Era.* New York: Routledge.

Daly, Herman E. editor. 1973. *Toward a Steady-State Economy.* New York: Freeman.

Daly, Herman E. 1977. *Steady-State Economics.* San Francisco: Freeman.

Dienst, Richard. 2011. *The Bonds of Debt.* London: Verso.

Dryzek, John S. 2005. *Politics of the Earth: Environmental Discourses.* Oxford: Oxford University Press.

Du Pisani, Jacobus A. 2006. "Sustainable Development – Historical Roots of the Concept." *Environmental Science* 3(2): 83–96.

Georgescu-Roegen, Nicholas. 1971. *The Entropy Law and the Economic Process.* Cambridge: Harvard Univ. Press.

Goodland, Robert, Herman Daly, and Salah Serafy. 1991. *Environmentally Sustainable Economic Development: Building on Brundtland.* Environment Department working paper, no. ENV 46. Washington, DC: World Bank.

Harding, R. 2006. "Ecologically Sustainable Development: Origins, Implementation and Challenges." *Desalination* 187(1–3): 229–239.

Harvey, David. 2006. *Spaces of Global Capitalism: Towards a Theory of Uneven Geographical Development.* New York: Verso.

Hawken, Paul. 1993. *The Ecology of Commerce: A Declaration of Sustainability.* New York: Harper Business.

Heinberg, Richard. 2003. *The Party's Over: Oil, War and the Fate of Industrial Societies.* Gabriola, BC: New Society Publishers.

Heinberg, Richard. 2010. *Peak Everything: Waking up to a Century of Declines.* Gabriola: New Society Publishers.

Heinberg, Richard. 2011. *The End of Growth: Adapting to Our New Economic Reality.* Gabriola, BC: New Society Publishers.

IMF (International Monetary Fund). 2012. *World Economic Outlook Database, September 2011*. Accessed July 27, 2016. www.imf.org/external/ns/cs.aspx?id=28.

IUCN. 1980. *World Conservation Strategy: Living Resource Conservation for Sustainable Development*. Gland, Switzerland: IUCN.

Jackson, Tim. 2009. *Prosperity Without Growth: Economics for a Finite Planet.* London: Earthscan.

Kallis, G., Kerschner, C., and Martinez-Alier, J. 2012. “The Economics of Degrowth.” *Ecological Economics* 84: 172–180.

Kennedy, Robert F. 1968. “Speech on 18 March 1968.” Accessed July 27, 2016.http://www.jfklibrary.org/Research/Research-Aids/Ready-Reference/RFK-Speeches/Remarks-of-Robert-F-Kennedy-at-the-University-of-Kansas-March-18-1968.aspx.

Klein, Naomi. 2007. *The Shock Doctrine: The Rise of Disaster Capitalism*. New York: Picador.

Kurlansky, Mark. 2010. *Cod: A Biography of the Fish that Changed the World*. Penguin Books.

Latouche, Serge. 2010. *Farewell to Growth*. Cambridge: Polity.

Lovins, Amory. 1977. *Soft Energy Paths: Towards a Durable Peace*. New York: Penguin.

Macekura, Stephen. 2015. *Of Limits and Growth: The Rise of Global Sustainable Development in the Twentieth Century.* Cambridge: Cambridge University Press.

Martinez-Alier, Joan, U. Pascual, F.-D. Vivien and E. Zaccai. 2014. “Sustainable Degrowth: Mapping the Context, Criticisms and Future Prospects of an Emergent Paradigm.” In *Sustainable Development: Critical Concepts in the Environment*, Vol. 4, edited by J. Blewitt, 77–94. New York: Routledge.

Mason, Paul. 2010. *Meltdown: The End of the Age of Greed*. New York: Verso.

McKibben, Bill. 1996. “Buzzless Buzzword.” *New York Times*, April 10.

McNeill, John R. 2000. *Something New Under the Sun: An Environmental History of the Twentieth-Century World.* W.W. Norton.

MEA (Millennium Ecosystem Assessment). 2005. *Ecosystems and Human Well-Being: Biodiversity Synthesis.* Washington, DC: World Resource Institute.

Meadows, D. H., Meadows, D. L., Randers, J., BehrensIII, W.W. 1972. *The Limits to Growth*. New York: Universe Books.

Mebratu, Desta. 1998 “Sustainability and Sustainable Development: Historical and Conceptual Review.” *Environmental Impact Assessment Review* 18(6): 493–520.

Mill, John. S. 1848. *Principles of Political Economy.* London: John W. Parker.

Mirowski, Philip and Dieter Plehwe. editors. 2009. *The Road from Mont Pèlerin: The Making of the Neoliberal Thought Collective.* Cambridge: Harvard University Press.

Mishan, E. J. 1967. *The Cost of Economic Growth*. London: Staples.

Mishan, E.F. 1977. *Economic Growth Debate: An Assessment*. London: Allen & Unwin.

Mitcham, C. 1995. “The Concept of Sustainable Development: Its Origins and Ambivalence.” *Technological Society* 17: 311–326.

Monbiot, George. 2009. *Heat: How to Stop the Planet from Burning*. New York: Random House.

Monbiot, George. 2015. “False Promise.” Accessed November 24, 2015. www.monbiot.com.

Muir, John. 1901. *Our National Parks.* New York: Houghton Mifflin.

Ocampo, José A. 2014. “The Latin American Debt Crisis in Historical Perspective.” In *Life After Debt: The Origins and Resolutions of Debt Crisis,* edited by Joseph Stiglitz and D. Heymann. London: Palgrave Macmillan.

Odum, H. T. and Odum, E. C. 1976. *Energy Basis for Man and Nature.* New York: McGraw-Hill.

O’Neil. Daniel W. 2012. “Measuring Progress in the Degrowth Transition to a Steady State Economy.” *Ecological Economics* 84: 221–231.

Rees, William E. and Wackernagel, Mathis. 1992. “Ecological Footprint and Appropriated Carrying Capacity: What Urban Economics Leaves Out.” *Environment and Urbanization* 4(2): 121–130.

Rice, James. 2009. “North-South Relations and the Ecological Debt: Asserting a Counter-Hegemonic Discourse.” *Critical Sociology* 35: 225–252.

Rist, Gilbert 2010. “Is ‘Development’ a Panacea? How to Think Beyond Obsolete Categories.” *Canadian Journal of Development Studies/Revue d’études du développement* 30: 345–354.

Robinson, John A. 2004. “Squaring the Circle? Some Thoughts on the Idea of Sustainable Development.” *Ecological Economics* 48(4): 369–384.

Rockström, Johan *et al.* 2014. “Planetary Boundaries: Exploring the Safe Operating Space for Humanity.” In *Sustainable Development.* Vol. 1, edited by J. Blewitt, 51–117. New York: Routledge.

Scheer, Robert. 2010. *The Great American Stickup: How Reagan Republicans and Clinton Democrats Enriched Wall Street While Mugging Main Street.* Nation Books.

Schneider, Francois, Kallis, Giorgos, and Martinez-Alier, Joan. 2010. “Crisis or Opportunity? Economic Degrowth for Social Equity and Ecological Sustainability. Introduction to this Special Issue.” *Journal of Cleaner Production* 18: 511–518.

Schumacher, E.F. 1973. *Small is Beautiful: Economics as If People Mattered.* New York: HarperCollins.

Skidelsky, Robert and Skidelsky, Edward. 2012. *How Much is Enough? Money and the Good Life.* New York: Other Press.

Stivers, Robert L. 1976. *The Sustainable Society: Ethics and Economic Growth.* Philadelphia: Westminster.

Turner, Graham M. 2008. “A Comparison of the Limits to Growth with 30 Years of Reality.” *Global Environmental Change* 18: 397–411.

Turner, Graham M. 2012. “On the Cusp of Global Collapse? Updated Comparison of the Limits to Growth with Historical Data.” *Gaia* 21: 116–124.

UN. 1992a. *Agenda 21.* New York: United Nations.

UN. 1992b. *Convention on Biological Diversity.* New York: United Nations.

UN. 1992c. *Framework Convention on Climate Change.* New York: United Nations.

UNPop (UN Population Division). 2010. *World Population Prospects: The 2010 Revision.* New York: United Nations.

UN. “Sustainable Development Goals.” 2015. AccessedJuly 27, 2016. http://sustainabledevelopment.un.org/?menu=1300.

US EPA. 2013. “The Causes of Climate Change.” Accessed April 1, 2013. http://www.epa.gov/climatechange/science/causes.html.

Victor, Peter A. 2008. *Managing Without Growth: Slower by Design, not Disaster.* Edward Elgar Publishing.

Victor, Peter A. 2012. "Growth, Degrowth and Climate Change: A Scenario Analysis." *Ecological Economics* 84: 206–212.

WCED (World Commission on Environment and Development). 1987. *Report of the World Commission on Environment and Development: Our Common Future*. New York: Oxford University Press.

Worster, Donald. 1993. *The Wealth of Nature: Environmental History and the Ecological Imagination*. Oxford: Oxford University Press.

8 Sustainable degrowth

Historical roots of the search for alternatives to growth in three regions

Barbara Muraca and Matthias Schmelzer

In September 2014, more than 3,000 people from all around the world gathered at the University of Leipzig for the *4th International Conference for Ecological Sustainability and Social Equity*. Bringing together academics spanning multiple disciplines – mostly from the social sciences, economics, and humanities, but also engineers and natural scientists – as well as practitioners working on bottom-up alternative economies and social activists involved in struggles around ecology, social justice, or globalization, this conference represented the provisional climax of the international degrowth debate. The Leipzig conference marked a significant step for what is increasingly called the international degrowth movement: it brought into dialogue different streams and traditions of growth critique and laid the ground for a stronger international network and for alliances with other movements (Brand 2014; Eversberg and Schmelzer 2016). Yet, how did the degrowth movement emerge and what historical roots and inspirations does it invoke?

In the wake of the recent world economic crisis from 2007/8 onwards a new wave of critique of economic growth and of the limits of GDP accounting, as well as proposals for post-growth economics have been put forward by scholars and activists in the context of a broad public debate about the merits and pitfalls of policies geared toward economic growth (Stiglitz et al. 2010; Enquete-Commission in Germany; Beyond Growth Initiative of the EU). Not all critiques of growth and the related processes of ecological destruction and increasing global inequalities are part of the degrowth debate. Rather, degrowth can be understood as the most radical strand of this discussion, which aims at a social-ecological transformation of high-income societies.

Degrowth is both a new academic and societal perspective and a social movement, which emerged in France ("décroissance") and other Southern European countries in the 2000s and in the following decade spread to the English-speaking world ("degrowth") and the German-speaking region ("Post-wachstum" or "Wachstumsrücknahme") and beyond. While including the traditional critique of growth as a monetary rate (measured by GDP) and as a material flow that increases the pressure on ecosystems (measured by HANPP or ecological footprint), the degrowth perspective focuses on the structural and cultural function that the fixation on economic growth has been playing in modern, capitalist societies and envisions a radical transformation of basic social institutions. At its core it revolves around alternatives *to* growth and economic development (rather than alternative growth paths), a repoliticization of economic debates, and the claim that global environmental justice demands a reduction of the economic output in high-income countries and a fundamental socio-economic transformation aimed at achieving a good life for all.

As other contributions in this book clearly show, the critique of economic growth is not new. Especially the scholarly debate is familiar with a long list of contributions that date back not only to the 1970s, but basically to the very emergence of the growth paradigm. While the critique of economic growth is largely well-known (see also the contributions by Macekura, Fioramonti, and Caradonna in this volume), we know relatively little about the historical precursors and roots of the current degrowth alternative. The established narrative within the degrowth discourse about the so-called "sources" of degrowth mainly highlights the intellectual origins of the French-inspired original *décroissance* debate and neglects other relevant references for the overall critique of growth that might have been less crucial for the original French discussion (Muraca 2013; Demaria et al. 2013; Kallis et al. 2014). While there are good historical reasons for this (the term "décroissance" originated in French and then spread to other regions also thanks to the research community around the network Research & Degrowth (R&D) based in Barcelona), proponents from other geographical areas have not focused to the same degree or not at all on making explicit their historical sources and on systematizing their contribution.

In a similar vein, British and Canadian economists Tim Jackson and Peter Victor, who both published groundbreaking books in 2009, have claimed that at that time they were the only economists working on the question of economies without growth, thus failing to acknowledge parallel discussions going on in other countries (and languages) at that time. It was only recently that, sparked by the international degrowth conferences in 2008 in Paris, 2010 in Barcelona, 2012 in Venice, 2014 in Leipzig, and 2016 in Budapest, these debates started to internationalize and bring different traditions into a fruitful dialogue. The internationalization of the degrowth debate demands a more accurate analysis of its different streams.

In this chapter we aim at reconstructing some key passages in the longer-term history of the precursors and roots of the current degrowth alternative along three main ideal-typical paths (both in a geographical and in substantial sense of the term): the English-speaking critique of economic growth; the Southern European degrowth perspective; and the German discussions about alternatives to growth. Of course the distinction is primarily analytical, as some lines of debates and some authors have played a major role in all three branches – a point we will come to later. Yet, identifying these three main types of degrowth debates in three geographically separate yet interlinked discursive spaces allows for a more nuanced and less one-sided historical reconstruction of the international degrowth perspective.

We deliberately limit our analysis to the period from the late 1960s onwards and to three regions in the global North. The late 1960s and the 1970s experienced a phenomenal wave of growth critiques, dozens of bestsellers were discussed by broad sections of society, and in combination with the "world revolution of 1968" the ideological foundations of the postwar compromise of embedded liberalism, growthism, and consumerism in countries around the world were shaken (Wallerstein 1989; Schmelzer 2016). Most prominently, the famous report to the Club of Rome *Limits to Growth* – published in 1972 with a staggering public relations campaign – made many aware that at least in the long term, unlimited growth was not possible on a finite planet (Meadows et al. 1972; Kupper 2004). The intense discussions critical of expansion, exploitation, and materialism, which developed in this period in the context of new social movements and the search for alternative ways of living, still form the ideological background of current degrowth debates (Nehring 2009; Hahn 2006; Nussbaum 1973). Furthermore, degrowth is explicitly a proposal *from* and *for* the global North. It rejects the idea of a universal societal path for all regions and aims at increasing the ecological space left for poor economies to develop independently of the growth imperative. In this vein, we also focus only on historical roots within debates in North America and Europe, knowing that this only provides a very partial picture of debates elsewhere as well as of transnational links (see for example Kothari et al. 2014; Martinez-Alier 2012; Escobar 2015; Barkin et al. 2012). While we cannot address in a detailed way all these developments here, our modest aim is to offer an overview of some different historical tracks of progressive and radical precursors to degrowth by showing their overlapping ground, differences, and possible future perspectives. Through this analysis we hope to disclose the specificity of the degrowth discourse within the larger family of growth-critiques.

Critiques of growth and the steady state economy: the debate in English-speaking countries

The Romanian-born American mathematician and economist Nicholas Georgescu-Roegen (1906–1994) not only laid some of the most crucial foundations for the degrowth movement, but can also be considered the liaison point of the different traditions of growth critique that we examine in this chapter. We thus start our analysis with a short examination of some of his key ideas.

After many years of groundbreaking work in econometrics, Georgescu-Roegen developed what can be considered the foundation of ecological economics and what he then called "bioeconomics" (Bonaiuti 2010). In the book *The Entropy Law and the Economic Process* (1971), he rethought the foundations of economics in terms of a social science that should be modeled on biology rather than (classical) physics. According to Georgescu-Roegen, economic processes are similar to biological "open systems" and are therefore creative, metabolic, and qualitatively transformative. Like biological processes, they feed on the low entropy of their environment. However, while biological organisms feed on the single "infinite" source of low entropy available on the planet, i.e. the solar energy as it is captured and rendered available by the Earth's surface (*Land*), economic processes – starting with the industrial revolution – deplete the so-called terrestrial stocks of low entropy (fossil fuels, mineral resources), which are not infinite in size and whose regeneration takes geological times. Whereas the flow rate of terrestrial stocks can be more or less adapted to society's needs, the flow of solar energy and of most renewable sources might be infinite in its amount, but not at our disposal with regard to the flow rate of its use.

In this perspective, the shift to non-renewable sources with the fossil-based industrial revolution has disentangled humans from the temporal limitation that the regeneration of renewable energies required, yet at the expense of an accelerated depletion of terrestrial stocks. Based on this analysis, which was backed up by thermodynamic thinking, Georgescu-Roegen pointed out the crucial importance of the so-called *maintenance flows* for the regeneration of what he called the *agents* of production or *Funds*, i.e. *Land, Capital* proper, and *Labour*. The continued reliance on non-renewable energy might enable an intensification of human production in some regions of the world for some time, but it necessarily jeopardizes this very option for the future and for other regions (Georgescu-Roegen 1971; Bonaiuti 2010; Muraca 2010; Petridis et al. 2015).

Georgescu-Roegen's analyses were far-reaching and revolutionary for his time: Even before the problem of the absorption capacity of sinks (such as soil, atmosphere, and water) was discussed besides the scarcity of resources, he showed that continuous economic growth is not compatible with the continuation of the human species on earth. In the years following the publication of his main book, he was a most welcomed guest for lectures in France, Italy, and Spain, where his bioeconomics attracted scholars and activists alike. However, with some notable exceptions, his later works did not meet with great attention within the English-speaking world, which was more interested in the rather technocratic and top-down perspective stemming from the advice of the Club of Rome than in his biophysical analysis of the impossibility of infinite growth (Hajer 1995). It was one of his students, the US economist Herman Daly, who had a stronger influence on how ecological economics developed throughout the coming decades. The controversy and differences between the two are key to understanding the particular thrust of degrowth thinking until today (see also Duverger 2011a).

The discipline of ecological economics was developed in the English-speaking world in the 1980s by a group of scholars aiming at integrating the academic disciplines of economics and environmental sciences (Costanza and Daly 1987). They generally shared a dissatisfaction with the flaws of national income accounting (Hueting 1980) and a strong interest in system theory. In particular, Kenneth Boulding's contributions to parallel economic and ecological systems and Howard T. Odum's *Environment, Power, and Society* (1971) inspired input-output analyses and ecological systems analyses. The controversies that Georgescu-Roegen outlined with respect to the function of mathematical modeling, technological optimism, and economic growth have characterized the discipline up to these days. According to Daly, ecological economics aimed at a "paradigm shift" in the Kuhnian sense within economics – to overcome the anomalies that were seen in "growthmania" and to provide a suitable alternative (Daly 1973a). Key issues were the biophysical constraints on economic growth, including population growth, a re-orientation toward ultimate values,[1] and an adjustment to a steady state.

While Daly's understanding of the steady state economy has changed over time, the emphasis on stable minimal throughput of matter/energy and on stabilizing population has remained constant. Daly's normative concept of a steady state is

> an economy with constant stocks of people and artifacts, maintained at some desired, sufficient levels by low rates of maintenance 'throughput', that is, by the lowest feasible flows of matter and energy from the first stage of production (depletion of low entropy materials from the environment) to the last stage of consumption (pollution of the environment with high entropy wastes and exotic materials).
>
> (Daly 1992, 16; see also Daly 1973b, 152)

Georgescu-Roegen vigorously opposed the concept of a "steady state" and instead promoted what he termed a "declining state," intended in Mill's positive sense as a chance for a better social life (Georgescu-Roegen 1977). In 1979, this term was translated – with Georgescu-Roegen's approval – into the French "décroissance" and the surrounding arguments proved decisive for the degrowth movement until today (Georgescu-Roegen 1979). In his perspective, the very idea of a steady state is not only physically impossible due to the constant increase in entropy and the dynamic process that characterize living beings, but also a rather cynical prospect for poor countries:

> Of course, the idea of getting into a steady state was greatly applauded in the advanced countries; indeed, those people would have been happy to go on living in the same kind of dwellings, to drive the same types of automobiles, and to eat the same appetizing food. But they did not realize that they were the victims of a great illusion. Strangely, very strangely, no priest of the steady state creed came to think that for the people from lands of scarcity – from Bangladesh, for example – the steady state prescription would certainly mean a life sentence to misery.
>
> (Georgescu-Roegen 1989, 167)

While reducing population growth remains an important goal from a thermodynamic perspective,[2] this should not divert attention from the mindless intensification of production and consumption in industrialized countries that does not serve what he calls the "enjoyment of life" (the real goal of the economy), but the profit and power machine (Georgescu-Roegen 1975, 378).[3]

On the same line of thought Georgescu-Roegen rejected the concept of "sustainable development," in which he saw a new alluring logo aimed at salvaging growth by means of a sustainable make-up, i.e. ultimately at maintaining the living standard of Western countries while formally acknowledging the needs of so-called developing countries, without realizing the immanent contradiction of this assumption (Georgescu-Roegen 1989). As we will argue in the next section, this attempt at avoiding this contradiction constitutes the basis for the Southern European degrowth-tradition, which also developed out of the rejection of "sustainable development" with the argument that this is not environmentally feasible and that, at least for the countries in the global North, economic downscaling is the only viable and globally just alternative to the current growthmania.

However, as argued above, in the 1980s and 1990s this more radical critique of growth had little influence in the English-speaking world. In conjunction with the worldwide discourse on sustainable development, a substantial critique of GDP – and GDP growth – as the main focus of public policy gained momentum and was rediscovered from the 1990s onwards. In particular, all over the world lists of sustainability indicators and dashboards appeared (Cassiers 2015). In a more recent renaissance of this critique, research on subjective indicators (Layard 2005) and mixed assessments (both subjective and objective, see NEF 2012) are being developed with moderate, yet increasing attention by policy makers. It was not before the late 2000s that the question of the end of growth and degrowth scenarios reemerged. In 2008 the Canadian economist Peter Victor developed a de-growth scenario for Canada (Victor 2008). One year later, the work of the British *Sustainable Development Commission*, initiated by the Labour Government in 2000, marked a pivotal step in the growth-critique-discourse when its Economics Commissioner, Tim Jackson, published the highly controversial study *Prosperity Without Growth: Economics for a Finite Planet*. Jackson's book, that develops a macroeconomic alternative to economic growth, that can keep and increase the quality of life, an alternative based on Sen's and Nussbaum's capabilities approach, spurred a new wave of growth critique not only in the English-speaking world, but internationally (Jackson 2009).

It is debatable whether Jackson can be considered a representative of degrowth or rather of the steady state à la Daly, as his position does not involve a radical critique of basic economic and social structures. The Southern European degrowth debate was at that time little known to the English-speaking world due to language barriers. Nevertheless, one of the endorsements of the book states: "Jackson's clear and practical vision leads the burgeoning De-Growth movement."[4]

Similarly, with the exception of Georgescu-Roegen, it is not clear whether the other positions in the English-speaking debate can be framed as part of the degrowth discourse in a strict sense. They share some common ground in the critique of growth-based economies, but diverge when it comes to consider drivers and alternatives. While – as discussed in the next section – several degrowth thinkers such as the French philosopher and economist Serge Latouche have clearly positioned the degrowth alternative politically within the left and emancipatory tradition, Daly has consistently framed the steady state economy as a third way and rejected a more straightforward critique of capitalism (Daly 1980). Nevertheless, both the earlier debate fostered by Daly and the more recent renaissance of growth critique share some common ground: both rely on a critique of GDP-accounting; both present in-depth analyses not only of the environmental costs of growth, including the difficulties of decoupling GDP growth from environmental impacts such as climate change, but also from the social costs of growth, including cross-sector and time-scale analyses of the relationships between GDP growth with objective and subjective well-being; both focus on concrete and accessible (macro-) economic proposals for change that are targeted at a wider community and at policy makers. Moreover, the focus on alternative ways of understanding well-being related to a no-longer growing economy complement the political-economic discussion. However, the degrowth discourse addresses also the structural role that growth has played for the stabilization of modern, capitalist societies (Petridis et al. 2015) and the symbolic-cultural pervasiveness with which the growth logic has permeated all spheres of social life.

Décroissance: the debate in Southern European countries

The French term "décroissance" first appeared in the political and cultural arena in the early 1970s in conjunction with the publication of *Limits to Growth* at the peak of the crisis of the growth paradigm and in the midst of a heated public debate (Meadows et al. 1972; Duverger 2011a). In 1972, French intellectual and political theorist André Gorz was the first to use the term in a positive and normative sense. While earlier uses can be found (e.g. Pierre Vilar in 1960, see Sutter 2016), in a lively debate organized in Paris by *Le Nouvel Observateur*, Gorz posed the fundamental question that still shapes debates today: "Is the earth's balance, for which no-growth – or even degrowth – of material production is a necessary condition, compatible with the survival of the capitalist system?" (cited in Kallis et al. 2014, 1; Asara 2015, 25).

Rooted in the public debate sparked by *Limits to Growth* and by the commissioner of the European Community Sicco Mansholt's public promotion of a planned democratic socialism not based on growth, in the following years the term "décroissance" was used by various French authors (Duverger 2011a). However, it was only with a collection of papers by Georgescu-Roegen translated into French and entitled *Demain la Décroissance: Entropie – Écologie – Économie* that the term was established in its more specific meaning as an alternative to steady state and to zero growth within the French debate (Georgescu-Roegen 1979; Grinevald 2011).

The French birth of the term "décroissance" reveals some key elements of its original meaning: from the very beginning it appeared on the scene as a twofold concept that merged a technical-economic critique of growth and of mainstream economics with a rather socio-cultural critique of the paradigmatic logic of late capitalism. The influence of the *Situationists* (an intellectual current of anti-authoritarian social revolutionaries, avant-garde artists, intellectuals, and political theorists prominent in Western Europe in the 1960s) in conjunction with a specific variant of heterodox Marxism strongly aware of ecological issues (Cornelius Castoriadis, André Gorz, Ivan Illich, Herbert Marcuse), French personalism (Jacques Ellul, Bernard Charbonneau), and finally neo-rural movements close to the French tradition of left-catholicism[5] played a major role in what scholars more recently called "degrowth à la Française" (Duverger 2011b; Martínez-Alier et al. 2010). Together with one novel element, also rooted in the antagonistic discourses of the 1970s, it were these currents that proved decisive for the renaissance of degrowth in the 1990s: the critique of the Western model of development as it has been framed by the no-global, or – as it was called in France – the *altermondialist* movement.

Between Gorz's diagnosis of limits to growth as a chance for a radical social transformation and the revival of growth critique in the late 1990s something happened that shifted the debate on growth: the expansion of those very limits in (at least) three important directions and the incorporation of environmental issues into the dominant paradigm of growth and development. Briefly, the three changes that boosted new possibilities for economic growth were the deregulation of the financial markets with the end of the Bretton Woods system, globalization as a model of territorial expansion without invading other countries that made available and accessible natural resources, and the implementation of a neoliberal culture of self-enhancement that contributed to what degrowth critics later called the "colonization of the imaginary."[6] However, the message of the Club of Rome did not completely go unheeded and was incorporated into a new framework to secure a model of development based on economic growth, while also including environmental and social concerns. The normative goal of a "sustainable development" was originally based on the Brundtland commission's report, which contained nuanced analyses and focused on redistribution, legal obligations, possible limits, and on closely linking social and ecological questions in a context of global inequalities (Borowy 2014). However, within governments and international organizations, this critical thrust was soon diluted: While environmental protection first appeared in the public as an issue that was seen to be in conflict with economic growth and could at best be balanced, this relationship was soon reversed. Economic growth and the environment did not have to be balanced, but could be integrated, it was argued (Hajer 1995; Schmelzer 2016). In spite of critical voices present at the Rio summit, the concept of sustainable development ultimately established itself in its mainstream version as a working compromise between environmentalists and developmentalists. More or less successfully, it became the overarching paradigm for alternative paths of (rather than replacements of) economic growth more consistent with ecological limits, as Georgescu-Roegen clearly spotted. The German framework on ecological modernization (see next section) represents one of the most successful variants of that very model. Sustainable development replaced for more than two decades the controversy on economic growth, which only remained present under the surface, albeit without significant public resonance. Against this background, it is rather indicative that the French translation of sustainable development ended up manifesting one specific direction of the Rio compromise: *développement durable* (literally, enduring development) clearly embodied the idea that what had to be sustained was ultimately economic growth.

Starting in Southern French ecological, anti-consumerist, anarchist, and non-violent activist circles, the term was again taken up in the late 1990s, and in July 2001, Lyon-based intellectuals Bruno Clémentin and Vincent Cheynet launched the term "sustainable degrowth." It is remarkable to notice here that "développement durable" was counteracted by "décroissance soutenable," where the term "sustainable" should explicitly refer to a degrowth path that guarantees social justice, thus echoing some of the more critical voices involved in the Rio summit. Moreover, as Serge Latouche, one key exponent of the French *décroissance*, repeatedly says, a key early event for the revival of radical growth critique was a colloquium at UNESCO in 2002 in Paris entitled "Défaire le développement, refaire le monde" (Undoing development, redoing the world), which brought together over 800 environmental activists and post-development scholars. The event marked the new visage of degrowth as a radical critique of development.

From France the term soon gained a strong foothold in Southern European countries, facilitated by the language familiarity and some common inspirational sources.

In the following years *décroissance, decrescita*, or *decrecimiento* developed not only into a vibrant concept in intellectual and scholarly debates, but also into an interpretative frame used by and for social movements engaged in initiatives for car-free cities or food cooperatives, in anti-globalization activities, in protests against large infrastructures or advertisement, and in environmental campaigns (Demaria et al. 2013; Martínez-Alier et al. 2010; Petridis et al. 2015).[7] In 2007 the academic collective *Research & Degrowth* was founded and promoted a series of international conferences that helped to further internationalize and institutionalize degrowth both as an academic concept and as an activist slogan, and which grew from 200 participants in Paris in 2008, over further conferences in Barcelona (2010), Montreal and Berlin (2011), Venice (2012), to 3,000 participants in Leipzig in 2014, and over 500 in Budapest in 2016. The degrowth community is a heterogeneous platform that summons different social movements, experiments, and more or less antagonistic initiatives under the common umbrella of a structural (economic and institutional) and socio-cultural (modes of subjectivation, social imaginary, colonization of the lifeworld) critique of economic growth as the main point of fixation of late capitalistic societies. As the French political thinker Paul Ariés once said, degrowth is a *mot obus* (Ariés 2005), a projectile word, because it has the power to hit modern growth-societies at their very core. While attempts at a right-wing appropriation of the degrowth-narrative in terms of encapsulated local, self-sufficient, culturally homogeneous communities can be observed in France (De Benoist 2007), these perspectives so far did not gain a foothold within the degrowth movement.

The Spanish degrowth tradition is more evidently inspired by a merging of political ecology with ecological economics. In this specific variant of degrowth, thermodynamic and metabolic analyses complement both economic and socio-political perspectives. A fruitful dialogue with steady state perspectives is ongoing: according to Martinez-Alier degrowth is considered a necessary step to reach a sustainable level for a steady-state economy, thus taking into account Georgescu-Roegen's critique of steady state economics and sustainable development as a cynical project to maintain the current economic path of industrialized countries. The main focus is here not so much on absolute limits of growth as scientifically given barriers, but on the catastrophic consequences of a continuous trend of pushing those limits further in the global North at the expense of countries of the global South in general and more specifically of marginalized social groups, indigenous people, small farmers, and the poor. Degrowth is envisioned as a biophysical and normative necessity from the point of view of global environmental justice, a perspective lacking in the English-speaking tradition. Martinez-Alier, around which the group R&D has formed, promotes an alliance between degrowth in the global North and environmental justice movements (which he frames under the concept of "environmentalism of the poor" to indicate the struggles *against* the Western model of development and the new extractivism offensive) (Martínez-Alier 2012).

In France and Italy the anthropological critique of *economism*[8] and of utilitarianism as it is embodied by mainstream economic thinking has played a key role in framing the local degrowth movements. The French scholar network inspired by the anthropologist Marcel Mauss and called accordingly the M.A.U.S.S. (*Mouvement Anti-Utilitariste dans les Sciences Sociales*) is an important terrain for Latouche, although it has never openly embraced degrowth. Its main exponent, Alain Caillé, has developed what he calls a third paradigm for social sciences, which counteracts both holism and individualism and is based on Mauss' core idea of the triadic structure of the gift (gift giving, gift receiving, and gift reciprocation) intended as the basic structure of the social bond, on which all kinds of rationally constructed social contracts rely (Caillé 2007). In line with this perspective, the French degrowth perspective is not limited to an economic analysis and critique of growth, but addresses the general socio-cultural paradigm that justifies growth as economic goal.

Caillé's elaboration plays a major role in Latouche's detailed critique of instrumental rationality and the performative power of the *utilitarian* paradigm: according to Latouche, the imposition of the Western model of development has implied the colonial exportation of instrumental rationality, which has replaced or threatened other forms of reasoning based on the awareness of reciprocity and relational dependency. In the logic of instrumental rationality, the means-goals relation is inverted. Forms of *rationalization*, which basically imply a more efficient allocation of services, lead to a reduction of diversity and autonomy – and thus of democratic power (Latouche 2001).

Common to both, the Spanish and French variants of degrowth, are – as already mentioned – political ecology and postdevelopment (Flipo 2009; Muraca 2013; Duverger 2011b), albeit in a slightly different understanding. The postdevelopment school, which became prominent under this heading from the 1990s onwards (Sachs 1992; Escobar 1995; Latouche 1993; Rist 1996), builds on the critique of development as a hegemonic, Western, and postcolonial idea. Accordingly, economic growth is not only *the* sole model of societal futures available for so-called underdeveloped countries that are expected to follow the normative path of the industrialized global North, but it also imposes itself in the mode of a pervasive imaginary that colonizes needs, desires, and relations (Muraca 2013). The Western logic of development reproduces itself by continuously recreating the basis for its self-legitimation (planned obsolescence, manipulation of desires, generation of the feeling of lack) and by driving people into a drug-addiction-like state, in which they lose their autonomy (i.e. the capacity to creatively deal with problems and find solutions adequate to the context) to the systemic and technical forces of the development machine (Illich 1978). Without romanticizing tradition and lifestyles in the global South, the postdevelopment critique seeks to identify alternatives *to* development rather than alternative development paths and emphasizes the key role of grass-roots and social movements in this process (Escobar 2015). While the French variant of degrowth focuses more on the critique of alienation, the Spanish stream exhibits a stronger proximity to anti-extractivism and environmental justice movements in Latin America.

Political ecology rejects apolitical explanations of environmental problems and re-politicizes the debate about how a society frames its relations to what it calls nature. As André Gorz has shown, the discourse about natural limits is perfectly compatible with an authoritarian path, in which scientifically proved ecological limits and other constraints serve to justify dictatorial political measures, thus undermining democracy. Political ecology, instead, critically analyzes the political process, in which society–nature relations are framed and – especially in its French tradition – fosters autonomy and ignites convivial practices against dominant technofascist paradigms (Gorz 1980). For Castoriadis (2010, 194–199) political ecology has the subversive power of questioning the capitalist imaginary of a constant increase of production and consumption and can implement a radical transformation of social institutions, i.e. radical change in the social imaginary. As a specific discipline, "political ecology studies the roots of social conflicts over access and use of the environment" and approaches environmental issues through the lens of social, distribution, and knowledge conflicts. Accordingly, costs and benefits in environmental change "are unevenly distributed along lines of class, race, ethnicity or gender" (www.politicalecology.eu). While the French *décroissance* is strongly indebted to Gorz and Castoriadis's theoretical framing of political ecology, the Spanish degrowth tradition is deeply rooted in the overlap between science and activism specific of the analysis of global environmental conflicts.[9]

Postgrowth: the debate in German-speaking countries

The broad debate criticizing growth that characterized the German public in the 1970s and 1980s has largely been forgotten. In particular in the early 1970s, growth criticisms were very articulate in Germany, stretching throughout the entire political spectrum. Highly controversial debates were waged even within churches and trade unions (Oltmans 1974; Steurer 2002). This literature – widely read and discussed at the time – testifies to the diversity of issues and motivations that shaped growth-critical debates in the 1970s, ranging from the distribution of work at a time of deindustrialization and continued mechanization, to antiauthoritarian self-determination, the critique of technology and expertocracy, and the safeguarding of the environment. Some of the more radical strands of these debates are taken up or echoed in the current post-growth discussion in Germany and will be discussed in this section.

Symptomatic for the depth of the debate about post-industrial societies beyond growth was the widely read book series aptly entitled *Technologie und Politik. Das Magazin zur Wachstumskrise* (Technology and Politics. The Journal on the Crisis of Growth) which was published between 1974 and 1985 by the publishing house Rowohlt. Edited by the politician and journalist Freimut Duve under consultation of various intellectual key figures of the international growth critical debate such as André Gorz, Ivan Illich, and Ernst von Weizäcker, its 22 volumes cover almost all the issues currently debated in the degrowth literature.[10] These issues ranged from several books on *Die Zukunft der Arbeit* (The Future of Work), starting with a collection of essays by Joachim Steffen, André Gorz, and others (1977), then publishing Hannah Arendt's *Vom Sinn der Arbeit* (The Meanig of Work) and Illich's *Nützliche Arbeitslosigkeit – eine gesellschaftliche Alternative* (Useful Unemployment – A Societal Alternative; 1978), to a series of essays by Gorz, Illich, Mike Cooley, and E. F. Schumacher under the title *Leben ohne Vollbeschäftigung* (Living without full employment, 1980), to the book *Frauen, die letzte Kolonie* (Women, the Last Colony) by Claudia v. Werlhof, Maria Mies, and Veronika Bennholdt-Thomsen (1983) (Duve 1974; see also Ullrich 1979). While only partly taken into account or cited in the current international or German degrowth literature, these works prefigured central arguments and could add not only historical, but also conceptual depth to current degrowth discussions, in particular in the areas of feminism, the role of work and employment, and non-capitalist forms of provisioning.

The critique of growth spanned the entire political spectrum. As in all times and places, conservative critiques of growth also flourished. To give just one example, the German writer and environmentalist Carl Amery demanded a fundamentally political understanding of nature (Amery 1985; on the conservative reactions more generally see Graf 2008).[11] More important for current degrowth debates were contributions from the left. For example, in 1972, the German Steel Workers Union (IG Metall) organized a large congress in Oberhausen entitled *Quality of Life: Task for the Future*, during which 1,200 international delegates discussed the environmental, resource, and growth crises as well as perspectives for a transformation that would overcome the focus on growth and lead to a "humanization of working life."[12]

Marxists and dissidents from the German Democratic Republic such as Wolfang Harich in his book *Kommunismus ohne Wachstum* (1975), Rudolf Bahro in his *Die Alternative* (1977), or Robert Havemann in his *Morgen. Die Industriegesellschaft am Scheideweg* (1980) – taking the limits to growth seriously – worked on a materialistically grounded revision of Marxism for the ecological era. While the official regime and the Socialist Unity Party interpreted the rise of environmental questions in the West as an ideological maneuver of the ruling classes, these intellectuals aimed at combining socialism with ecology by reviving the notion of utopia to strive toward (Amberger 2014). Nowadays largely forgotten – and also ignored in current discussions about degrowth economies – these thinkers further developed their ideas and practices in broad public debates during the 1970s and included cooperative, pacifist, and eco-feminist strands into their utopias (Harich 2015; on the development of Harich's ecological thinking see Heyer 2015).[13]

Further influential discussions were advanced by feminists and eco-feminists, most famously the subsistence perspective developed by Claudia v. Werlhof, Maria Mies, and Veronika Bennholdt-Thomsen from the so-called Bielefeld school. These authors and activists explain the social and ecological crises by analyzing the patriarchal capitalist exploitation of (female) reproductive work, of nature, and of the (postcolonial) economies in the global South. Building on the long-standing feminist critique of GDP-accounting that has been developed since the early 1970s, which has demonstrated how powerfully the growth paradigm devalues (monetarily and in terms of human values) all non-market forms of work, the subsistence perspective put the activities that are most essential to sustain life itself (those directly related to human needs, most importantly care work) at the center of economics and society. Key principles of this perspective are precaution, cooperation, and the orientation toward what is necessary for sustaining life (Werlhof et al. 1983; Bennholdt-Thomsen 2010; Waring 1989).

What is most striking is that within the entire degrowth discussion – not just in Germany, but generally – only few are aware of the fact that many of the arguments and proposals of the current degrowth agenda were essentially already discussed and promoted by the early German Green Party (Pueyo 2015). From their foundation in 1980 until the so-called "Fundis" (fundamentalists) left the party in the early 1990s, the critique of industrialism, technocracy, and economic growth formed a core of the economic discussions and in particular some of the economic programs of *Die Grünen* (for more details on these programs see Riechmann 1993). For instance, the economic program adopted in 1983 (*Sinnvoll arbeiten – solidarisch leben. Gegen Arbeitslosigkeit und Sozialabbau* – Working Meaningfully, Living in Solidarity: Against Unemployment and Social Cutbacks), already claimed that "The GREENS are determined that within the Federal Republic of Germany, as in the other industrial nations, there is not too little industrial production, but too much." Highly concordant with degrowth arguments some 25 years later, the party argued that the "gains from further industrial growth are already outweighed by the ecological damages," criticized large-scale technologies, the gendered division of labor, and the devaluing of unpaid work. It also demanded the selective reduction in certain sectors of the economy (resource and energy-intensive mass production, toxic production, plastics, cement, armament, and atomic energy) and the focus on those parts of the economy more directly linked to human needs such as alternative energies, public transport, dignified housing, and organic food crops (Die Grünen 1983, 3).[14]

A particular focus was the reduction of working time and the Greens even joined arms with some colleagues from the trade unions to form an initiative demanding the 35-hour working week (Die Grünen 1984). During the following years, these ideas were developed into concrete legislative proposals within the German Parliament. In 1990, for example, a draft law stated: "The goal of ecologically and socially friendly development will take the place of the traditional global goal of promoting economic growth [...] The [...] goal of 'steady and appropriate growth' is a relic of a phase of global and undifferentiated growth thinking in economic politics" (Deutscher Bundestag 1990, 20). These proposals and discussions are still highly illuminating and – in many respects – more advanced than current degrowth proposals. However, during the 1990s, the Greens in Germany – in line with ecological movements in most Western countries and in the context of efforts to move into positions of political power – abandoned this search for policies and legislation beyond economic growth and started to endorse the idea of sustainable development and, more particularly, the idea of ecological modernization (Japs 2008; Nishida 2005).

In German-speaking countries the most recent wave of growth critiques emerged in the wake of the economic crisis of 2008, which became visible with the 2011 conference *Jenseits des Wachstums?!* (Beyond growth?!). This conference, which drew more than 2,500 people to Berlin, was organized by the network for another globalization *Attac*, which cooperated with many ecological, development-aid-related, and social foundations. Already in the years before, several authors had written about the need for alternatives to growth. One can distinguish various thematic strands, ranging from a sufficiency-oriented growth critique most prominently presented by Niko Paech (2005;

2012), a social-reformist branch strongly connected to environmental groups (Seidl and Zahrnt 2010), an anti-capitalist critique rooted in the alter-globalization movement and solidarity economies (Exner et al. 2008; Rätz et al. 2011), and finally a feminist strand whose arguments go back to the subsistence debates of the Bielefeld School in the 1970s (Bennholdt-Thomsen 2010; for an overview of these currents of the German degrowth debate see Schmelzer 2015). While the term "postgrowth" ("Postwachstumsgesellschaft" or "Postwachstumsökonomie") is more established – which largely stems from the fact that linguistically it is not possible in German to construct a neologism in parallel to "de-growth" – in substance the positions are at least partly congruent with the original degrowth perspective (in particular regarding the latter three perspectives). After the 2014 international degrowth conference in Leipzig, there are several organizational hubs, including an ongoing seminar at the University of Oldenburg, several websites and blogs, a large network linking researchers, grassroots activists, and bottom-up initiatives called *Netzwerk Wachstumswende,* and some think tanks.[15] Recently, degrowth actors have started a structured networking process with over thirty other social movements and alternative economy currents ranging from commons to transition towns and trade unions (http://www.degrowth.de/de/dib).

Generally, the German-speaking debate is characterized by a large heterogeneity of positions, the strong involvement of political groups and initiatives from the solidarity economy, an intense exchange with more traditional organization such as trade unions or political associations and – maybe most importantly – a strong focus on discussing macroeconomic policies for non-growing economies (Adler and Schachtschneider 2010; Eversberg and Schmelzer 2016; Schneidewind and Zahrnt 2013). In contrast to the rather explicit and well-developed invocation of historical roots in the Southern European and the clear focus on ecological and welfare economics in the English tradition, the historical sources referred to by degrowth or postgrowth actors in Germany are more vague and wide, ranging from some of the authors so crucial to the Southern European *décroissance* (mostly filtered through French texts to Germany) to thinkers from the altermondialista current, ecological economics, theories of money and interest, and to feminist debates.

Conclusion

Skepticism of economic growth and the search for alternatives are on the rise. In his new ecological encyclical "Laudatio Si," presented in June 2015, even Pope Francis joined the debate, criticized luxury and consumption and demanded economic decline in rich countries:

> if in some cases sustainable development were to involve new forms of growth, then in other cases, given the insatiable and irresponsible growth produced over many decades, we need also to think of containing growth by setting some reasonable limits and even retracing our steps before it is

> too late. We know how unsustainable is the behavior of those who constantly consume and destroy, while others are not yet able to live in a way worthy of their human dignity. That is why the time has come to accept decreased growth in some parts of the world, in order to provide resources for other places to experience healthy growth.
>
> (Francis 2014, 141)

The ambiguous term of "decreased growth" is the English translation of "decrescita" in the Italian original. Francis thus deliberately used a political neologism that has been at the forefront of a new academic and societal debate and social movement that spread during the last 10 years from France ("décroissance") and other Southern European countries ("decrescimiento") to the English-speaking world ("degrowth") and the German-speaking region ("Postwachstum" or "Wachstumsrücknahme"; see also Krüger 2015). This practical utopian perspective aims at the development of more equitable and sustainable lifestyles through the planned contraction of the current mode of economic activity, while also challenging its ideological legitimation such as productivism, economism, and developmentalism.

In this chapter we have presented three main lines of development and classified them as three models in three geographically separate yet interlinked discursive spaces. Common to the different traditions of degrowth is a radical critique of growth as the main gravitation point of policies, institutional settings, and economic structures of modern, capitalistic societies.

The English-speaking debate on economic growth has particularly been shaped by ecological economists. While Georgescu-Roegen's writings on thermodynamics, economics, and alternatives from the 1970s proved highly influential for the original French *décroissance* in the 2000s, his arguments were and still tend to be partially ignored in the English-speaking world. This seems to still effect current growth critiques. In contrast to the Southern European strand, concepts in the US and England are less politically radical, more technocratic, and more strongly focused on economic, social, and environmental reforms, while also neglecting philosophical or anthropological perspectives and a general questioning of economism.

The Southern European tradition has a very broad thematic focus that not only includes social, economic, and environmental issues, but also strongly emphasizes the cultural dimension and issues of democracy and autonomy and – at least in some currents – a quite radical questioning of capitalism, industrialism, and modernity. A continuous engagement with historical roots and allied perspectives – such as political ecology, post-development, and environmental justice – plays a key role. New streams of thought are being integrated, appropriated, and interpreted in a degrowth-like manner. For example, Bataille's concept of *dépense* (literally: expenditure) has recently been re-read from a degrowth perspective as a mode of collective and communal "squandering" of excessive wealth that re-equilibrates social inequalities (D'Alisa et al. 2014).

Lastly, the German strand of growth critiques has been particularly shaped by the strong sustainability debate critiques of green growth, and by its organizational base in the environmental and anti-globalization movements. Longer-term historical roots are not explicitly invoked and do not seem to play an important role in current discussions. Nonetheless, a closer look reveals lively discussions in the 1970s that spanned large segments of society and involved not only trade unions, but also the emerging Green Party. Next to a series of highly influential books – most of which would certainly deserve more attention in current degrowth or "Postwachstums" debates – in both Eastern and Western Germany, in particular the policy and legislative debates among the Green Party in the 1980s are highly instructive. Also, the materialist eco-feminist perspective of the Bielefeld school has played a major role in unmasking the patriarchal-capitalistic logic that sustains the logic of growth and in articulating visions for a radical social transformation. Finally a more analytic perspective of the structural role of economic growth for modern societies plays a significant role within the German Debate. This perspective is particularly prominent in a research group on "Post-Growth Societies" at the University of Jena that focuses on how capitalist societies are dynamically stabilizing through economic growth, and what democratic alternatives exist.

To conclude, the historical analysis of precursors of current degrowth debates in three language regions prove both long-term path dependencies, national idiosyncrasies, and separated debates, as well as influential cross-fertilizations across barriers – but even more so the great potential for future processes of transnational exchange and learning. The case of the growth critical debates of the German Greens in the 1980s is only one case in point: The French-inspired degrowth discussions could indeed spark a renewed interest – also in Germany – in these older debates. In a similar vein, several streams of the radical English-speaking critique of growth from the 1970s onwards have become crucial to the Southern European degrowth debate, but did not meet with much attention in the current English-speaking discussion. Moreover, further English-speaking influences such as the nineteenth-century American philosopher and naturalist Henry David Thoreau, or the writings of libertarian eco-socialist Murray Bookchin or the Austro-American economist and political theorist Leopold Kohr, both highly influential in the US environmental and social discourse in the latter half of the twentieth century, are not part of current prominent English-speaking variants of growth critique.

By focusing on the precursors of radical growth critiques in these three cultural regions, we aim at facilitating the dialogue about a historically grounded and transnationalized degrowth movement. Within the larger family of growth critique, the degrowth movement is characterized by a stronger focus on structural and socio-cultural dimensions of economic growth and engages in a more radical critique of the status quo. For this reason, it plays an important role as a common platform for different types of social movements (environmentalism, altermondialismo, social justice) and social experiments (urban gardening, social cooperatives, self-managed communities, etc.). With this chapter, we not only aimed at unraveling the historical depth underlying current degrowth debates, but also at facilitating future collaboration in the development of more coherent conceptions that build on rather than reinvent debates of the past.

Notes

1 By this, Daly does not only mean a re-embedding of the economy into a normative sphere, which is not rooted in market transactions and the assumptions of "economic man," but also that values need an objective grounding, which he often sees represented in established religious traditions, as he writes: "an enduring ethic must be more than a social convention. It must have some objective transcendental authority" (Daly 2014, 170). While Georgescu-Roegen would partly agree on the first part, he was definitely more skeptical about the idea of some transcendentally given ultimate values. He propagated re-embedding economic analysis into dialectical reasoning, i.e. into a socio-political deliberation about concepts that – like justice – do not have clear-cut boundaries, but are surrounded by what he called a "dialectical penumbra" (Georgescu-Roegen 1971, 44).

2 Georgescu-Roegen states that while Daly's concept of steady state had nothing to offer in terms of size of population or the level of the standard of living, a thermodynamic analysis would instead make clear that "the desirable size of population is that which can be fed by organic agriculture alone" (Georgescu-Roegen 1977, 270).

3 Inter alia due to Georgescu-Roegen's critique, in later works Daly reformulated this idea in terms of the new leading concept established worldwide at the beginning of the 1990s, sustainable development, that he redefined in terms of "qualitative improvement without quantitative growth" (Daly 2007, 159), but never gave up on the idea of the steady state economy (Daly 2014).

4 Jackson (2009, book cover). Endorsement by Dr. Robert Goodland, former environmental and social advisor to the world bank group and close collaborator of Herman Daly.

5 A strong movement especially in France and Italy that combines the socialist critique of the market-driven economy and of social inequalities with a critique of competition and productivism rooted in Christian anthropology and in the social doctrine of the Church.

6 For the latter see Foucault's reconstruction of American neoliberalism as a mode of subjectiv(iz)ation according to the model of the enterprise (becoming entrepreneur of oneself) and Boltanski and Chiapello's analysis of the incorporation of the so-called artists' critique into late capitalism in terms of self-realization, creativity, and self-enhancement (Foucault 2008; Boltanski & Chiapello 2006).

7 In 2004, the magazine *La Décroissance, le journal de la joie de vivre* was founded, which today sells 30,000 copies each month.

8 *Economism* is the imperialistic and pervasive dominance of economic mode of explanation of social reality, including agency, relations, and behavioral drivers. Caillé and the M.A.U.S.S. expose and reject the Chicago School's overarching economization of all social phenomena.

9 The quotes above are taken from a current EU-funded Initial Training Network on political ecology coordinated by the Autonomous University of Barcelona and more specifically by members of Research & Degrowth.

10 Gorz and Illich are important liaisons between the German and the French debate.

11 The Austrian philosopher Gunther Anders diagnosed in his *Antiquiertheit des Menschen* (The Outdatedness of Human Beings; originally 1956; second volume

1990) a fundamental contradiction between the fallibility and imperfection of humans and the increasing perfection of machines, putting the critique of technics and technology to the forefront of conservative growth critiques.

12 Although 10 volumes document this fascinating event, it has not been analyzed in the historical literature and is largely forgotten, even within trade union circles (Friedrichs 1975; Klitzke 2011). Nonetheless, the discussions between degrowth proponents and union activists are much stronger in Germany then in other countries, see below.

13 Harich's book is widely regarded as the first Marxist account of a communism without growth, a debate that would take off internationally from the 1970s onwards. However, already an earlier draft from 1972 contained the core ideas of Harich's thinking on this issue, as recently shown (Heyer 2015, 13). See also for a more recent account Blauwhof (2012).

14 One could go to lengths in showing the similarities. The GREENS also demanded the dismantling of large industries; decentralized small-scale production; a reduction of national and international division of labor and a localization of production; more long-living products, more recycling; critique of GDP; creation of more free time for social and artistic activities; the strengthening of cooperatives; redirection of technological research to serve human needs; repair cafés; income independently from labor; a just global economic system; just distribution of available work to all; societal ownership of land, natural resources, means of production and banks, self-organized basic democracy, etc. (Die Grünen 1983, 4–8).

15 See in particular www.degrowth.de; www.postwachstum.de; www.wachstumswende.de; 4 July 2016.

References

Adler, Frank and Ulrich Schachtschneider. 2010. *Green New Deal, Suffizienz oder Ökosozialismus? Konzepte für gesellschaftliche Wege aus der Ökokrise*. München: oekom verlag.

Amberger, Alexander. 2014. *Bahro – Harich – Havemann. Marxistische Systemkritik und politische Utopie in der DDR*. Paderborn: Verlag Ferdinand Schöningh.

Amery, Carl. 1985. *Natur als Politik. Die ökologische Chance des Menschen*. Reinbek bei Hamburg: Rowohlt.

Anders, Gunther. 1956. *Die Antiquiertheit des Menschen. Band I: Über die Seele im Zeitalter der zweiten industriellen Revolution*. München: C. H. Beck.

Ariés, Paul. 2005. "La décroissance, un mot-obus," *La Décroissance*, April 26.

Asara, Viviana. 2015. "Democracy without Growth: The Political Ecology of the Indignados Movement." *PhD thesis*, Barcelona: Universitat Autònoma.

Bahro, Rudolf. 1977. *Die Alternative. Zur Kritik des real existierenden Sozialismus*. Köln: Europäische Verlagsanstalt.

Barkin, David, Mario E. Fuente Carrasco, and Daniel Tagle Zamora. 2012. "La significación de una Economía Ecológica radical." *Revista Iberoamericana de Economía Ecológica* 19: 1–14.

Bennholdt-Thomsen, Veronika. 2010. *Geld oder Leben: Was uns wirklich reich macht*. München: Oekom.

Blauwhof, Frederik Berend. 2012. "Overcoming Accumulation: Is a Capitalist Steady-State Economy Possible?" *Ecological Economics* 84: 254–261.

Boltanski, Luc, and Eve Chiapello. *The New Spirit of Capitalism*. London: Verso, 2006.

Bonaiuti, Mauro. 2010. "Conclusion: From Bieconomics to Degrowth." In *From Bioeconomics to Degrowth: Georgescu-Roegen's 'New Economics' in Eight Essays*, by Nicolas Georgescu-Roegen, 171–194. New York: Routledge.

Bookchin, Murray. 1971. *Post-Scarcity Anarchism*. Montreal: Black Rose Books.

Borowy, Iris. 2014. *Defining Sustainable Development: The World Commission on Environment and Development (Brundtland Commission)*. London and New York: Routledge.

Boulding, Kenneth. 1966. "The Economics of the Coming Spaceship Earth." In *Environmental Quality in a Growing Economy*, 3–14. Baltimore: Johns Hopkins University Press.

Brand, Ulrich. 2014. "Degrowth: Der Beginn einer Bewegung?" *Blätter für deutsche und internationale Politik* 10: 29–32.

Caillé, Alain. 2007. *Anthropologie du don. Le tiers paradigm*. Paris: Édition La Découverte.

Cassiers, Isabelle, ed. 2015. *Redefining Prosperity*. New York: Routledge.

Castoriadis, Cornelius. 2010. *A Society Adrift: Interviews and Debates, 1974-1997*. New York: Fordham University Press.

Costanza, R. and H. E. Daly. 1987. "Toward an Ecological Economics," *Ecological Modelling* 38: 1–7.

D'Alisa, Giacomo, Federico Demaria, and Giorgos Kallis, eds. 2014. *Degrowth: A Vocabulary for a New Era*. London and New York: Routledge.

Daly, Herman E 1973a. "Introduction." In *Toward a Steady-State Economy*, edited by Herman E. Daly, 1–29. San Francisco: W.H. Freeman and Company.

Daly, Herman E 1973b. "The Steady-State Economy: Toward a Political Economy of Biophysical Equilbrium and Moral Growth." In *Toward a Steady-State Economy*, edited by Herman E. Daly, 149–174. San Francisco: W.H. Freeman and Company.

Daly, Herman E., ed. 1980. *Economics, Ecology, Ethics. Essays toward a Steady-State Economy*. San Francisco: W.H. Freeman and Company.

Daly, Herman E. 1992. *Steady-State Economics*. London: Earthscan.

Daly, Herman E. 2007. *Ecological Economics and Sustainable Development*. Cheltenham/ Northhamption: Edward Elgar Publishing.

Daly, Herman 2014. "Integrating Ecology and Economics," *The Daly News*, June 5. Accessed October 17, 2016. http://dalynews.org/learn/blog/page/7.

De Benoist, Alain. 2007. *Demain, la décroissance!: penser l'ecologie jusqu'au bout*. Paris: Édite.

Demaria, Federico, Francois Schneider, Filka Sekulova, and Joan Martinez-Alier. 2013. "What Is Degrowth? From an Activist Slogan to a Social Movement." *Environmental Values* 22(2): 191–215.

Deutscher Bundestag. 1990. "Entwurf eines Gesetzes für eine ökologisch-soziale Wirtschaft – Drucksache 11/7607."

Die Grünen. 1983. *Sinnvoll arbeiten – solidarisch leben. Gegen Arbeitslosigkeit und Sozialabbau. Verabschiedet auf der Bundesdelegiertenversammlung am 15./16. Januar 1983 in Stuttgart-Sindelfingen*. Bonn: Die Grünen.

Die Grünen – Arbeitskreise Wirtschaft und Arbeit/Soziales der Grünen im Bundestag. 1984. *Arbeitszeitpolitik der Grünen*. Bonn: Die Grünen.

Duve, Freimut, ed. 1974. *Technologie und Politik. Das Magazin zur Wachstumskrise*. Reinbek bei Hamburg: Rowohlt.

Duverger, Timothée. 2011a. "De Meadows à Mansholt: L'invention du 'zégisme.'" *Entropia* 10: 114–123.

Duverger, Timothée 2011b. *La décroissance, une idée pour demain: Une alternative au capitalisme Synthèse des mouvements.* Paris: Le Sang de la Terre.

Escobar, Arturo. 1995. *Encountering Development: The Making and Unmaking of the Third World.* Princeton: Princeton University Press.

Escobar, Arturo. 2015. "Degrowth, Postdevelopment, and Transitions: A Preliminary Conversation." *Sustainability Science* 10(3): 451–462.

Eversberg, Dennis, and Matthias Schmelzer. 2016. "Über die Selbstproblematisierung zur Kapitalismuskritik. Vier Thesen zur entstehenden Degrowth-Bewegung.": *Forschungsjournal Soziale Bewegungen* 1: 9–17.

Exner, Andreas, Christian Lauk, and Konstantin Kulterer. 2008. *Die Grenzen des Kapitalismus. Wie wir am Wachstum Scheitern.* Wien: Ueberreuter.

Flipo, Fabrice. 2009. "Les racines conceptuelles de la décroissance." In *La décroissance économique pour la soutenabilité écologique et l'équité sociale*, edited by Baptiste Mylondo, 19–32. Bellecombe-en-Bauges: Croquant.

Foucault, Michel. 2008. *The Birth of Biopolitics: Lectures at the Collège de France, 1978–1979.* New York: Palgrave Macmillan.

Fournier, Valérie. 2008. "Escaping from the Economy: The Politics of Degrowth." *International Journal of Sociology and Social Policy* 28(11/12): 528–545.

Francis, Pope. 2014. *Encyclical Letter Laudato Si' Of The Holy Father Francis On Care For Our Common Home.* Rome: Vatican Press.

Friedrichs, Günter. 1975. *Aufgabe Zukunft. Qualität des Lebens. Beiträge zur vierten internationalen Arbeitstagung der Industriegewerkschaft Metall für die Bundesrepublik Deutschland 11. bis 14. April 1972 in Oberhausen.* 10 vols. Frankfurt am Main: Europäische Verlagsanstalt.

Georgescu-Roegen, Nicholas. 1971. *The Entropy Law and the Economic Process.* Cambridge, Mass.: Harvard University Press.

Georgescu-Roegen, Nicholas. 1975. "Energy and Economic Myths." *Southern Economic Journal* 41(3): 347–381.

Georgescu-Roegen, Nicholas. 1977. "The Steady State and Ecological Salvation: A Thermodynamic Analysis." *BioScience* 27(4): 266–270.

Georgescu-Roegen, Nicholas. 1979. *Demain la décroissance: entropie, écologie, économie.* Translated by Ivo Rens and Jacques Grinevald. Paris: P.-M. Favre.

Georgescu-Roegen, Nicholas. 1980. "Selections from 'Energy and Economic Myths.'" In *Economics, Ecology, Ethics. Essays toward a Steady-State Economy*, edited by Herman E. Daly, 61–81. San Francisco: W.H. Freeman and Company.

Georgescu-Roegen, Nicholas. 1989. "Quo Vadis Homo sapiens sapiens." In: Georgescu-Roegen, Nicolas. *From Bioeconomics to Degrowth: Georgescu-Roegen's "New Economics" in Eight Essays.* Edited by Mauro Bonaiuti. New York: Routledge, 2011, 158–170.

Gorz, Andre. 1980. *Ecology as Politics.* Boston: South End Press.

Gorz, Andre. 1994. *Capitalism, Socialism, Ecology.* London: Verso.

Graf, Rüdiger. 2008. "Die Grenzen des Wachstums und die Grenzen des Staates. Konservative und die ökologischen Bedrohungsszenarien der frühen 1970er Jahre." In *Streit um den Staat. Intellektuelle Debatten in der Bundesrepublik*, edited by Dominik Geppert and Jens Hacke, 207–228. Göttingen: Vandenhoeck & Ruprecht.

Grinevald, Jacques. 2011. "Nicholas Georgescu-Roegen et Le 'Message Terrestre' de La Décroissance." *Entropia* 10: 135–154.

Hahn, Friedemann. 2006. "Von Unsinn bis Untergang: Rezeption des Club of Rome und der Grenzen des Wachstums in der Bundesrepublik der frühen 1970er Jahre." *Ph.D. thesis*, Universität Freiburg.

Hajer, Maarten A. 1995. *The Politics of Environmental Discourse: Ecological Modernization and the Policy Process.* Oxford: Oxford University Press.

Harich, Wolfgang. 1975. *Kommunismus ohne Wachstum? Babeuf und der Club of Rome.* Reinbek bei Hamburg: Rowohlt.

Harich, Wolfgang 2015. *Ökologie, Frieden, Wachstumskritik.* Edited by Andreas Heyer. Schriften aus dem Nachlass Wolfgang Harichs8. Marburg: Tectum.

Havemann, Robert. 1980. *Morgen: Die Industriegesellschaft am Scheideweg.* Frankfurt a.M.: Fischer Taschenbuch.

Heinberg, Richard. 2011. *The End of Growth: Adopting to Our New Economic Reality.* Gabriola Island, Canada: New Society Publishers.

Heyer, Andreas. 2015. "Die Entwicklung von Harichs ökologischem Konzept." In *Ökologie, Frieden, Wachstumskritik*, by Wolfgang Harich, 9–100. Schriften aus dem Nachlass Wolfgang Harichs8. Marburg: Tectum.

Hueting, Roefie. 1980. *New Scarcity and Economic Growth.* Amsterdam: North-Holland Publishing Company.

Illich, Ivan. 1978. *Toward a History of Needs.* New York: Pantheon Books.

Jackson, Tim. 2009. *Prosperity without Growth: Economics for a Finite Planet.* London: Earthscan.

Japs, Simon. 2008. *Etablierung durch Anpassung. Programmatischer und inhaltlicher Wandel der Grünen.* Saarbrücken: VDM Verlag Dr. Müller.

Kallis, Giorgos, Federico Demaria, and Giacomo D'Alisa, eds. 2014. "Introduction." In *Degrowth: A Vocabulary for a New Era*, 1–17. London and New York: Routledge.

Kerschner, Christian. 2010. "Economic de-Growth vs. Steady-State Economy." *Journal of Cleaner Production* 18(6): 544–551.

Klitzke, Udo. 2011. "Zur Frage von gewerkschaftlicher Gesellschafts- und Betriebspolitik: der Aspekt der Nachhaltigkeit." *Das Argument* 294(5): 723–733.

Kohr, Leopold. 1957. *The Breakdown of Nations.* Reprint. London and New York: Routledge.

Kohr, Leopold. 1978. *The Overdeveloped Nations: The Diseconomies of Scale.* New York: Schocken Books.

Kothari, Ashish, Federico Demaria, and Alberto Acosta. 2014. "Buen Vivir, Degrowth and Ecological Swaraj: Alternatives to Sustainable Development and the Green Economy." *Development* 57(3–4): 362–375.

Kreschner, Christian. 2010. "Economic De-growth vs. Steady-state Economy." *Journal of Cleaner Production* 18(6): 544–551.

Krüger, Oscar. 2015. "Laudato Si‘ as signalling towards Degrowth." Accessed July 1, 2016. http://www.degrowth.de/de/2015/06/laudato-si-as-signalling-towards-degrowth.

Kubiszewski, Ida, Robert Costanza, Carol Franco, Philip Lawn, John Talberth, Tim Jackson, and Camille Aylmer. 2013. "Beyond GDP: Measuring and Achieving Global Genuine Progress." *Ecological Economics* 93: 57–68.

Kupper, Patrick. 2004. "'Weltuntergangs-Vision aus dem Computer'. Zur Geschichte der Studie 'Die Grenzen des Wachstums' von 1972." In *Wird Kassandra heiser? Die Geschichte falscher Ökoalarme*, edited by Frank Uekötter and Jens Hohensee, 98–111. Stuttgart: Steiner.

Latouche, Serge. 1993. *In the Wake of the Affluent Society: An Exploration of Post-Development.* London: Zed Books.

Latouche, Serge. 2001. *La Déraison de la raison économique: de l'efficacité au principe de précaution.* Michel: Paris.

Latouche, Serge. 2010a. *Farewell to Growth*. Cambridge: Polity.

Latouche, Serge. 2010b. "Degrowth." *Journal of Cleaner Production* 18(6): 519–522.

Layard, P., Richard, G. 2005. *Happiness: Lessons from a New Science*. New York: Penguin Press.

Luks, Fred. 2001. *Die Zukunft des Wachstums. Theoriegeschichte, Nachhaltigkeit und die Perspektiven einer neuen Wirtschaft*. Marburg: Metropolis.

Martínez-Alier, Joan. 2012. "Environmental Justice and Economic Degrowth: An Alliance between Two Movements." *Capitalism Nature Socialism* 23: 51–73.

Martínez-Alier, Joan, Unai Pascual, Franck-Dominique Vivien, and Edwin Zaccai. 2010. "Sustainable de-Growth: Mapping the Context, Criticisms and Future Prospects of an Emergent Paradigm." *Ecological Economics* 69(9): 1741–1747.

Meadows, Donella H., Dennis L. Meadows, Jorgen Randers, and William W. Behrens. 1972. *The Limits to Growth: A Report for the Club of Rome's Project on the Predicament of Mankind*. Washington: Potomac Associates.

Mende, Silke. 2011. *"Nicht rechts, nicht links, sondern vorn": Eine Geschichte der Gründungsgrünen*. München: Oldenbourg Wissenschaftsverlag.

Mill, John Stuart. 1909. *Principles of Political Economy, with Some of Their Applications to Social Philosophy*. London: Longmans, Green, Reader, and Dyer.

Muraca, Barbara. 2010. *Denken in Grenzgebiet: prozessphilosophische Grundlagen einer Theorie starker Nachhaltigkeit*. Freiburg: Karl Alber.

Muraca, Barbara. 2013. "Decroissance: A Project for a Radical Transformation of Society." *Environmental Values* 22(2): 147–169.

NEF (New Economic Foundation). 2012. Happy Planet Index. Accessed July 12, 2016. http://www.happyplanetindex.org/assets/happy-planet-index-report.pdf.

Nehring, Holger. 2009. "Genealogies of the Ecological Movement. Planning, Complexity, and the Environment of 'the Environment'." In *Nature's End. History and the Environment*, edited by Sverker Sörlin and Paul Warde, 115–138. New York: Houndsmills.

Nishida, Makoto. 2005. *Strömungen in den Grünen (1980–2003): Eine Analyse über informell-organisierte Gruppen innerhalb der Grünen*. Münster: Lit-Verlag.

Nussbaum, Henrich von. 1973. *Die Zukunft Des Wachstums*. Düsseldorf: Bertelsmann Universitätsverlag.

O'Connor. 1995. *Is Capitalism Sustainable: Political Economy and the Politics of Ecology*. New York: Guilford Press.

O'Connor, James R. 1998. *Natural Causes: Essays in Ecological Marxism*. New York: Guilford Press.

Odum, Howard T. 1971. *Environment, Power, and Society*, New York: John Wiley and Sons.

Oltmans, Willem L., ed. 1974. *Grenzen des Wachstums: Pro und Contra*. Reinbek bei Hamburg: Rowohlt.

Paech, Niko. 2005. *Nachhaltiges Wirtschaften jenseits von Innovationsorientierung und Wachstum. Eine unternehmensbezogene Transformationstheorie*. Marburg: Metropolis-Verlag.

Paech, Niko 2012. *Befreiung vom Überfluss: Auf dem Weg in die Postwachstumsökonomie*. München: oekom verlag.

Petridis, Panos, Barbara Muraca, and Giorgos Kallis, "Degrowth: Between a Scientific Concept and a Slogan for a Social Movement." In: Joan Martinez-Alier and Roldan Muradian, eds., *Handbook of Ecological Economics*, 176–200. Cheltenham: Edward Elgar.

Pueyo, Salvador. 2015. "Forgotten Economic Programmes for a Degrowing Future." Accessed on April 4, 2016. https://grunentodegrowth.wordpress.com.

Rätz, Werner, Tanja von Egan-Krieger, Barbara Muraca, Alexis Passadakis, Matthias Schmelzer, and Andrea Vetter, eds. 2011. *Ausgewachsen! Ökologische Gerechtigkeit, soziale Rechte, gutes Leben*. Hamburg: VSA-Verlag.

Riechmann, Jorge. 1993. "Otra Forma de Trabajar, Producir Y Consumir: Los Programas Económicos de Die Grünen." *Ecologia Politica* 6(2): 59–89.

Rist, Gilbert. 1996. *The History of Development: From Western Origins to Global Faith*. London: Zed Books.

Sachs, Wolfgang, ed. 1992. *The Development Dictionary: A Guide to Knowledge as Power*. London: Zed Books.

Schmelzer, Matthias. 2015. "Gutes Leben statt Wachstum: Degrowth, Klimagerechtigkeit, Subsistenz – Eine Einführung in die Begriffe und Ansätze der Postwachstumsbewegung." In *Atlas der Globalisierung: Weniger wird Mehr*, 116–121. Berlin: Le Monde Diplomatique.

Schmelzer, Matthias. 2016. *The Hegemony of Growth. The OECD and the Making of the Economic Growth Paradigm*. Cambridge: Cambridge University Press.

Schneidewind, Uwe and Angelika Zahrnt. 2013. *Damit gutes Leben einfacher wird: Perspektiven einer Suffizienzpolitik*. Munich: oekom verlag.

Seidl, Irmi and Angelika Zahrnt, eds. 2010. *Postwachstumsgesellschaft: Neue Konzepte für die Zukunft*. Marburg: Metropolis-Verlag.

Skidelsky, Robert, and Edward Skidelsky. 2012. *How Much Is Enough? Money and the Good Life*. New York: Other Press.

Steurer, Reinhard. 2002. *Der Wachstumsdiskurs in Wissenschaft und Politik: Von der Wachstumseuphorie über "Grenzen des Wachstums" zur Nachhaltigkeit*. Berlin: Verlag für Wissenschaft und Forschung.

Stiglitz, Joseph, Amartya Sen, and Jean-Paul Fitoussi. 2010. *Mismeasuring Our Lives: Why GDP Doesn't Add Up*. New York: New Press.

Sutter, Andrew J. 2016. Review of Degrowth: A Vocabulary for a New Era. Giacomo D'Alisa, Federico Demaria, and Giorgos Kallis, eds. Routledge, Abingdon, 2014, personal correspondence.

Ullrich, Otto. 1979. *Weltniveau – In der Sackgasse des Industriesystems*. Berlin: Rotbuch.

Victor, Peter A. 2008. *Managing Without Growth: Slower by Design, Not Disaster*. Advances in Ecological Economics. Cheltenham: Edward Elgar.

Wallerstein, Immanuel. 1989. "1968, Revolution in the World-System. Theses and Queries." *Theory and Society* 18(4): 431–449.

Waring, Marilyn. 1989. *If Women Counted: A New Feminist Economics*. London: Macmillan.

Werlhof, Claudia von, Maria Mies, and Veronika Bennholdt-Thomsen. 1983. *Frauen, die letzte Kolonie*. Reinbek bei Hamburg: Rowohlt.

Index

For Product Safety Concerns and Information please contact our EU
representative GPSR@taylorandfrancis.com
Taylor & Francis Verlag GmbH, Kaufingerstraße 24, 80331 München, Germany

www.ingramcontent.com/pod-product-compliance
Ingram Content Group UK Ltd.
Pitfield, Milton Keynes, MK11 3LW, UK
UKHW021612240425
457818UK00018B/514

* 9 7 8 1 1 3 8 4 9 9 6 7 6 *